A Guide to Research
in
Music Education

A Guide to Research
in
Music Education

■

Roger P. Phelps
New York University

WM. C. BROWN COMPANY PUBLISHERS
Dubuque, Iowa

MUSIC SERIES

Consulting Editor
    FREDERICK W. WESTPHAL
    Sacramento State College

Copyright © 1969 by
Wm. C. Brown Company Publishers

Library of Congress Catalog Card Number: 69-11127

Printed in the United States of America

To my wife, Mildred,
and our sons,
Roger and Homer

Preface

This textbook is designed to be a practical guide for those who wish to become familiar with the basic concepts and techniques of research methodology as they apply specifically to music education. The increased demand for post-baccalaureate and advanced graduate instruction has resulted in the addition of courses in research methodology in music education by many graduate schools because some type of culminating experience in research usually is a concomitant of receiving a graduate degree. Yet because of lack of general agreement regarding what the term "music education research" connotes, these courses have varied in content both qualitatively and quantitatively. The object of this book is to present a concise, practical, and logical approach to the fundamental principles and methods of research which can be readily understood and applied by the music educator who, because of his usual preoccupation with the development and maintenance of performing skills, is often unfamiliar with the philosophical and pragmatical connotations of research. The concepts and techniques described in this treatise are those which are generally accepted and used successfully by researchers in various disciplines.

Largely an outgrowth of this writer's experience in presenting the materials contained herein to graduate students in music education research methodology classes, this book is designed to be used for courses in the fundamentals of music education research, in thesis seminars, and by researchers who may be engaged independently in research in music education or the arts and humanities. Although most of the individuals who will use this book undoubtedly will be students in pursuit of either a master's or a doctoral degree, the postdoctoral researcher also should find it to be of value. In addition, it is anticipated that a graduate adviser can use it for reference purposes.

At present there are several excellent publications relating to the concepts and techniques of educational research, but their utility to music education has often been disappointing to music research tyros. It was at the urging of several of his students who had expressed the conviction a book was needed which concentrated specifically on problems peculiar to music education research that the writer first gave serious attention to writing *A Guide to Research in Music Education.*

Various titles are in print relating to music research, but they are either bibliographically- and stylistically-oriented or devised for use in conjunction with musicological studies. *A Guide to Research in Music Education* represents the first textbook designed especially with the precepts and procedures of music education research in mind. The concept of including analytical research as a separate and distinct type of music education research also is novel. Admittedly the book does not represent the only approach to music education research. On the other hand, it has been utilized successfully for many research studies which either have been or are being completed under the writer's direction. Points emphasized throughout the book are those in which a persistent deficiency has been evident.

This treatise can be especially useful when the principles and methods discussed within its pages are translated into the formulation of an acceptable research design, its adequate implementation, and the eventual dissemination of the research findings. This is the central theme of the book and its principal reason for being written.

The writer is appreciative of and indebted to the following for their contributions as noted: William P. Sears, Jr., Professor of Education, New York University, for his incisive and salutary appraisal of the entire manuscript; Mrs. Barbara Marks, Education Librarian, New York University, for her helpful suggestions to strengthen Chapter 4; Joseph Azzarelli, Director, Educational Research Services, New York University, for his constructive criticism of Chapter 12; Walter Kob, Associate Professor of Music Education, New York University, for his lucid and competent preparation of Chapter 9; and to his wife, Mildred Wade Phelps, Professor of Music, The King's College, who carefully read the entire manuscript and offered many trenchant suggestions to improve its readability. The writer also is grateful to the many publishers, noted throughout the treatise, who graciously gave permission to utilize quotations from their publications. Finally, a debt of gratitude is due to New York University for granting the sabbatical leave which made completion of this book possible.

Roger P. Phelps

Contents

· 1 ·

The Setting for Research in Music Education

The rise and fall of civilization have been a chronicle of man's attempts to find solutions to problems. Man has not always been concerned with a formalized plan to seek his way out of a dilemma as is frequently the case today; rather, the process of trial and error often has been his *modus operandi*. Recall that some of the greatest discoveries of the world have been the result of serendipity. That marvelous antibiotic penicillin was discovered by Alexander Fleming (1881-1955) quite by accident, and X-rays, which are so widely used today, were revealed in much the same way to Wilhelm Roentgen (1845-1923). The telephone, perhaps more closely allied to music than penicillin and X-rays, is generally accepted as having been discovered by chance when Alexander Graham Bell (1847-1922) was experimenting with a device to enable his deaf wife to hear better. It must be recognized, however, that most discoveries do not come about by serendipity. They result from careful and deliberate planning followed by precise experimentation and critique. Frequently this cycle is repeated several times before significant results are achieved. Problems, it seems, have always confronted man and will probably continue to challenge his ingenuity. The continuum is endless because as answers to questions are formulated experimentally and philosophically, new and additional challenges arise as man has moved up the ladder of progress.

Man, by instinct, is dedicated to change, since without it survival is not possible for long. The same is true in the animal realm. Witness the demise of the large prehistoric brontosaurus and the renowned dodo, a more contemporary but awkward flightless bird formerly inhabiting

1

certain islands in the Indian Ocean. Their disappearance from the face of the earth has been attributed to an inability to adjust to environmental changes which took place. As a possible explanation of this evolutionary process, Charles Darwin (1809-1882) engendered the principle of "survival of the fittest" in his *Origin of the Species,* a publication which has continued to arouse controversy since it first appeared in 1859. Since man is regarded as the most intelligent of all creatures, it is not unreasonable to expect that he will continue seeking diligently to perpetuate himself by finding answers to his perplexities in an intelligent and rational way, something which many fauna apparently have been unable to do.

The process of metamorphosis has extended, as everyone knows, to the tools and devices which man uses not only for his survival but also for his enjoyment. Certain musical instruments are appropriate for illustrative purposes at this point. Even a cursory glance at a music history textbook will reveal names of many instruments which are no longer contemporaneous. The ancient Greek cithara, the medieval shawm, and the ophicleide of the last century, to cite a few, are no longer found in the standard symphony orchestra. Reasons for their obsolescence are beyond the scope of this book, but in common with the brontosaurus and the dodo they evidently outlived their usefulness. It might be added, parenthetically, that the current disuse of these instruments, however, should be no comfort to the music educator. Any well-read person in music, as well as in any other discipline, is expected to be knowledgeable regarding significant developments and events pertinent to his field. A knowledge of the past is essential in enabling one to understand the present better. Acquisition of this information by a music educator will in part be due to his "research" into many sources. The connotation of "research" is used more loosely in this instance than it will be throughout the remainder of this book. Even in this illustration, however, it does imply a "seeking of information," although not necessarily in depth.

The quest for solutions to problems, as already suggested, may properly be called research. The sequence seemingly is endless because change brings with it new riddles which often defy immediate resolution. Alteration then frequently is attended by some organized type of research to cope with the deficiency which has become evident. Some solutions to problems obviously result from procedures which are less formally organized, because as Kelley avers, "the essence of research is evolution."[1] In the realm of music, Johann C. Denner's clumsy eighteenth-century clarinet of five keys would be repugnant to the contemporary clarinetist

---

[1]Truman Lee Kelley, *Scientific Method,* p. 1. © Truman Lee Kelley, 1932. Used by permission of The Macmillan Co., New York.

who performs on an instrument containing up to twenty keys and seven rings. One can scarcely fail to wonder whether or not the aforementioned cithara, shawm, or ophicleide likewise could have been modified and improved to keep pace with changing esthetic and musical concepts. This conjectural query hardly seems appropriate at this juncture because the record is clear. Obsolescence or utility are both dependent on change, but for different reasons, many of which will never be known. It should be noted, however, that research may hasten either one or the other. From a practical standpoint it normally is concerned with utility, although for historical perspective obsolescence would provide appropriate topics for study.

THE CONNOTATION OF RESEARCH

In its simplest meaning "research" has several manifestations. It is a carefully organized plan which can result in the discovery of new knowledge, the substantiation of previously held concepts, or the rejection of tenets which have been widely acclaimed. Sound research, in logical sequence, consists of organization, execution, and dissemination. Research obviously cannot be conducted properly without a good plan of operation. On the other hand a well-organized prospectus may not be effectively implemented, resulting in insufficient data. It is thus important that both organization and execution be of the highest caliber. In scientific research dissemination is almost universally a concomitant aspect of a project. This is not usually the case, unfortunately, in research in education and the humanities. If research in music education is worthy of the name, the results should be shared graciously with members of the profession.

It hardly seems necessary to mention that the investigator is crucial to the success of all research. He must include among his virtues the ability to be both critical and inquisitive and also the capacity to determine what type of research is feasible for him to implement, as Barzun and Graff so clearly point out.[2]

To the musician, largely trained in non-verbal skills, the idea of undertaking research may seem repulsive. If he is a teacher, he frequently finds it difficult to justify the rationale of the researcher's carefully organized approach as the method which will help him receive practical answers to his problems. Yet the increasing demand on the part of state departments of education for a minimum of a master's degree as the requisite for permanent certification has resulted in a phenomenal

---

[2]Jacques Barzun and Henry F. Graff, *The Modern Researcher* (New York: Harcourt, Brace and World, Inc., 1962), p. 88.

growth in graduate programs of music education all over the nation. While some master's degree programs are organized so the student automatically substitutes extra course work in lieu of a written project, there are others where some type of creative endeavor (composition, arrangement, thesis, recital, or field project) is mandated as partial fulfillment of degree requirements. The option of either extra course work or a project exists in some master's degree curricula, a discretionary arrangement which has some advantages. The experience of this writer in advising students at both the master's and doctoral levels, however, suggests that graduate schools should consider very strongly the feasibility of making some type of culminating written requirement mandatory for all master's matriculants. Not only can the intellectual acuity to organize and implement a research proposal be most beneficial to the student, but he will also have had some practical research experience should he eventually pursue a doctorate.

The demand for an academic standing above the baccalaureate degree began in the 1920's. Until the advent of World War II the master's degree generally was considered to be adequate for music teachers, even on the college or university level. In the past twenty years, however, the pressure by administrators on music teachers at the college and university level has caused a rethinking of graduate music education with the result that many beginning post-baccalaureate students now anticipate that a master's degree may only be a transitory step to a terminal degree. An aspirant for a teaching position at the college or university level now can hardly hope to rise above the rank of assistant professor without an earned doctorate except in a few isolated situations. A by-product of this coercion has been the demand for doctorates with different emphases than the traditional Ph.D. and Ed.D. have presented. The D.M.A. (Doctor of Musical Arts) and the Mus.D. (Doctor of Music) may now be earned at several colleges and universities in the United States. These degrees are often reserved for individuals who desire a doctorate in performance or composition, whereas the Ph.D. and the Ed.D. still are largely utilized for areas in music and music education.

Since all earned doctorates at present are based upon the acceptance of some type of "creative" project, students in music education as well as other disciplines find themselves faced with the reality of engaging in research. Selection of an acceptable topic for research many times becomes an unnecessarily long and tedious process which might be considerably shortened if the student initially were to use reflective thinking to help him locate and develop a subject which will be meaningful and interesting to him. The necessity for a researcher to be able to do his own thinking is emphasized by Koefod, who also observes that an excellent research report is the hallmark of this kind of investigator.[3]

SELECTION OF A TOPIC

Fortunately many students give considerable thought to potential projects prior to enrollment in a graduate program. Others, regretfully, depend on expediency, mandate, or suggestions from an adviser, or some other extrinsic factor in the choice of a topic. Such ambivalence can hardly result in anything more than inferior productivity. The researcher should choose a topic for investigation in which he not only has an intense interest but also can lay claim as being "his own." It is inconceivable that any individual can involve himself effectively in a research topic in which he is neither totally engrossed nor in general agreement with philosophically. School administrators generally recognize that personnel perform most efficiently in the areas where they are most competent and interested. In the interest of educational efficiency, good administrative practice dictates that such predilections be honored whenever possible through appropriate assignments. Why should the conduct of research operate under a different concept? As if in reply, Kelley notes that the conduct of worthwhile research is not easy and he also deplores those who dismiss its importance too lightly.[4] Although the selection of an appropriate topic is very significant for the researcher, no further attention will be given to it here because it will be treated more comprehensively in the next chapter.

While most of the research in music education is conducted by graduate students for pragmatical purposes, a gratifying trend is evident in the ever-increasing number of postdoctoral research titles which are appearing. Many of these projects are supported by governmental or philanthropic agencies. They are subsidized, moreover, only after a very careful review of the research procedures proposed. It would be ridiculous, of course, to imply that a person who has become skilled in research techniques during the period of his graduate instruction is thus better equipped than his counterpart without this experience and automatically will have any plan he submits accepted. Still the experience he has received in developing and pursuing a graduate project successfully ought to make it easier to prepare an acceptable proposal for funding. On the other hand it would not be accurate to infer that all research plans which are rejected for funding are deficient in organization. Many

---

[3]Paul E. Koefod, *The Writing Requirements for Graduate Degrees* (Englewood Cliffs, N. J.: Prentice-Hall, Inc., 1964), p. 11.

[4]Kelley, *op. cit.,* p. 3.

excellent proposals cannot be subsidized because of limited funds available. On an encouraging note, it will be observed in Chapter 12 that music education is well represented by federally-supported research which either has been completed or is in progress.

The quality of research in music education, like that of education in general, has been open to question in many quarters. Unfortunately some of this criticism has been justifiable. Frequently a research study consists of a rather superficial treatment of some insignificant topic which the busy music educator who normally has little time to read an extended account of research anyway may not even find pertinent to him. Actually there is a virtual myriad of significant problems which need to be solved in music education. Might it not be more useful to concentrate first on those which are of immediate concern and practical value to the profession? When realistic solutions have been found to these then some attention may be given to those areas which are of less import to music educators. Realistically it must be admitted that some of the most crucial areas do not lend themselves readily to easy and quick solutions. Time of a researcher and his financial subsidization both are frequently limited. Since times change, as indicated earlier, some solutions may neither be found nor needed for certain perplexities. Rhetorically it might be queried why engage in research if it will not be beneficial or if the results will be inconclusive? Significant research rarely results when answers to problems are obtained expeditiously. In addition, such findings may even be erroneous or impractical, notes Borg.[5]

One of the factors which has affected both the quality and kind of research conducted in music education is the dichotomy to which this writer called attention in 1960.[6] On the one hand there are those educators who feel that music is a practice or skill and as such does not lend itself readily to research techniques. This group is opposed by those who recognize that music can and does properly adapt itself to the recognized criteria for research but who feel that it has not been conducted in as much depth as desirable. The recent encouraging increase in research projects being undertaken by musicians and music educators suggests that at last the climate for research activity may be changing. Even a casual glance at titles of some of the research currently in progress will substantiate this optimistic observation. Noting the apathy and indifference to which reference has just been made, Glenn

---

[5]Walter R. Borg, *Educational Research: An Introduction* (New York: David McKay Co., Inc., 1963), p. 2.

[6]Roger P. Phelps, "Research in Music and Music Education," *Music Educators Journal*, XLV (June-July, 1960), 51-53.

poignantly states: "Music school faculty members have little sympathy with a topic that has educational implications. Professional education and psychology might consider us ignorant when it comes to designing an experimental study. There is no easy answer to this dilemma. It seems to me that the answer will be found when all parties concerned study very carefully the purposes for a graduate program in music education."[7] Perhaps the solution lies in a more careful structuring of research projects in music education with a subsequent meticulous implementation of the research plan to bring about valid and objective results which, when disseminated, will be meaningful and practical to members of the profession.

CATEGORIES OF MUSIC EDUCATION RESEARCH

Most research studies in music education basically fall under one of the following categories: historical, experimental, descriptive, philosophical, or analytical. A purview of any standard textbook in educational research likely will include a discussion of the first three types. Philosophical will be contained in a few, but many educational researchers either deny its existence as a separate kind of research or suggest that its use in education is so extremely limited as to be hardly worth serious consideration. Yet in music education philosophical research can be a very fruitful area for investigation. The last type, analytical, is a designation which is being used in this textbook to include a rather sizable group of studies which are undertaken by music students. Analytical research usually is concerned with the study and analysis of certain compositions of a composer, including his role in the mainstream of music history. It may be regarded quite properly as quasi-musicological in scope. Many possibilities exist in this type of research for the music educator who has a good theoretical and musicological background.

Since the techniques, procedures, and characteristics of each of these kinds of research as they are relevant to music education will be presented in detail in subsequent chapters, attention only will be called to them here. Any one study, of course, may incorporate some aspects of the other types, but its emphasis basically will be centered in one of the areas just listed. The organization of a study largely determines the format under which the research will be conducted. In view of this it may be expected that a historical study will emphasize the design for a historical study, the descriptive study the aspects of that kind of

---

[7]Neal E. Glenn, "Current Issues in Graduate Music Education," *Music Educators Journal*, XLIX (April-May, 1963), 39. Used by permission of the *Music Educators Journal*.

project, and so on. A fetish should not be made of the labels associated with a given research study, however, because the essential factor is the *information included in the study*. Categorization, on the other hand, is helpful in determining procedures which will be or have been followed in a research study.

Just as most research studies are not constituted exclusively in one area at the expense of the others, so by analogy no person is completely an introvert or an extrovert. His personality traits label him as being predominantly inclined in one direction or the other. To cite another example, a musical tone which an observer identifies as "A" may have a frequency of 220 cycles per second. When the sound is analyzed by an oscilloscope it may be found also to possess minor amounts of energy present for E (660 cycles per second) or C♯ (1100 cycles per second), yet the listener perceives only the note A because it is the dominant sound. Likewise, an experimental study could include both historical and philosophical concepts, yet basically be regarded as an experimental project because it is organized and implemented as an experimental study. Regardless of the kind of organization, the research must meet certain rigid criteria if it is to be sound. Many of these are totally dependent on the attitude of the researcher, not on the organization, *per se*, because even the best organized research plan is virtually meaningless unless it is implemented carefully by an investigator who is acclimatized to research techniques.

THE RESEARCH CLIMATE

If music education research is to gain and maintain the respect of the academic community that it should, mere motivation to receive an advanced degree or a promotion to a higher professorial rank is not enough. The investigator, as noted earlier, usually is the key to the ultimate success or failure of a research project. Is it not logical, then, to expect that the researcher be in the proper frame of mind while planning, executing, and reporting his investigation if it is to be successful? This mental condition can be appropriately called the "research climate" because it implies that the person will involve himself wholeheartedly in the task before him. Certain traits or characteristics are essential and need either to be present or developed if a researcher is to complete his project successfully. Ideally each person should possess the maximum of all of them, but realistically each individual has his own limitations. While by no means exhaustive, the following ten adjectives are indicative of characteristics which need to be possessed by a successful investigator in music education. He should be inquisitive, perceptive, objective, discriminative, impartial, candid, diligent, persistent, creative, and erudite.

The *inquisitive* mind is the first requisite for research. Without a passion on the part of an investigator to uncover or learn new information, research is not possible. Once the desire to seek new information has been met, a *perceptive* mind is necessary to formulate the plan which will be used most effectively for the duration of the research. This format, obviously, should not be immutable, but subject to modification as the need for emendation arises. The individual who lacks a perceptive mind can hardly be expected to pursue research in depth. After the research plan has been established, the investigator needs to obtain his information with an *objective* viewpoint. He must be willing to accept the results of his research even though they may prove to be contrary to what he has believed up to this point. When the point of objectivity has been realized, the researcher should be *discriminative* in determining what material will be useful in the formulation of a written account detailing the results of his research. Discrimination also implies that the investigator ought to be *impartial* and not biased one way or the other in his reporting. He should avoid the tendency to weight his evidence because of some prejudice which he may have. A *candid* accounting, of course, suggests that the investigator must be forthright and frank with his presentation. This means that he accepts and reports accurately all his research findings. If research is to be successful and complete, *diligent* attention to all details is necessary. Diligence alone, unfortunately, is not enough to guarantee good research. A diligent researcher also needs to be *persistent*. Persistence implies that an investigator will carry on his project despite obstacles which may either appear to impede his progress or possibly intimate that he may be obtaining negative information. The skillful researcher also should be *creative*. He must not only organize his project in a manner which shows originality but also execute and disseminate the results in a manner which is refreshing and different. Finally, a researcher ought to be *erudite*. As a result of having reached this final step an investigator should be more knowledgeable than he was prior to the research; however, he will very likely also have accumulated some basic knowledge in the several disciplines that go into the making of an "educated" person, sometimes referred to as "basic general education" or "general cultural education." Music graduates frequently are handicapped in this regard, especially if they have pursued a conservatory approach in their previous education where skills often are emphasized at the expense of general culture. This writer has found, as a result of advising doctoral students for several years, that the "narrow" concept, to which reference has just been made, frequently is a handicap to ultimate success in a doctoral program. Such students, by inclination or training, sometimes do not have the intellectual foundation to successfully organize and execute a doctoral project. When institutions which prepare students at the undergraduate level fail to provide curricula which not only train future musicians professionally but also intellectually, they must share some of the blame when their graduates experience difficulty in completing post-baccalaureate work successfully.

The quintessence of the factors just enumerated is embodied succinctly in these words of Barzun and Graff: "The reason why research is like sculpturing from memory is that in neither is there a concrete subject to copy directly. The subject—as sculptors themselves are fond of saying—is hidden in the block of material."[8]

RESEARCH CONCEPTS

The researcher in music education may expect to encounter certain terms or concepts which relate to the conduct of research. Those which refer only to specific areas or types of research will be discussed in the appropriate chapters in this book. Others, which are common to all types of research, follow. An understanding of these items is important to any researcher who desires to organize his study logically, and presumably everyone does. When matriculated, especially at the doctoral level, a candidate often is required to make a distinction in his program of studies between an emphasis which will enable him to acceptably produce a project of *pure* research as opposed to one which may be called *applied*. The former, sometimes known as "basic" or "fundamental" research, is based on the accurate reporting of results without any attempt to incorporate practical applications of the findings in the study. An individual who reads the report is expected to make whatever use of the data seems appropriate to his own situation. *Pure* research is desirable in almost all fields of endeavor but frequently it is not the type which will produce answers to the questions perplexing music educators daily in the classroom. *Applied,* sometimes called "action" research, is conducted and reported in such a way that the investigator includes practical suggestions for applying data of his study to a teaching situation. In this connection a distinction sometimes is erroneously made by referring to the Ph.D. as a superior "research" degree because of its emphasis on the "basic" concept of research and to the Ed.D. as a somewhat inferior "teaching" degree, in which an investigator is expected to indicate ex-

[8]Barzun and Graff, *op. cit.*, p. 22. Used by permission of Harcourt, Brace and World, Inc.

plicitly how the results of his research may be utilized. To elevate one degree over the other indeed is unfortunate. It must be admitted, however, that in some graduate programs the Ed.D. really is inferior to the Ph.D. due to differences in acceptable minimum standards between them. The unfortunate result then is that not as much is expected academically, musically, or from a research standpoint from the former as from the latter. Both types of degree programs should be predicated on sound research procedures. It is the emphasis which properly ought to be the essential difference between the two, not the academic or intellectual demands on the investigator. A history of eighteenth-century English secular choral music, for instance, most likely would be regarded as pure research, providing the study was conducted according to the concepts of "basic" research. On the other hand, an anthology of eighteenth-century English secular choral music could be classified as "applied," because an anthology, by implication, may consist of compositions which have been collected and edited by an investigator for a specific group, with rehearsal suggestions also incorporated in the study. The anthology quite properly needs to contain a history section, but this factor alone should not be important enough to change the character of the study, since the intent of an investigator in this type of research basically is to present practical suggestions for utilizing this research.

Of the five kinds of research enumerated earlier in this chapter, historical, experimental, and philosophical most characteristically fall under the heading of "pure" research, and descriptive and analytical research might best be described as "applied." It should be noted, however, that any attempt to assign arbitrarily any kind of research to one category or the other is risky at best. The data and the purpose of a research study ought to be the determining factors in regard to whether a given study is classified under one area or the other. Pigeonholing can be very hazardous, but a researcher who, during the process of planning, considers his research with either a "pure" or an "applied" emphasis in mind will find his project easier to organize objectively for implementation.

Qualitative and *quantitative* research refers to degrees of involvement rather than to the extent or depth with which research is conducted. The former merely indicates the presence or absence of certain qualities, attributes, or data, whereas the latter details how much of any one quality, attribute, or datum is present. Travers is among those authorities who point out that qualitative generalizations eventually may lead to pronouncements which are substantiated quantitatively.[9] Ideally every

9Robert M. W. Travers, *An Introduction to Educational Research* (Second Edition; New York: The Macmillan Co., 1964), p. 44.

research study should include both qualitative and quantitative data. On the other hand, while it is possible for a research project to be so organized that it would contain only qualitative data, it would be impossible for a study to contain quantitative but not qualitative data, because specific amounts only can be identified after it has been established that the condition is present in the first place. It is not uncommon to examine research studies in music education which contain qualitative data only and quantitative data have been omitted when every indication was present that they should have been included. Studies of this caliber must be categorized as ineffective and weak research because the investigator did not proceed in a thorough and careful manner to the next significant step of quantifying information. For example, a qualitative study might be undertaken to learn which school systems in a given state have instrumental music programs. This information could be readily obtained by a questionnaire or other means. By itself this collection of data could be useful to a school administrator who does not have an instrumental program in his system, to enable him to report to his Board of Education that such a program is needed if children in the community are to receive the same type of cultural advantages as youngsters in school systems which replied in the affirmative. To the music teacher, by contrast, these data would be relatively useless because they give no indication of the actual content of the instrumental programs surveyed. They merely signify presence or absence of instrumental music in school systems investigated. The music supervisor more likely would be interested in determining *how* his curricular offerings compare with those of the other schools. In other words, he might be interested to learn that a certain school had two orchestras, two bands, or two choruses in the senior high school, when these designations are specified, and thus try to convince his superiors that this pattern should be emulated in that school system. Since music is largely concerned with skills, still unanswered is the question of performing competency of the groups under consideration. This problem also would be quantitative and answers obtained would be dependent on the utilization of a specialized type of measurement in conjunction with the questionnaire. Such an investigation would be proper under certain conditions. The investigator, in this instance, would need to establish criteria for comparison in order to ascertain how well the groups performed. A researcher who organizes his project so quantitative data may be obtained is in a better position initially to produce a significant research study than is one who merely scratches the surface by only seeking qualitative information. Music education has suffered too long from an abundance of studies which largely contain only qualitative data, with the attendant poor regard generally for research in the field. Research in music education should be structured so that not only qualitative but also quantitative data may be obtained whenever possible.

THE SCIENTIFIC METHOD

Although the precepts of the scientific method were initiated and originally utilized by researchers in the natural sciences, the principles now have been applied to almost all disciplines of research. Unfortunately there is confusion at times on the part of music educators who feel that the scientific method should be used only with certain types of research. This misconception evidently is due to a misunderstanding of what the scientific method connotes. Each of the five types of research enumerated earlier in this chapter ought to be based on an application of the scientific method with the understanding, of course, that because of differences in techniques of the various types, some modifications will be necessary.

Stated in its simplest terms, any investigation which is logically organized, objectively implemented, and precisely interpreted may be said to meet the conditions of the scientific method. Almack succinctly defines the scientific method as *"the expert pursuit of knowledge."*[10] A more complex definition, which is more acceptable to behavioral scientists, is given by Kerlinger: *"scientific research is systematic, controlled, empirical, and critical investigation of hypothetical propositions about the presumed relations among natural phenomena."*[11] This explanation includes the concept of natural assumptions which long have served as the basis for scientific research. Since these assumptions generally were accepted without question, they were regarded as the logical point of departure for scientific research, because there was no need to prove the existence of these phenomena.

In both quotations just cited is it not noteworthy that emphasis in the scientific method is placed on *objectivity* rather than on subjectivity? The onus is upon every researcher to organize his study so that objectivity will always be the foremost and ultimate goal. The scientist's basis for objectivity, as just observed, originally stemmed from certain assumptions regarding natural phenomena. The philosopher, as well as the scientist, in describing these "natural phenomena" might regard them as "com-

---

[10]John C. Almack, *Research and Thesis Writing* (Boston: Houghton Mifflin Co., 1930), p. 57. Used by permission of the Houghton Mifflin Co.

[11]Fred N. Kerlinger, *Foundations of Behavioral Research* (New York: Holt, Rinehart and Winston, Inc., 1965), p. 13. Used by permission of Holt, Rinehart and Winston, Inc.

mon sense" assumptions. To give an oversimplified example, the scientist and philosopher assume that the sun will rise and set at certain specified times on any given day in the future because of past experience. They cannot prove, however, that this *will* take place. An assumption can be made only because it has happened in the past. In the design and production of a machine or piece of equipment the manufacturer normally does not *prove* beforehand that the object will respond the way it should if certain conditions relative to its operation are met. He can only *assume* that such will occur in view of previous experience with this product under comparable conditions. Such assumptions are valid and may serve as the focal point of departure for the researcher using the scientific method. He has to accept the validity of these assumptions, comments Van Dalen, if his research is going to be conducted in accordance with the precepts of the scientific method.[12]

Even the music educator who understandably finds the realm of science to be an anathema should find no difficulty in making application of the scientific method. Many researchers in music actually have been utilizing some of these concepts without realizing that they were based on what is designated as the "scientific method." Science and philosophy basically are compatible in regard to the premises on which knowledge is based, even though the techniques for obtaining data often vary between them. Unfortunately, the philosophical aspect of the scientific method has not been used as widely in music education research as it should be. Note these two rather simple illustrations. How many students who write conventional four-part harmony exercises understand the philosophical and acoustical reasoning behind the axiom prohibiting the writing of parallel fifths? The student may write exercises which are technically perfect but is it thus logical to assume that he understands why they sound well without the use of parallel fifths? Again, in the realm of instrumental music, may it be presumed that the bassoonist who is trying to develop a "resonant" tone really understands the scientific ramifications of timbre? His teacher may give him certain practical suggestions for embouchure development which subsequently result in his achieving a significant improvement in tone quality but he still may be unable to analyze why this transformation took place. Now it will be argued by some music educators that the development of practical skills should come first, Then, if there is time and inclination after the perfection of technical skills, philosophical and theoretical concepts are reflectively introduced. Consequently many researchers in the humanities area suddenly find themselves confronted with the necessity

[12]Deobald B. Van Dalen, *Understanding Educational Research* (Enlarged and Revised Edition; New York: McGraw-Hill Book Co., Inc., 1966), pp. 33-34.

of formulating some philosophical bases to assist in the solution of the problem at hand. In the natural and physical sciences, where reflective thinking and an "intellectual" approach normally are an adjunct to instruction, the scientific method is not strangely new to graduate students who initiate a research project. Observing this desirable fusion of skills and theory, Good states that "science without philosophy is blind, while philosophy without science is empty."[13]

The intellectual handicap frequently confronting a graduate student in music education is pinpointed by Robert W. House who wrote these words in a letter to this writer: "The plain fact is that music education is not a research discipline, in the sense that the various natural and social sciences are; music education is essentially a practice. Members of the profession accordingly interest themselves primarily in how to do better what they are doing, and not in any systematic uncovering of facts relating to their task."[14]

The scientific method is not something which should cause trepidity in a researcher in music education; rather it needs to be understood and then utilized. In this day and time when so much emphasis is being placed on research in music education an investigator can ill afford to proceed with a project which is not logically organized, objectively implemented, and precisely interpreted. He may need considerable assistance and guidance to realize these objectives, especially if his undergraduate training has emphasized "skills" at the expense of the "systematic" and "intellectual" approach to learning. A college or university which does not provide the intelligent and perceptive leadership required to give graduate students in music education the kind of information and stimulation they need to pursue a research project objectively to a successful conclusion is derelict in its duty of training tomorrow's leaders in music education. This does not imply, of course, that an adviser should do all the thinking and planning for his advisees, nor does it infer that any graduate student who complies with certain academic requirements automatically will receive his degree. The determining factor simply should be whether or not an individual has been able to produce a piece of research which at least meets the minimum standards prescribed by the institution granting him his degree. He is entitled to competent advice and guidance to reach this goal.

Involvement in research can be a most gratifying and uplifting experience, especially if an understanding and application of the con-

[13]Carter V. Good, *Essentials of Educational Research* (New York: Appleton-Century-Crofts, 1966), p. 19. Used by permission of Appleton-Century-Crofts.

[14]Quoted by Phelps, *op. cit.,* p. 51. Used by permission of the *Music Educators Journal.*

cepts of the scientific method are uppermost in the mind of the researcher. Since the setting for research actually begins with a problem which may need to be clarified or refined before it can be solved, this most momentous and absorbing initial phase of research will be discussed in the next chapter.

QUESTIONS FOR REVIEW AND DISCUSSION

1. What is research? Sound research connotes what steps?
2. Discuss factors which are important in the selection of a research topic.
3. Consider some of the problems which are of immediate concern to you and make some type of preliminary investigation to determine whether or not you will be able to reach a solution to some of them.
4. Why is a proper "research climate" important for music education research? What characteristics are essential for a researcher to possess in order that the conditions of a proper "research climate" be met?
5. What is the difference between pure and applied research? Give synonyms for each of these terms.
6. Differentiate between qualitative and quantitative research.
7. In succinct terms, what does the term "scientific method" imply? Why is the scientific method so important for music education research?

SUPPLEMENTARY READINGS

ALMACK, JOHN C. *Research and Thesis Writing*. Boston: Houghton Mifflin Co., 1930. Chapter III.

BEST, JOHN W. *Research in Education*. Englewood Cliffs, N. J.: Prentice-Hall, Inc., 1959. Chapter 1.

BORG, WALTER R. *Educational Research: An Introduction*. New York: David McKay Co., Inc., 1963. Chapter 1.

CHOATE, ROBERT A. "Research in Music Education," *Journal of Research in Music Education*, XIII (Summer, 1965), 67-86.

COOK, DAVID R. *A Guide to Educational Research*. Boston: Allyn and Bacon, Inc., 1965. Chapter I.

COURTNEY, E. WAYNE (ed.). *Applied Research in Education*. Totowa, N. J.: Littlefield, Adams and Co., 1965. pp. 50-93, 159-161.

GASTON, E. THAYER. "A Symposium on Research: Factors Which Underlie the Development of a Research Program," *Journal of Research in Music Education*, III (Spring, 1955), 21-22.

GLENN, NEAL E. "Current Issues in Graduate Music Education Programs," *Music Educators Journal*, XLIX (April-May, 1963), 37-39, 51-52.

———, and TURRENTINE, EDGAR M. *Introduction to Advanced Study in Music Education*. Dubuque, Iowa: Wm. C. Brown Company Publishers, 1968. pp. 93-95.

GOOD, CARTER V. *Essentials of Educational Research*. New York: Appleton-Century-Crofts, 1966. Chapter 1.

————, and SCATES, DOUGLAS E. *Methods of Research*. New York: Appleton-Century-Crofts, 1954. Chapter 1.

HILLWAY, TYRUS. *Introduction to Research*. Second Edition. Boston: Houghton Mifflin Co., 1964. Chapters 1, 2, 7, and 17.

KERLINGER, FRED N. *Foundations of Behavioral Research*. New York: Holt, Rinehart and Winston, Inc., 1965. Chapter 1.

McGRATH, G. D., JELINEK, JAMES E., and WOCHNER, RAYMOND E. *Educational Research Methods*. New York: The Ronald Press Co., 1963. Chapters 1, 4, and 10.

MORGAN, HAZEL B., and BURMEISTER, CLIFTON A. *Music Research Handbook*. Evanston, Ill.: The Instrumentalist Co., 1962. Chapter I.

MOULY, GEORGE J. *The Science of Educational Research*. New York: American Book Co., 1963. Chapters 4 and 8.

PETZOLD, ROBERT G. "Directions for Research in Music Education," *Bulletin of Council for Research in Music Education*, I (Summer, 1963), 18-23.

PHELPS, ROGER F. [P.] "Current Status of Research in Musical Education," *School Music News*, XXV (April, 1962), 29-30.

————. "Research in Music and Music Education," *Music Educators Journal*, XLVI (June-July, 1960), 51-53.

RUMMEL, J. FRANCIS. *An Introduction to Research Procedures in Education*. Second Edition. New York: Harper and Row, Publishers, 1964. Chapter I.

TRAVERS, ROBERT M. W. *An Introduction to Educational Research*. Second Edition. New York: The Macmillan Co., 1964. Chapter 1.

VAN DALEN, DEOBALD B. *Understanding Educational Research*. Enlarged and Revised Edition. New York: McGraw-Hill Book Co., Inc., 1966. Chapters 1 and 3.

WATANABE, RUTH T. *Introduction to Music Research*. Englewood Cliffs, N. J.: Prentice-Hall, Inc., 1967. Chapter 1.

WHITNEY, FREDERICK L. *The Elements of Research*. Third Edition. Englewood Cliffs, N. J.: Prentice-Hall, Inc., 1950. Chapters I and II.

WISE, JOHN E., NORDBERG, ROBERT B., and REITZ, DONALD J. *Methods of Research in Education*. Boston: D. C. Heath and Co., 1967. Chapter I.

• 2 •

Formulating the Problem

It would be no understatement to assert that the adequate formulation of the problem is unquestionably the most important initial step in research. As noted in the previous chapter, a problem which utilizes the concepts of the scientific method is much easier to translate into a satisfactory solution than one which does not. The most profound as well as the least significant problem may prove to be disconcerting to a music educator, but if a way is found to resolve this dilemma, his teaching will be more effective. The realization that many problems still remain for the researcher in music education has both good and bad aspects. Most impelling, perhaps, is the negative connotation, because it suggests that conditions, however they may be defined, could be better for those concerned if solutions were forthcoming to these problems. On the positive side, a graduate student frequently may become unduly apprehensive and consequently apply himself diligently lest someone else "preempt" his topic and complete the proposed research first. Such misapprehensions usually are needless because, as most research studies will bear out, the same problem could be approached differently by two individuals. In addition, when one problem seems to be solved others appear which were not manifest previously.

Even though research activity in music education seems to have reached an all-time high, and although solutions to many previously disturbing problems have been reached in recent years by an ever-increasing number of investigators, there are other perplexities in which the explanations obtained either have been inconclusive or not very convincing. Perhaps it is one of the ironies of research that frequently indecisive answers result when a researcher fails to give enough careful thought to the organization and formulation of his problem into a workable research design. In the desire to begin collecting research data as soon as possible, investigators have begun the actual research process before comprehending its significance. An unorganized accumulation of data can be the result of this kind of impulsive action. Unfortunately research data by themselves are virtually worthless unless there is a rationale for using and interpreting them. Commenting on the importance of circumspect attention to the problem, Borg relates that the distinction between an outstanding project and one which is unscholarly does not rest on the "amount of work required to carry it out but the amount of thought that the student applies in the selection and definition of his problem."[1]

SOURCES OF INFORMATION

In the formulation of a problem application of the time-worn "who, when, where, what, why, how" concept can be most beneficial to an investigator in organizing a study to obtain valid data. Quite frequently a graduate student, in a sincere and diligent endeavor to ferret out unique information for a research topic, overlooks some of the most obvious sources available to him. Some of the most significant ideas for research projects in music education may come from the following, not necessarily listed in order of importance: (1) textbooks relating to various phases of music; (2) professional and privately printed journals for music educators; (3) lists of graduate theses, dissertations, and projects; (4) reports of subsidized research; (5) graduate seminars and classes; (6) conferences with advisers and professors; (7) discussions with fellow graduate students; (8) difficulties pinpointed in the classroom; (9) speeches and lecture-demonstrations at national, regional, and state meetings of music educators; and (10) visits to libraries, archives, museums, etc.

Textbooks are an unusually good source of potential research topics because quite often a reader may find statements with which he disagrees. Even more important, a perusal of textbooks enables a person to be in a better position to know what has been consummated in his own field and thus be more knowledgeable about what areas remain as fertile fields for research.

---

[1]Walter R. Borg, *Educational Research: An Introduction* (New York: David McKay Co., Inc., 1963), p. 26. Used by permission of David McKay Co., Inc. Inc.

Whereas the concepts and ideas incorporated in a textbook may be outmoded by the time a textbook is actually printed, if an investigator keeps current in his reading, periodicals enable him to keep up-to-date on the latest trends and ideas in his field. Professional organs such as the *Journal of Research in Music Education* and the *Music Educators Journal* are excellent in this regard. In addition there are numerous state journals published by music educators' associations which may be helpful, as well as privately-oriented publications such as *The Instrumentalist, The Music Journal,* and many periodicals in other disciplines which contain articles, book reviews, and other items relating to music education. Some of these, like the *Music Educators Journal,* contain accounts by individuals who report on successful techniques they have used to surmount some of the perplexities with which they have been faced. Others, such as *The Instrumentalist,* often include articles provocative in nature, which usually provide nascent possibilities for research topics.

One of the most effective ways for a student to learn what has been done in the field of music education is to examine lists of theses, dissertations, and projects which are either in progress or have been completed. After scrutinizing these a researcher frequently can observe neglected areas in which he may feel confident to pursue research. On the other hand he may discover that his "red-hot" idea already has been competently investigated by others. This, of course, does not rule out his prerogative to continue research in the same area, but a very careful examination of studies already completed should certainly be given maximum priority so an early determination can be made regarding whether the idea should be implemented or abandoned. Since specific references will be made to bibliographical and other sources in Chapter 4, no further presentation will be given here.

The unprecedented increase in federal, state, and private subsidies for research in music education just in the past five years has opened up a whole new realm of possibilities for investigators, especially at the postgraduate level. Lists of projects are made available at periodic intervals and reference will be made to them in subsequent chapters. Since many of these reports contain suggestions of research needed to follow up the studies which have been completed, they usually are a lucrative source of information for investigators seeking a topic.

Interaction between professors and students in graduate seminars and classes often proves to be an unexpected origin of potential subjects for research. Frequently possibilities of which the student was unaware or had only considered lightly manifest themselves in graduate seminars. This is especially true when emphasis in the class is placed on the type of reflective thinking that can result either in a person's clarifying a topic which he already may have in mind or in compelling him to analytically begin the search for one. It has commonly been said, however, that every person has problems, although he may not always be aware of them. The process of interaction may assist him to delineate some of them. In the classroom the instructor's comments or remarks often point out areas or problems which are in need of diligent attention.

The role of the graduate adviser should be more than that of just affixing a signature to a student's course program card. To take the other extreme, a true "adviser" does not arbitrarily assign a topic to one of his advisees. The student must feel that the subject which he eventually selects and then implements is his own personal property. How can he spontaneously generate a "personal feeling" about something which has been forced upon him? An adviser, when he assumes the role, should express a sense of obligation by making suggestions and assisting each of his advisees in the formulation and development of his research topic. Quite naturally an adviser or professor, because of his experience in the field, may have definite ideas about research that is needed and he should not hesitate to express them. An adviser, however, must be careful lest he mandate rather than propose.

Graduate students not infrequently engage in periods of informal discussion among themselves. Strange as it may seem, these often result in some rather tangible suggestions for research topics. Quite often an especially perceptive individual will pinpoint the need for research in a certain area in which he himself does not feel capable. Another person whose interests and capabilities may lie here perhaps had never regarded this as a possibility, or may have initially rejected it as being impractical. As a result of discussions with some of his peers he may redirect his thinking to a previously discarded subject.

On the surface it would appear as though a cataloging of problems encountered in teaching might seem to be a profitable source of research subjects. A more careful study of the prospective topics, however, will very likely reveal that many of them indeed are in need of study, but the practicability of defining them clearly so they can be studied in an objective manner tends to exclude many. Nevertheless, the dilemmas confronting one serve as a natural point of departure for the identification of potential research topics.

Remarks made by speakers, either informally or in prepared lectures and demonstrations, sometimes constitute the origin of research topics. This is especially true if points of disagreement are manifest, because they can serve as nascent possibilities for research. The graduate music education student who is seeking a topic and wants to keep his "ear to the ground" would do well to attend meetings of professional associations such as the Music Educators National Conference and the Music Teachers National Association and their affiliated and associated organizations. Although he normally would expect to find as the most productive of ideas for research the meetings in which he is primarily interested, he should not overlook the possibility also of obtaining stimulation in an area which ostensibly has little interest to him.

Visits to libraries, archives, and museums can be especially beneficial providing a researcher is interested in more than just becoming familiar with the holdings. An examination of the writings and effects of an individual, for example, could reveal the need for studies in depth about that person. A musician could approach the matter from the standpoint of the contributions this individual has made to music, especially as his claim to fame rests other than in music. For instance, the involvement in and contributions to music of Benjamin Franklin (1706-1790) or Thomas Jefferson (1743-1826) might prove to be intriguing to some investigator after examining personal effects and writings of these esteemed patriots at the Free Library of Philadelphia and at Monticello, Virginia, respectively.

The eager, dedicated, and inquisitive person should experience little difficulty in finding a subject for research in music of particular interest to him. The list of possibilities is virtually legion, and a constantly changing society and new methods and resources are continually opening up other possibilities.

REFLECTIVE THINKING

Correct formulation of a problem into a pliable and workable format necessitates reflective thinking on the part of an investigator. As indicated earlier, this initial phase of research unquestionably is one of the most important, yet it frequently is treated in an insipid manner. Several educational researchers, including Travers, aver that the ultimate success of a research project is often related to the manner in which the problem is formulated.[2]

Concepts of reflective thinking may be traced as far back as the deductive method used by Aristotle (384-322 B.C.) and other early Greek thinkers. Deduction is reasoning from the general to the specific (or particular). This type of reasoning marked one of man's earliest attempts to think through problems. As an example of deduction, note the music teacher who is in the process of buying a box of clarinet reeds. Upon

---

[2]Robert M. W. Travers, *An Introduction to Educational Research* (Second Edition; New York: The Macmillan Co., 1964), p. 75.

examination of three or four, which he finds to be entirely satisfactory, he concludes that the entire box is of equivalent quality, hence purchases all of them. For centuries this type of reasoning was virtually the only one used to obtain knowledge. Syllogism is an example of this deductive Greek concept of problem solving. In syllogism the formula of an argument consists of three propositions. The first two, known as major and minor premises, have one aspect in common, which furnishes a logical connection between these two premises and the third proposition, known as the conclusion. An example of syllogism follows:

Major premise: all musicians are talented
Minor premise: conductors are musicians
Conclusion: conductors are talented.

Such a system of logic assumes, of course, that the major premise is true. In this type of reasoning no attempt is made either to prove or disprove the major assumption. This method of reasoning served as the basis for the scientific method which, as was noted in the previous chapter, was originally developed by researchers in the natural sciences.

Many classic anecdotes exist which indicate that those who dared to utilize a concept of logic different from this deductive method were reprimanded severely even as late as the seventeenth century. For example, the announcement by Galileo (1564-1642) that, while searching the heavens with his new telescope, he had discovered four moons revolving around Jupiter was received skeptically by many of his peers. One fellow professor even stated that since Aristotle had not mentioned these moons, they could not possibly exist. Others declared that since they were not visible to the naked eye they did not exist at all. Such was the stranglehold which the Greek system of Aristotelian logic had on scholars up to the time of Francis Bacon (1561-1626), who disagreed with the prevailing concept of blindly accepting deductive theories merely because they were being passed on as truth by the authorities.

This uncertainty of whether or not a generalization was true led Bacon to develop the type of thinking known as induction, which is reasoning from the specific (or particular) to the general. It was assumed that reasoning which was based on specific items would result in more valid generalizations. On the basis of these specifics, generalizations could then be made about similar or related but unobserved facts or events. This type of reasoning occasionally is used by music teachers. For instance, a band director may come to the conclusion that his group will perform badly as the consequence of noting several specific deficiencies. First, it may be evident that the oboists do not have their reeds completely inserted in the casing, which will result in intonation which is consistently flat. He then observes that some of the French horns obviously are using the E♭ slide when the music is written for F horn. The percussion section may then be found to have the wrong music in front of them. The example is absurd, of course, but it illustrates that a music teacher can use inductive reasoning to reach the generalization that an unsatisfactory sound will result if his musicians were to perform under the conditions just described, even though he has not heard them play one note of music yet.

More recently research has been predicated on a combination of the two concepts and commonly referred to as the "deductive-inductive" process. Charles R. Darwin (1809-1882) is generally acclaimed as the individual who first successfully combined the ideas of Aristotelian deduction with those of Baconian induction. According to Best, Darwin, in stating his theory of origin of the species, formulated through deductive-inductive procedures, a process which now serves as the basis of the scientific method.[3] To illustrate this concept simply, when a music teacher hears his beginning string class is performing badly he analyzes the performance of each student, observing deficiencies and correcting them when necessary. As a result of his diagnosis of each student's performance, he may then prognosticate what will result if changes are effected. As if to clinch the idea of the deductive-inductive process, Cook relates that any type of investigation organized to uncover new knowledge must "follow these twin lines of reasoning, from the general to the particular and back to the general again."[4] Through application of this deductive-inductive process an investigator is in a much more favorable position to adequately formulate and then pursue his topic than he would be without it. This concept of logic makes it relatively easy to organize research reflectively.

The large number of textbooks on research methodology which use as the basis for reflective thinking the five steps originally proposed by John Dewey (1859-1952) signifies the high regard with which research leaders in virtually all areas of education generally hold this distinguished educational philosopher. Dewey's five steps, as paraphrased, are: (1) recognition of need, (2) isolation of the problem, (3) postulation of solution, (4) accumulation and codification of data, and (5) confirmation and experimental substantiation of hypothesis.[5] To these original five, other educational philosophers, such as Kelley, have added another

---

[3]John W. Best, *Research in Education* (Englewood Cliffs, N. J.: Prentice-Hall, Inc., 1959), p. 3.

[4]David R. Cook, *A Guide to Educational Research* (Boston: Allyn and Bacon, Inc., 1965), pp. 3-4. Used by permission of Allyn and Bacon, Inc.

[5]John Dewey, *How We Think* (Boston: D. C. Heath and Co., 1933), p. 107.

—appraisal of the solution in light of future needs.[6] Not only do these six precepts form the *ipso facto* basis for the delineation of a problem, but they may also be employed for implementation of the research. In view of the current emphasis on distributing research findings to the public, the resolution and completion of the research suggests an additional step, dissemination of the data, which might be proposed as a seventh step. Attention was called in the previous chapter to this serious deficiency in much of the research which has been completed in music education. Many excellent reports at present are of no value to those who may be looking unsuccessfully for the specific solutions contained in these research studies because the investigator has been either unable or unwilling to share his results with others. Research which is worthy of the name certainly ought to be worth disseminating. Even research of a superficial nature has value for potential researchers because they not only may be able to avoid the mistakes made by their predecessors but also may be in a better position to determine areas which need more intensive investigation. These seven steps, in essence, form the basis for the formulation, implementation, and promulgation of a research topic and appropriately may constitute a "method" for research.

VULNERABILITY OF MUSIC EDUCATION RESEARCH

Music education research has been especially vulnerable to attacks not only from leaders in other disciplines but also from members of the profession. In many instances the claims have been justified; in others, not so. Music basically is a skill and this, no doubt, makes it difficult for a researcher to state in objective terms what actually transpires while the skill is being performed. In addition, as already noted, skills frequently do not lend themselves as well to philosophizing or reflective thinking as do the natural or behavioral sciences. How can one, to cite an obvious example, objectively measure the effectiveness of a teacher of violin in a private studio as against his performance in a classroom with a group of violinists? To be sure, certain subjective judgments can be made, based on an evaluation of the performance of his students, but this is an indirect type of measurement for a researcher who might have as his topic "A Study to Compare the Effectiveness of a Violin Teacher in Private Studio Teaching as Contrasted to Classroom Violin Teaching." This indirect measurement results in a determination of pupil performance rather than the direct evaluation of the effectiveness of the teacher himself. It may be argued, however, that pupil performance to some

---

[6]Truman Lee Kelley, *Scientific Method* (New York: The Macmillan Co., 1932), p. 24.

extent is governed by teacher effectiveness and this is valid reasoning. The distinction, then, between the subjective measurement of teacher skill and the objective measurement of pupil performance is a rather tenuous one. Is the latter a result of the former or in spite of it? Several studies similar to this suggested topic have been undertaken by researchers in music education and other areas, often with the presentation of results that are not too convincing.

Realizing that research in music education generally had been suffering from what properly might be termed a "research malnutrition syndrome," a committee on Graduate Studies in Music Education was appointed a few years ago by the Music Educators National Conference to evaluate research studies in music education which had appeared up to that time. The incisive and candid report prepared by this committee still represents the most complete of its kind to appear up to the time of this writing. One or more of the ten deficiencies noted then are still evident in projects which are being submitted "in partial fulfillment" of degree requirements. In paraphrased version these shortcomings are: (1) a topic which is relatively insignificant; (2) the tabulation of a large amount of miscellaneous data without the conscientious and serious projection of logical conclusions; (3) a project which requires little or no background in music and conceivably could have been completed by a musically illiterate scholar; (4) a study containing errors which might have been eliminated by recourse to original source material; (5) presentation of erroneous conclusions because the investigator did not adequately prepare, collect, and analyze data; (6) obvious shortcomings in musical taste and understanding; (7) an inability of the investigator to express himself concisely and clearly; (8) a failure to reveal intellectual curiosity which suggests a greater concern in meeting formal course requirements than in becoming involved reflectively in the quest for knowledge; (9) a lack of understanding regarding the practical problems and potentialities of music education; and (10) noteworthy indications of inadequate preparation and understanding of proper research techniques.[7]

Although some studies are still being undertaken which seemingly are not significant, a heartening increase has been observed in research which is not only organized and conducted well but also is focused on a subject which could have considerable import for the profession. Topics such as "A Study to Compare the Effectiveness of the Dry Lip as Opposed to the Wet Lip Approach to Trumpet Playing" are being replaced by those with titles such as "A Study to Determine the Effec-

---

[7]"Graduate Study in Music Education," *Journal of Research in Music Education,* II (Fall, 1954), 168.

tiveness of Teaching Beginning Trumpet Students with a Teaching Machine." Each one has its merits, no doubt, but the former is concerned with a concept which is highly subjective and does not even arouse much curiosity among brass players today, whereas the latter is related to an idea that is receiving increasing attention on the part of music educators, partially because this device offers certain objectivity in the evaluation of teaching procedures.

The tabulation of large amounts of miscellaneous data without appropriate interpretations and projection of logical conclusions still appears to be an area which needs considerable attention. Weaknesses of this kind frequently can be diminished by correctly formulating and implementing hypotheses which are logical. Interpretation of these data also requires a researcher who possesses a perceptive and creative mind.

Research which requires little or no background in music fortunately does not seem to be as prevalent in music education today as it formerly was. It would appear that those charged with the responsibility of advising graduate students in music are not only competent musically but also, equally important, have an understanding of research techniques and procedures. Individuals from other disciplines who are interested in pursuing a study in the area of music evidently are either being discouraged if they do not have an adequate musical background, or are being required to strengthen their knowledge of music before proceeding with their research.

Studies containing errors due to the failure of the investigator to ferret out original source material still seem to be more abundant than they should be. In the pressure incumbent with receiving a degree as expeditiously as possible such is to be expected. It is unfortunate that a graduate student must be more often concerned with meeting certain deadlines than with the quality of research which he describes. As larger amounts of financial support become available, it is to be hoped that the direct result will be research of a better quality. With some type of subsidy, a student may be in a position to be less concerned with financial pressures which frequently necessitate the completion of a project within a specified time limit, and be more preoccupied with production and dissemination of quality research.

Closely related to the previous research deficiency is the proffering of erroneous conclusions because the researcher did not adequately prepare, collect, and analyze data. Many studies still evidence serious weaknesses in this area. Unfortunately, it is easy to rationalize that this inadequacy also is largely due to the pressure incumbent on an individual to receive his degree as quickly as possible. In several of the studies in music education which display shortcomings in this area the explanation lies elsewhere. Sometimes the fault appears to be with a candidate's sponsoring committee, but more often it is the result of his own intellectual shortcomings. A project which is organized according to the scientific method and implemented accordingly should rarely exhibit the weaknesses just mentioned. In this connection Van Dalen appropriately remarks that proper organization of a research proposal is really the most significant step in research, and implementation is "largely a mechanical process which requires more persistence than profundity."[8]

Studies in which shortcomings in musical taste and understanding are evident fortunately do not seem to be as prevalent as they once were. In common with the third deficiency, which was discussed above, it appears that students with inadequate background who may have proposed to engage in some type of nebulous research bearing a general relationship to music are either being encouraged to pursue their topics in greater depth or are being urged to abandon them entirely.

The inability of an investigator to express himself concisely and clearly still seems to be a perpetual problem for many music education students. It is a syndrome for which satisfactory answers may never be found. Presumably a graduate student, prior to his matriculation for an advanced degree, already has had adequate courses which prepare him to express himself in an intelligent manner through writing. Many colleges and universities, however, do find it necessary to offer special courses in remedial writing for graduate students who have obvious deficiencies in this regard. A question should be raised at this point as to whether a remedial course of one or two semesters can enable a student to overcome a deficiency that evidently has persisted at least since high school. It is rather difficult to imagine that a one or two semester remedial course in music theory, for instance, can enable a student to amply compensate for a minimum of two to three years of college or university theory instruction which he either has not had or which was taught so ineffectively that it was meaningless. Some serious reservations exist about the advisability of permitting a student who is unable to express himself adequately in the English language to matriculate for a graduate degree. Might not this serious deficiency also be a syndrome of other indications of inadequate preparation which would make the successful completion of graduate study extremely improbable?

The failure to reveal intellectual curiosity is a weakness of most serious consequence, and one which still prevails in many graduate music research projects more than it should. It seems rather apparent

---

[8]Deobald B. Van Dalen, *Understanding Educational Research* (Enlarged and Revised Edition; New York: McGraw-Hill Book Co., Inc., 1966), p. 120. Used by permission of the McGraw-Hill Book Co., Inc.

that there is a definite relationship between this defect and some of the others previously discussed, notably the second, fifth, sixth, and seventh. It is a matter of record that in most states it is now mandatory for a teacher in the public schools to earn a master's degree or its equivalent in order to qualify for permanent certification and subsequent advances in salary schedule. Whether or not this "pressure" has resulted in a lowering of graduate standards is a debatable question which is beyond the scope of this book. It is an issue, however, which cannot be resolved by subterfuge. A thorough, objective, and impartial reappraisal of the entire graduate program in music education, especially at the master's level, is implicit. One can only wonder how realistic a grading system is in graduate schools which recognize only "A" and "B" as passing grades. Does an "average" student suddenly become "good" or "excellent" when he reaches graduate school? It frequently is contended by proponents of this system that "average" students on the undergraduate level are not admitted to graduate study, so therefore only those who are "good" or "excellent" remain. Unfortunately, this concept is not shared by all graduate schools, many of which admit a student according to other criteria, even when a student does not possess the requisite "B" average for admission. It seems rather likely that there will be more rather than less relaxing of the prerequisite "B" requirement for graduate admission in the future coupled with increased emphasis on other factors which may be more truly indicative of a student's probable success in graduate study. It is possible that some of these factors, such as a natural curiosity or motivation, which may not always be apparent in a student's grades, can be utilized to advantage in determining the admissibility of a student to graduate study. This individual may become so engrossed in his subject that he will experience less difficulty in pursuing his research to a logical and successful conclusion than will another who does not have this motivation. The performance of veterans who enter college or university with previous unspectacular records is a case in point.

Some students enroll in graduate music education programs for expediency who have neither the background nor understanding of the discipline. Prospective doctoral candidates often remark candidly that it is "easier to get a doctoral degree in music education than in other areas of music." If this indictment be true, it is time for a review of doctoral programs in music education to determine areas which need strengthening. With the increased demand for teachers to meet the needs of an exploding population has come a large increase in the number of students who enter graduate study in music education with an undergraduate liberal arts background. Many of these individuals have not had general and specific methodology courses, psychological principles of education, some skill in several performing areas of music, and student teaching. To engender an understanding of the philosophies, principles, and problems of music education is not easily accomplished in two or three semesters of graduate instruction. Is it then not reasonable to assume that the person who has taught in the public schools is in a much better position to cope with practical problems and potentialities in the field when he enrolls in a graduate program of music education than is one who is devoid of such experience?

Fortunately, the increase in graduate courses in music education has been accompanied by a corresponding acceptance of the responsibility on the part of institutions awarding advanced degrees to offer courses which devote some attention to an understanding and application of research techniques. This factor, perhaps more than any other, has resulted in a gradual increase not only in quantity but also, even more important, in quality of research studies in music education. There seems to be an unanimous agreement among researchers that good research usually does not just happen, as already noted. Addressing themselves to this point Barzun and Graff affirm that: "reading, writing, *and thinking* are the three activities of research."[9]

INITIAL CONSIDERATIONS IN THE SELECTION OF A RESEARCH PROBLEM

Most textbooks on research methodology contain detailed and helpful suggestions of a general nature pertaining to the selection of a problem. One of the most concise accounts, moreover, is that by Chambers in the journal of a professional education fraternity for men.[10] Some of the most important considerations listed therein are concerned with the cordial relationships which should exist between the student and his advisers as the former seeks to formulate a problem for research. The proposals of Chambers, in paraphrased version, indicate that the potential researcher should: (1) avoid asking his adviser for an "assigned" topic, but rather seek one which is in accord with his own interests and initiative; (2) select a subject which is in harmony with his interests and background instead of one which is suited to the "predilections" of his adviser; (3) manifest erudition by not expecting his adviser to serve as an "intellectual nursemaid"; (4) define his prob-

[9]Jacques Barzun and Henry F. Graff, *The Modern Researcher* (New York: Harcourt, Brace and World, Inc., 1962), p. 21. Used by permission of Harcourt, Brace and World, Inc.

[10]M. M. Chambers, "Selection, Definition, and Delimitation of a Doctoral Research Problem," *Phi Delta Kappan,* XLII (November, 1960), 71-73.

lem clearly; (5) become familiar with literature in his field to serve as a basis for ascertaining what has or has not been done; (6) determine what methods, techniques, equipment, or instruments will be needed; and (7) find out whether field trips or visits to museums, libraries, private archives, and other repositories of information are necessary. After continuing with suggestions for student adviser conferences and for writing up the study, Chambers concludes by stating: "Research is not necessarily as complex, difficult, mysterious, or esoteric as a pedantic attitude can make it seem. In common with all things that are really great, it is essentially simple in concept. It has been comprehensively and simply defined in eight words as 'the orderly treatment of data to answer questions.' "[11]

In elaborating on these points, it should be noted that a topic which is "assigned" by an adviser has validity for the investigator *only if he is interested in the subject and can involve himself wholeheartedly in it.* By analogy, there are too many exercises in theory which result in a mediocre or mechanical sound because the person writing them has not been given the freedom to express himself in a manner which is meaningful and significant to him. This, obviously, is not to imply that all principles and rules should be abrogated. They certainly are needed as guidelines, but a student needs to be encouraged to express himself in a manner which is in accord with his own initiative and concepts of creativity. All too prevalent are research projects in a "series," usually at the master's level, which unfortunately are "assigned" by an adviser to certain of his students. A group of studies of this type might center around a general title such as a survey of elementary private method instruction books for specific instruments, with materials being examined and compared for each instrument of the band and orchestra. No doubt such projects, if well organized and implemented, can be very beneficial to students in instrumental techniques classes who are unfamiliar with these publications. It is in this spirit, no doubt, that advisers make such assignments. A less optimistic viewpoint is taken by Koefod, who reports: "Too many students do nothing but plead for assignment of projects by faculty supervisors, apparently having been somehow conditioned by the 'system' to do this."[12] Whether the "assignment" is solicited or whether it is involuntary, the results will usually be the same unless a student is interested and completely dedicated to the subject. The process of reflective thinking discussed earlier in this chapter will be most effective when the choice of a topic is the result of a student's

---

[11]*Ibid.*, p. 73. Used by permission of Phi Delta Kappa, Inc.
[12] Paul E. Koefod, *The Writing Requirements for Graduate Degrees*, p. 74. © 1964, Prentice-Hall, Inc., Englewood Cliffs, N. J.

initiative, since this decision undoubtedly will be one of the most important he will make in his educational career, and thus should be predicated on something in which he is intensely interested.

Chambers' reference to an adviser's serving as an "intellectual nurse-maid" is both amusing and tragic. The implication is that a student will merely put the "flesh" on a "skeleton" which may be constructed by his adviser. An adviser cannot do a student's reflective thinking for him any more than he would be expected to take his examinations. He should serve in a capacity which suggests a literal meaning of his title; namely, one who "advises" or "guides." In this role he is expected to direct attention to erroneous concepts of thinking and organization of materials. His suggestions should be practical, relevant, and within the framework of the research proposal, providing it is sound. His remarks ought to be regarded as suggestions, not mandates, with full responsibility for accepting or rejecting them resting with the investigator, upon whom the onus also eventually falls for defending his research.

Clearly stating the problem has been discussed earlier in this chapter and needs no additional elaboration here other than to again reiterate its importance.

It is incumbent on the researcher, as already indicated, to familiarize himself with the literature in his field. Many advisers continue to be distressed by an inordinately large number of students who come to them for advice regarding a "red-hot" idea before they obviously have examined the literature to determine whether or not the proposal is feasible. Many projected subjects would soon be eliminated by application of this procedure and the student would then be free to devote his energies, and those of his adviser, to something which is within the realm of possibility. It is, of course, always possible that two individuals, in good conscience, may be proceeding with the same topic unbeknown to one another. Although the likelihood of this happening is rare, Good and Scates give an account of two research studies in music education on the same national organization although they were not done at the same time. The projects were completed in different sections of the country even though the institutions were only 300 miles apart, but the initial study, which was finished five years before the second, could easily have been located by the second investigator in *Doctoral Dissertations Accepted by American Universities*.[13]

With the assistance of his adviser, an investigator, after his topic has been tentatively accepted, should carefully consider and make a projection of the methods, techniques, equipment, and instruments he will use to bring his study to successful fruition. This might involve the

---

[13]Carter V. Good and Douglas E. Scates, *Methods of Research* (New York: Appleton-Century-Crofts, 1954), p. 51.

use of certain standardized tests, instruments of the investigator's own devising, questionnaires, and special equipment such as teaching machines or computers, and other devices. Need for these items, in turn, will be determined partially by the methods or techniques chosen by the researcher. Normally an investigation based on the experimental method, for example, would not utilize the questionnaire technique, whereas one based on a descriptive study would rarely use the concept of the single variable, which will be discussed in a later chapter.

An investigator involved with a historical, and frequently a philosophical or analytical study, will need information which may be obtained from various repositories of information (libraries, museums, archives, historical societies, private collections, etc.). Since this will be treated in greater detail in Chapter 5, mention only will be made here in passing. The researcher obviously will need to know where specific items which he is seeking are located. If visits are involved they must be planned according to such considerations as an investigator's financial resources, time available, and hours when visitation is possible. Frequently it is next to impossible to conduct systematic and exhaustive historical research without this kind of scrutiny. Field studies, in the form of visits to other schools or colleges and universities, often are necessary for an individual involved in a descriptive study when comparisons are being made between curricular offerings or programs of music education. To determine why a string program may be successful in one school system but not in others can hardly be done properly by means of a questionnaire only. Interviews, personal visitation, and a questionnaire might be needed to garner enough information to make valid statements when comparing schools. Reference will be made to these techniques in the chapter on descriptive research.

STEPS IN THE FORMULATION OF A RESEARCH PROBLEM

An investigator who has a general subject in mind must proceed through several steps before he reaches a point where he has defined a research topic which is not only practical but also capable of being implemented to a successful conclusion. Numerous excellent suggestions are offered in almost every textbook relating to educational research. For instance, Rummel states that: "personal interest, personal capabilities, value of the topic, and availability of data" are the important principles to consider in the formulation of a research problem.[14] Slightly different precepts are indicated by Almack, including what already is

---

[14]J. Francis Rummel, *An Introduction to Research Procedures in Education* (Second Edition; New York: Harper and Row, Publishers, 1964), p. 29. Used by permission of Harper and Row, Publishers.

known and what needs to be learned, inconsistencies evident, and implementing suggestions received from various sources.[15]

A researcher may properly ask himself certain questions regarding the problem which he has under consideration. The correct answers to these queries will go a long way toward determining whether he should proceed with his plan, modify it, or discard it entirely. For example, Hillway poses five questions, of which the first four should be answered in the affirmative and the last one in the negative, if a researcher is to have a sound base for the formulation of his problem. He advises an investigator to determine whether his proposed topic is interesting, novel, requisite to advance knowledge, practicable, and already investigated.[16]

By posing and answering general questions similar to those just related by Hillway a music educator may then proceed to more specific queries and by reflection more clearly attempt to delineate the problem. He might, for purposes of illustration, begin with a topic such as "A History of Music in the United States." At first glance the subject may appear to be a good one for a graduate student, especially at the doctoral level. Before proceeding, however, a researcher would need to ask himself such specific questions as: (1) Will all phases of music be covered (instrumental, vocal, opera, symphony, chamber music, music education, etc.)? (2) Will the study be concerned with performances, teaching, or both? (3) What years will serve as the terminal limits of the study? (4) What kind of information will be sought? (5) Where may the desired information be best obtained? (6) How will the term "Music in the United States" be interpreted? (7) Will the study involve only native-born American musicians? (8) Will the role of music publishers be included? (9) Will consideration be given to an analysis of the compositions mentioned or to an identification of them only without comment? (10) Will the study include artists and performing groups from other countries? (11) What distinction, if any, will be made between amateur and professional groups? (12) Will manuscripts or facsimile copies of works by American composers be collected and cataloged? (13) What attention will be given to reviews of performances presented by artists in various cities? and (14) How will it be determined what gaps still remain in American musical history?

Almost immediately it should be apparent that "A History of Music in the United States" is a subject of such magnitude that it properly

[15]John C. Almack, *Research and Thesis Writing* (Boston: Houghton Mifflin Co., 1930), p. 48.

[16]Tyrus Hillway, *Introduction to Research* (Second Edition; Boston: Houghton Mifflin Co., 1964), p. 114.

consists of several other topics, all of which might be feasible for investigation. This matter of delimitation is one which is very significant for successful research, yet it frequently is not accorded enough attention by investigators in music education. There actually are enough topics to go around for all who desire to pursue research. Graduate students, however, frequently are unduly apprehensive about the possibility that all areas in which they are interested soon will be explored because of the ever-increasing number of individuals who are engaged in research. Actually, as research studies are completed they commonly suggest new areas needing investigation which may not have been evident before. It goes without saying that a study which is organized well and implemented in depth can make a much more significant and meaningful contribution to man's cultural knowledge than one which is so broad that the generalizations reached only result in superficial information.

The foregoing fourteen questions then connote certain sequential steps which must be considered and kept in mind as a researcher attempts to focus his attention on a research problem and then implement it. The feasibility of any topic may be evident only after these steps have been carried out. In other instances the impracticality of proceeding with a plan as originally conceived will be readily apparent earlier. After revisions the same procedures will be repeated until a satisfactory proposal has been developed which may then be pursued to bring about the objectives anticipated. This process of continually returning to the beginning and repeating the steps until satisfactory results are obtained is reminiscent of the looping technique used in certain phases of programing for the digital computer, where a program is repeated in successive steps until the information sought is received. In both instances the same questions may be asked over and over again, but with different objectives in mind.

Sequential steps in the actual formulation and implementation of a problem are to: (1) determine an area of need to which answers are not obvious; (2) ascertain whether or not the idea contains more than one basic problem; (3) delimit the subject to a topic which may be solved according to the background and training of the investigator; (4) develop basic assumptions and/or hypotheses; (5) locate existing information relating to the topic; (6) ascertain what instruments, tools, or equipment will be needed and whether or not such items are readily available or may be devised expeditiously; (7) postulate tentative conclusions; (8) implement the plan and accumulate preliminary data; (9) reconstitute and revise the research plan in view of inaccuracies appearing as a result of the preceding step; (10) accumulate and assimilate additional data; (11) interpret data accumulated; (12) draw up conclusions, recommendations, and suggestions for additional research; (13) obtain an evaluation of the research from peers and associates; and (14) disseminate results to the general public.

In commenting on these sequential steps, to determine an area of need to which answers are not obvious may seem to be redundant, but it is only through this type of intellectual inquiry that an investigator really can determine whether or not he has the basis for a research topic. Answers to many questions a person is concerned about frequently are abundantly available in many sources, although he may be unaware of them. The need for a detailed study in one of these areas thus may not be as critical as the researcher had originally believed. An instrumental music teacher, for instance, who is interested in obtaining background material on Berlioz to serve as motivation for introducing his high school orchestra to the composer's *King Lear Overture* hardly needs to go beyond Jullien's biography or Boult's *Berlioz's Life as Written by Himself in His Letters and Memoirs,* to cite two important sources of information. The endeavor to locate some new or little known fact of the composer's life, although it could prove interesting, would hardly be worth the time and effort necessary in preparing for this orchestra rehearsal and might in addition prove to be fruitless. If, on the other hand, a researcher was concerned with one specific aspect of Berlioz's life then the research, although time consuming, might result in a noteworthy contribution, such as Barzun's publication of some previously unknown Berlioz letters.[17] An experienced researcher like Barzun, of course, usually finds it easier to obtain research data because he knows what he is seeking, whereas an inexperienced researcher often does not. Hillway is among the many writers who stress the importance of an investigator's approaching research with a good idea of what he hopes to find.[18]

After careful scrutiny a researcher's initial idea frequently may be subdivided into several problems, each of which might constitute a topic in itself. The example listed earlier in this chapter, "A History of Music in the United States," obviously needs to be further split into several topics before it may be considered as feasible and practical to implement in depth. It has already been observed that it is very difficult to apply the techniques of sound research to a topic which is too broad in scope. Such a subject requires a researcher to have his energies dispersed in several directions, like the probing tentacles of an octopus. The diagram which follows serves as an illustration of this process of delineation.

---

[17]Jacques Barzun, *New Letters of Berlioz 1830-1868* (New York: Columbia University Press, 1954).
[18]Hillway, *op. cit.,* p. 116.

Tentative Title	*How Delimited From Previous Listing*
A History of Music in the United States	
A History of Instrumental Music in the United States	Delimited to instrumental music
A History of Instrumental Music in the Southern United States	Further delimited to one region of the United States
A History of Instrumental Music in the Southern United States from Earliest Times up to 1965	Additional chronological delimitation
The Development of Municipal Symphony Orchestras in the Southern United States from Earliest Times up to 1965	Slight change of title and further delimitation to specific form of instrumental ensemble
The Development of Municipal Professional Symphony Orchestras in the State of Florida from Earliest Times up to 1965.	Additional delimitation to exclude amateur groups but to include a specific state of the United States

As a result of successive delimitations, "The Development of Municipal Professional Symphony Orchestras in the State of Florida from Earliest Times up to 1965" is a subject for research which conceivably could be pursued by a student with appropriate background, training, and motivation to engage in this study. The title, as finally constituted, not only helps to confine the study to certain specific objectives but also enables the investigator to proceed with his research once he has established his *modus operandi*. The term "professional," as used in this illustration, might be defined differently for Florida than it would be for New York City, but the study could be just as valid in either instance if the research were properly constituted and implemented.

Assuming that the feasibility of the topic has been determined, at least tentatively, it is then necessary to consider certain steps in the plan of implementation; namely, basic assumptions and/or basic hypotheses, terms which will be discussed in greater detail in the next chapter. It should be noted, however, that they serve as the core around which a study revolves. A basic assumption refers to what an investigator assumes to be true, and thus does not need to be verified. On the other hand, a basic hypothesis is an educated guess of something which will need to be confirmed by experimentation, rationalism, or other means.

After basic assumptions and/or hypotheses have been formulated, the kind of research plan or methodology best suited to the nature of the research problem must be determined. It is at this point that a researcher in music education will decide whether his study will be essentially historical, experimental, descriptive, philosophical, analytical, or a combination of these. The ultimate determination is largely predicated on the previous steps.

A knowledge of relevant information is a most important next step. Cognizance of this may result in a recasting of the problem or even its abandonment altogether if careful scrutiny should reveal that the topic already has been adequately investigated. Resources include those which are both published and unpublished. A paucity of information, of course, suggests fertile areas for investigation which eventually might result in meaningful contributions to man's knowledge. Moreover, a veritable wealth of material about a subject might enable an investigator possibly to concentrate on a more specialized or infinitesimal phase of a problem. The methodology to be employed will be governed to some extent by the kind of data sought. An experimental project, which would have as its end result the formulation of conclusions to carefully controlled observations, would necessitate the quest for a different type of data than would a historical study which might rely rather heavily on original manuscripts or documents found in archives. In either instance the information sought must be pertinent to the topic at hand.

Experimental and descriptive studies, in particular, frequently make use of tests, special equipment, or questionnaires. Sometimes it is necessary for tests or special equipment to be devised by the researcher with the specific purposes of his research in mind; in others standard items may be used. Questionnaires, almost without exception, are devised by an investigator to fit the particular needs of his study, usually descriptive. Unlike a test which may be standardized, a questionnaire rarely can be used by more than one researcher unless another one is investigating the same problem under comparable conditions. Standardized tests in music and other areas may be used to supplement those devised by the researcher. When tests, equipment, or instruments are not available, the investigator must either develop them himself, or, if this proves impractical, revise his methodology to use those in existence.

The postulation of tentative conclusions can be very beneficial to an investigator by assisting him to logically anticipate the outcomes of his research. To paraphrase a well-known cliché, if a researcher does not know what he is seeking, how will he know when he locates the information? Tentative conclusions essentially are postulated from the basic hypotheses.

Implementation of the plan and accumulation of preliminary data are most significant phases because it is through their application that the hypotheses are really tested. The investigator is then in a position to know whether and to what extent his research plan needs to be revised should inaccuracies be evident. After necessary revisions, additional data are accumulated and assimilated.

Mere accumulation of data, however, is not enough. They will need to be interpreted in light of objectives of the study. It may be of little practical value, for instance, to find out that there are 200 school-owned oboes in the public schools of a certain state. More important is knowledge regarding whether or not these instruments are in playing condition, how many of them are being utilized and by whom, and the proficiency level of the students playing them. Moreover, the accumulation of additional data may be necessary in order that logical and valid interpretations may result.

Conclusions, recommendations, and suggestions for additional study are commonly grouped together in the final chapter of a research report. This really is not illogical when it is realized that final conclusions, although they may be similar to the tentative conclusions identified earlier, are deduced after the data have been accumulated and interpreted. Recommendations and suggestions for additional research then follow in normal sequence after the conclusions have been drawn. The recommendations usually include areas which, as he reflects on the project, the researcher feels might have been either approached differently or pursued in greater depth. On the basis of these, suggestions are offered for the benefit of future researchers. Often the final chapter of a research report is the most vital one to someone searching for a topic. It is here that he may find areas which, in the opinion of the investigator, are in need of careful study.

Although not always *fait accompli* in educational circles, a critique of the completed research by peers and associates can be most helpful. An investigator who earnestly desires to avoid the usual redundancies which characterize the creative efforts of most persons should welcome the opportunity to have an outside observer examine the completed project objectively and impartially. Because of his natural preoccupation with the project, a researcher frequently cannot do this. Critique of research by peers and associates is fairly standard practice in medical and scientific research but in music and other areas of education its use has been rather limited. It is for this reason that additional members are usually added to a doctoral candidate's examining committee at the time of his final oral examination, when basically he must defend his research.

An area of serious weakness in music education has been the dissemination of research results to the general public. A large number of completed doctoral projects in music education eventually are listed in *Dissertation Abstracts,* but only a very small percentage of the musical public who might be able to use these findings has access to them. Some reports do appear in various national and state music educators' journals, although usually only as a result of the investigator's initiative in preparing an abstract of his research for publication. Unquestionably much useful research remains virtually unknown because the researcher either does not take the time to write an interesting account of it or feels that his responsibilities have been discharged once the project is completed. This final step in the research process deserves much greater emphasis than it has received up to the present time. Through this means some of the better master's theses in music education which usually are overlooked could be made available to the musical public. On a more limited scale *Master's Abstracts* containing brief accounts of research by master's degree candidates is a companion to *Dissertation Abstracts,* but circulation is again largely limited to libraries.

Other resources will be mentioned in Chapter 4 of this book. It is encouraging, however, to note that many music educators have been distressed by the sparse amount of research information which has been disseminated in a form palatable to the general musical public. Petzold patently emphasizes this when he urges that the results of research be shared with the "practicing music teacher, using terminology that is readily understandable, so that any implications the study may have for practices in music education are evident. The teacher is seldom enthusiastic about reading an article presented in the typical research jargon that contains an overwhelming amount of technical information. He wants, and deserves, the *Reader's Digest* approach which summarizes the essentials in a straightforward manner."[19]

It hardly seems necessary to repeat that the finished research project is the result of careful planning and implementation on the part of an investigator. In emphasizing this Koefod states that the researcher must "establish beyond doubt that he has conceived a meaningful intellectual exercise and carried it through gestation to fruition."[20]

Just as the blueprint of an architect guides a building contractor, so a research proposal serves as the design which points the way for a researcher. It is the purpose of the next chapter to discuss this plan or proposal.

QUESTIONS FOR REVIEW AND DISCUSSION

1. Give some of the most likely sources of ideas for research projects in music education.

---

[19]Robert G. Petzold, "Directions for Research in Music Education," *Music Educators Journal,* L (January, 1964), 40. Used by permission of the *Music Educators Journal.*
[20]Paul E. Koefod, *The Writing Requirements for Graduate Degrees,* p. 107. © 1964, Prentice-Hall, Inc., Englewood Cliffs, N. J.

2. Discuss reflective thinking. What differences exist between the deductive and inductive methods of reasoning? How do they differ from deductive-inductive reasoning?
3. What is syllogism? Why is syllogism significant to research?
4. Name and discuss the seven steps of reflective thinking presented in this chapter.
5. In what ways has music education research been vulnerable in the past?
6. Discuss suggestions of a general nature to be used in the selection of a research problem.
7. The formulation of a research problem is dependent upon what general steps or procedures? What are some of the specific questions an investigator might ask himself as he gives consideration to his problem?
8. What sequential steps are involved in the formulation and implementation of a problem?

SUPPLEMENTARY READINGS

ALMACK, JOHN C. Research and Thesis Writing. Boston: Houghton Mifflin Co., 1930. Chapters II and IV.

BARZUN, JACQUES, and GRAFF, HENRY F. The Modern Researcher. New York: Harcourt, Brace and World, Inc., 1962. Chapter 2.

BEST, JOHN W. Research in Education. Englewood Cliffs, N. J.: Prentice-Hall, Inc., 1959. Chapter 2.

BORG, WALTER R. Educational Research: An Introduction. New York: David McKay Co., Inc., 1963. Chapter 2.

CHAMBERS, M. M. "Selection, Definition, and Delimitation of a Doctoral Research Problem," Phi Delta Kappan, XLII (November, 1960), 71-73.

COOK, DAVID R. A Guide to Educational Research. Boston: Allyn and Bacon, Inc., 1965. Chapter V.

COURTNEY, E. WAYNE (ed.). Applied Research in Education. Totowa, N. J.: Littlefield, Adams and Co., 1965. pp. 94-135.

DEIHL, NED C. "Research: Confined to Ivory Towers?" Music Educators Journal, LII (April-May, 1966), 70, 73.

DEWEY, JOHN. How We Think. Boston: D. C. Heath and Co., 1933. Chapter Seven.

GAGE, N. L. (ed.). Handbook of Research on Teaching. Chicago: Rand McNally and Co., 1963. Chapter 2.

GLENN, NEAL E. and TURRENTINE, EDGAR M. Introduction to Advanced Study in Music Education. Dubuque, Iowa: Wm. C. Brown Company Publishers, 1968. pp. 96-102.

GOOD, CARTER V. Essentials of Educational Research. New York: Appleton-Century-Crofts, 1966. Chapter 2.

———, and SCATES, DOUGLAS E. Methods of Research. New York: Appleton-Century-Crofts, 1954. Chapter 2.

"Graduate Study in Music Education," Journal of Research in Music Education, II (Fall, 1954), 157-170.

HILLWAY, TYRUS. *Introduction to Research*. Second Edition. Boston: Houghton Mifflin Co., 1964. Chapter 8.

KOEFOD, PAUL E. *The Writing Requirements for Graduate Degrees*. Englewood Cliffs, N. J.: Prentice-Hall, Inc., 1964. Chapter 1.

MCASHAN, HILDRETH H. *Elements of Educational Research*. New York: McGraw-Hill Book Co., Inc., 1963. Chapter 3.

MCGRATH, G. D., JELINEK, JAMES E., and WOCHNER, RAYMOND E. *Educational Research Methods*. New York: The Ronald Press Co., 1963. Chapter 3.

MORGAN, HAZEL B., "First Steps in Research for Graduate Students," *Music Educators Journal*, LII (September-October, 1965), 76, 81-82.

———, and BURMEISTER, CLIFTON A. *Music Research Handbook*. Evanston, Ill.: The Instrumentalist Co., 1962. Chapter II.

PETZOLD, ROBERT G. "Directions for Research in Music Education," *Music Educators Journal*, L (January, 1964), 39-42.

REIMER, BENNETT. "Effects of Music Education: Implications from a Review of Research," *Journal of Research in Music Education*, XIII (Fall, 1965), 147-158.

RUMMEL, J. FRANCIS. *An Introduction to Research Procedures in Education*. Second Edition. New York: Harper and Row, Publishers, 1964. Chapter II.

SAX, GILBERT. *Empirical Foundations of Educational Research*. Englewood Cliffs, N. J.: Prentice-Hall, Inc., 1968. Chapter 3.

TRAVERS, ROBERT M. W. *An Introduction to Educational Research*. Second Edition. New York: The Macmillan Co., 1964. Chapter 3.

VAN DALEN, DEOBALD B. *Understanding Educational Research*. Enlarged and Revised Edition. New York: McGraw-Hill Book Co., Inc., 1966. Chapters 2 and 7.

WATANABE, RUTH T. *Introduction to Music Research*. Englewood Cliffs, N. J.: Prentice-Hall, Inc., 1967. Chapter 8.

WHITNEY, FREDERICK L. *The Elements of Research*. Third Edition. Englewood Cliffs, N. J.: Prentice-Hall, Inc., 1950. Chapter III.

• 3 •

Organizing the
Research Proposal

The prospectus submitted for approval by a graduate student before he officially undertakes his research is known by various terms as thesis proposal, thesis outline, research agendum, or research design. Regardless of the nomenclature, the purpose is the same—for the investigator to indicate systematically, in writing, the plan whereby he proposes to collect, organize, and interpret the data of his research. It is imperative that the researcher give very careful thought and consideration to the preparation of his proposal because as Cook has so well indicated: "the more thought and effort the student puts into his proposal, the more likely will be the successful execution of the research itself."[1]

Subsequent to official acceptance by a committee or an individual especially designated to evaluate such proposals, a researcher's plan functions as the outline or guide as he proceeds with his research. The approved design also serves as the instrument a researcher will use to obtain additional assistance and guidance from his adviser or sponsoring committee.[2] Best is among those writers who consider the research design as being analogous to the architect's blueprint which must be prepared before construction can begin on a building.[3]

---

[1]David R. Cook, *A Guide to Educational Research* (Boston: Allyn and Bacon, Inc., 1965), p. 185. Used by permission of Allyn and Bacon, Inc.

[2]A committee, usually numbering three faculty members, selected by the candidate and approved by the administrator of graduate programs at a college or university, for the purpose of advising and guiding a student in the organization and implementation of his research plan.

[3]John W. Best, *Research in Education* (Englewood Cliffs, N. J.: Prentice-Hall, Inc., 1959), p. 22.

The research proposal, even after it has been officially accepted, should not be considered as immutable, for changes may prove to be advisable as the actual collection of data proceeds. These modifications might be only of minor significance such as a slight change in title, or they could assume major proportions, resulting in extensive alterations. As an example, subsequent to the acceptance of "An Experimental Study to Determine the Effectiveness of Teaching Beginning Violin Students by Means of a Teaching Machine," it might be deemed advisable to change the title to "An Experimental Study to Determine the Effectiveness of Teaching Beginning Class Violin Students by Means of a Teaching Machine." In the original title no suggestion is given that the teaching will be for a class situation, even though it may be so delineated in the actual body of the proposal itself. The subsequent revision clearly indicates this clarification. A research title, about which more will be said later in this chapter, needs to be a succinct and direct statement of the exact nature of the proposed study.

Other changes may assume greater import even to the point, in extreme instances, of a radical change in methodology. For example, in neither of the titles just proposed relating to violin teaching is the methodology explicit. It is implicit, however, to the extent that some kind of comparison is suggested. It is in the actual plan, as previously connoted, that methodological changes may take place. These in turn may suggest some modification of the title, although this is not always the case. As a hypothetical illustration, let it be assumed that an investigator has determined that it is not feasible to conduct an experimental study to compare the effectiveness of class violin teaching by means of a teaching machine. Instead, he may decide to compare experimentally a technique or concept of teaching utilizing the parallel group technique of research, to be treated in a subsequent chapter. The specific experimental technique in this instance may be an evaluation of the effects of prestudy, which on the one hand involves prior study of notes and fingering patterns before actual playing begins and on the other of reading at sight and playing material simultaneously without any preview. This change obviously necessitates a revision not only in methodology from the previous one involving a teaching machine, but also one in title.

Although there is no universally accepted format for a research design,[4] the one utilized in the School of Education at New York University includes the elements usually found in plans in effect elsewhere.

---

[4] The term research design will be used in subsequent references to thesis proposal, thesis outline, or research agendum, because it not only results in consistency but also it distinctly expresses the nature and functions of the prospectus.

This is not to suggest that the format used for research proposals at other institutions is less significant than the one to be discussed shortly, but simply that the writer considers this to be one of the better plans with which he has worked and also, parenthetically, is more familiar with it. The scheme to be related is not inflexible so the kind of research will largely determine whether all or only certain points will be utilized. Although many of the items will be identical in format with those at other institutions, modifications and changes obviously are in order when and where the occasion demands. The plan which follows is *suggestive* of the kinds of information to be included in a research design. Examples of research which are listed from New York University are representative of already completed projects or studies in progress which have been organized according to the plan which follows.

Suggestions for preparation of a research design may be found in *Standards for Written Work*.[5] The format follows:

The Problem	Procedure in Treating Data
General Statement	Bibliography
Specific Problems	Personal Qualifications
Definition of Terms	Education
Delimitations	Degrees
Basic Assumptions	Courses Taken
Basic Hypotheses	Professional Experience
The Need for the Study	Other Experience
Incidence of the Problem	Writing and Research
Related Literature	Appendix.[6]
Procedure in Collecting Data	

Quite properly neither recommended minimum nor maximum lengths are indicated. The student is discreetly enjoined to observe that his design should contain as many pages as are necessary to properly develop his research proposal[7]. Such decisions as those regarding length of the study should be left to the discretion of the student's adviser or his sponsoring committee. A discussion of each of the components of a research design now follows.

THE PROBLEM

General Statement

Since the general statement or problem is essentially a rewording of the title of the research, it is important that this exposition be a clear

---

[5]*Standards for Written Work* (Revised Edition; New York: New York University Campus Stores, 1963).

[6]*Ibid.*, pp. 32-35.

[7]*Ibid.*, p. 35.

and accurate indication of the nature and scope of the study as envisioned by the researcher. During the course of collecting data, however, it may be found desirable to effect a change in title, as noted previously. Whitney appropriately voices a generally accepted principle that an alteration of both research design and title should result when it is evident that the research is proceeding differently than originally proposed.[8]

When further clarification of the general title is necessary a subtitle may be used. The subtitle, however, normally does not appear in bibliographical listings of research topics, therefore serious consideration should be given to the desirability of utilizing a single, inclusive title. An example of a general title and a subtitle is the doctoral study on Ravel's piano music completed by Dubbiosi.[9] In this instance the simple statement "The Piano Music of Maurice Ravel" suggests that the study is one involving some type of analysis. The title becomes more definitive, however, when the subtitle "An Analysis of the Technical and Interpretive Problems Inherent in the Pianistic Style of Maurice Ravel" is added.

Specific Problems

Sometimes known as "subordinate" or "sub-problems," the specific problems state either in declarative or interrogatory form the more precise aspects of the general statement. In other words, the title is broken down into more definitive components. Specific problems, however, are not to be confused with subtitle. The title and subtitle are general in nature; the sub-problems, or specific problems, are explicit. The specific problems are the parts that make up the whole, or a Gestalt, as it were. The researcher must find answers to these sub-problems in order to be able to resolve the main problem. For some research studies it may be necessary to formulate several specific problems; for others only a few. Pruitt, in a doctoral study relating to withdrawals of beginning instrumental music students, listed ten subordinate or sub-problems.[10] He endeavored to determine the extent to which withdrawals from the beginning instrumental program were related to the: (1) number of students in beginning instrumental classes, (2) frequency of class meetings, (3) length of the beginning instrumental program class period, (4) condition of the musical instrument, (5) relationship

[8]Frederick W. Whitney, *The Elements of Research* (Third Edition; Englewood Cliffs, N. J.: Prentice-Hall, Inc., 1950), p. 123.

[9]Stelio Dubbiosi, "The Piano Music of Maurice Ravel," (unpublished doctoral dissertation, New York University, 1967).

[10]Jack S. Pruitt, "A Study of Withdrawals in the Beginning Instrumental Music Programs of Selected Schools in the School District of Greenville, South Carolina," (unpublished doctoral dissertation, New York University, 1966).

between the scores of students on the *Gaston Test of Musicality*, (6) relationship between scores of students on the *Kwalwasser Music Talent Test*, (7) relationship between the intelligence scores of students, (8) relationship between the scores of instrumental instructors on the *Minnesota Teacher Attitude Inventory*, (9) display or lack of display of communication between the instrumental instructor and parents, and (10) display or lack of display of communication between the instrumental instructor and students.[11]

At the other end of the spectrum, McGarry's doctoral study describing vocalization techniques used experimentally with instrumental groups contains only three specific or subordinate problems.[12] The purpose of the research becomes clearer with the addition of this subtitle: "A Comparison of the Effectiveness of Two Teaching Techniques on Instrumental Music Performance Utilizing the Watkins-Farnum Performance Scale." His sub-problems were to: (1) select and pair two groups of students to be taught by the techniques being compared in the study, (2) devise teaching procedures which will embody a control and experimental method, and (3) determine the extent, if any, to which vocalization improves performance skill. Preceding these is this general statement which indicates that his study purported to find out the extent to which vocalization assists in the development of selected skills in instrumental music performance.[13]

It is of consequence to recall that even though the specific problems are a further clarification of the title of the research, they too are stated in general terms. Also to be noted is that specific problems are not to be stated as procedures. They are merely questions or statements for which solutions must be obtained. Furthermore, they must not be regarded as synonymous with basic hypotheses, which will be discussed subsequently.

Definition of Terms

Any terms used in the statement of the problem, the sub-problems, or throughout the study should be defined if they might be construed to be ambiguous or technical in nature. In addition, terminology used to connote a meaning differing from that usually accepted should be clarified. This would be true not only for terms such as *gebrauchsmusik*,[14]

---

[11]*Ibid.*
[12]Robert J. McGarry, "A Teaching Experiment to Measure the Extent to Which Vocalization Contributes to the Development of Selected Instrumental Music Performance Skills," (unpublished doctoral dissertation, New York University, 1967).
[13]*Ibid.*
[14]Music designed essentially for use by amateurs, characterized by simplicity of parts and in length of movements, and written to be utilitarian.

which might not be understood by any except the well-read musician, but also for such seemingly well-known terms as "chorus," when the investigator wishes to employ a specific meaning. This is not to suggest that a researcher has license to utilize a definition which is manipulated to meet the express purposes of the study or to employ one which is not generally accepted by authorities in the field. The sole purpose of including terminology should be to bring about clarity. The terms, as McAshan so appropriately notes, must be both utilitarian and sensible.[15] A researcher, moreover, must not affront his readers by defining terms which are obvious. On the other hand, he must not assume that all of his readers are as familiar and as well versed in his subject as he is, which might account for his failure to define terms that need explanation or clarification. It is this desirable balance between the obvious and the too readily assumed for which the researcher must constantly strive.

Delimitations

A research plan which is open-ended will rarely result in the most expeditious accumulation and interpretation of data. In his understandable enthusiasm and zeal to make a significant contribution to the world's knowledge, the novice in research, note Good and Scates, frequently "chooses too broad a topic, which in reality may include many problems large enough for separate investigation."[16] Actually the upshot of such ambivalence may be an investigator's inability to resolve the research problem which he has formulated. It is for this reason that the limits of the problem must be delineated. Some of the factors which might determine the extent of an investigator's delimitations include time and money available, his personal qualifications to conduct the particular research, and availability of special equipment or tools needed for the project. One of the most important of these is the element of time. This is not to imply that the researcher should delimit his topic so much, ostensibly because of the pressure of time, that his design virtually is emasculated before the study has begun. The delimitations must be those which will enable the researcher to organize his study in such a manner that he can effectively and efficiently obtain as complete data as possible. By contrast, there are not many occasions when a researcher will find it necessary to expand his topic. Such a dilemma

---

[15]Hildreth H. McAshan, *Elements of Educational Research* (New York: McGraw-Hill Book Co., Inc., 1963), p. 59.

[16]Carter V. Good and Douglas E. Scates, *Methods of Research* (New York: Appleton-Century-Crofts, 1954), p. 178. Used by permission of Appleton-Century-Crofts.

may suggest poignantly that the topic is too insignificant to be implemented.

An example of delimitation was noted earlier in this chapter in connection with the selection of the problem. For purposes of illustration another one will be given here. Thus, "A Critical Evaluation of Textbooks Relating to Elementary School Music Teaching" almost certainly would be too ambiguous. The proposal needs to be further delineated as follows: (1) statement as to whether the textbooks are for the music specialist or the classroom teacher, (2) the inclusive dates of publications to be examined, (3) identification of country or countries to which publications will be restricted, and (4) purpose for which information will be obtained. Following these circumscriptions the resultant title might read: "A Critical Evaluation of Music Textbooks Written in the United States Since 1930 to Identify Common Objectives Related to the Training of Elementary School Music Specialists." These reconstituted delineations, in general terms, tell: (1) for whom the textbooks were written, (2) inclusive dates of the publications, (3) country to which publications will be restricted, and (4) purpose for which the study will be pursued—to identify common objectives. Although the title may seem unnecessarily long, it does indicate in clear and precise manner what the investigator purports to do. It should be obvious by now that the sections relating to title and delimitations must be very closely related.

When stated in specific terms delimitations may be either negative or positive. To consider the term negatively, delimitations explicitly prescribe areas in which a study will *not* be concerned. Consequently the investigator has a better idea not only of what he hopes to effect positively in his research but also with what he will not be concerned. For instance, in the example relating to the evaluation of music textbooks cited above, it would be appropriate to include in the delimitations a statement to the effect that: "This study will not be concerned with textbooks which essentially are guides for the teacher in conjunction with a particular textbook series."

Positive delimitations are not used as frequently as those stated negatively because it is easy to confuse them with objectives of the study. When expressed positively, delimitations succinctly and clearly circumscribe limits of the study from an affirmative standpoint. Referring again to the title just cited, a positive delimitation might read: "This study will be delimited to the philosophical precepts included in American music textbooks written for the music specialist since 1930." Although such a statement may appear to be an oversimplification, and even possibly a redundancy, such lucid delineation is to the advantage of the investigator. Kerlinger circumspectly sums this up in these words: "*Design research to answer the research questions.*"[17]

BASIC ASSUMPTIONS

Almost all research is predicated upon certain principles or propositions for which no proof is necessary or even possible in some instances. The researcher is not expected to prove his basic assumptions, but he should give a rationale for them. He merely presents precepts that according to Rummel usually are "*axiomatic* in that they are propositions that virtually every reasonable person is ready to adopt but which cannot be proven."[18]

Careful formulation and wording of basic assumptions is imperative if the research is to proceed logically in subsequent steps. The next phase of a research design, basic hypotheses, for instance, is contingent upon sound basic assumptions.

Occasionally a graduate student, in his haste to get a design approved in order to proceed with the actual accumulation of data, will present assumptions that he ecstatically believes should exist but for which there seem to be no valid bases. As already stated, while basic assumptions do not need to be validated, some reasonable justification for their existence should be given. It is not enough, for example, merely to state: "It is assumed that instrumental music is making a greater impact than is vocal music on the students in Hill City High School." While the investigator may be convinced that he could prove this philosophically and musically, the mere presentation of comparative registration figures for vocal and instrumental music in Hill City High School would suffice. His assumption, moreover, might not be a valid one if applied to another school. If it should be reported that in Hill City High School 876 students were registered in instrumental music as compared to 368 in vocal music, it could readily be assumed, from the standpoint of enrollment, that instrumental music is making a greater impact on students in that school. On the other hand, if the researcher were to *demonstrate* that instrumental music was making a greater impact on the students than vocal music, he would then be concerned with a hypothesis, or something which needs verification. Basic assumptions, it should be added, are

---

[17]Fred N. Kerlinger, *Foundations of Behavioral Research* (New York: Holt, Rinehart and Winston, Inc., 1965), p. 298. Used by permission of Holt, Rinehart and Winston, Inc.

[18]J. Francis Rummel, *An Introduction to Research Procedures in Education* (Second Edition; New York: Harper and Row, Publishers, 1964), p. 60. Used by permission of Harper and Row, Publishers.

predicated on a common sense basis, and without their acceptance it will be all but impossible to proceed with the next step, derivation of the basic hypotheses.

BASIC HYPOTHESES

Although basic assumptions normally will be a part of every standard research design, not all proposals will contain basic hypotheses. Research projects organized on a historical, philosophical, or analytical basis might not include them, whereas those which are experimental or descriptive most likely would. Basic hypotheses, sometimes known as "working hypotheses," are indications of a researcher's guess as to the probable outcomes of his study. The basic theory underlying the hypotheses should be given to prevent the appearance of false and wild hypotheses. Hypotheses remain tentative until the research has been completed and they are either confirmed or rejected.

Various types of hypotheses are utilized in research but two kinds are useful for most music education research; namely, the *deductive* or positive and the *null* or negative hypothesis. When using the deductive type certain items of information about a subject are compared by analogy resulting in the confirmation or rejection of each hypothesis. The consequences of the hypothesis rather than the hypothesis itself are tested. Although this type of hypothesis testing is indirect, it nevertheless should not be regarded as insignificant. Van Dalen avers "deducing consequences from hypotheses that can be empirically verified cannot be a hurried or casual procedure."[19]

To cite an example of how a deductive hypothesis might be employed, an investigator could utilize such comparative elements as enrollment figures in music, percentage of students winning a first division rating at solo and ensemble contests, and the number of individuals continuing to participate actively in musical activities after graduation to show that the music program in Midtown is more effective today than it was twenty years ago.

The *null* hypothesis, commonly used in experimental research, simply states that no difference may be expected between two or more variables when measured statistically. Although this procedure usually results in a direct testing of the hypothesis, it nonetheless is constructed with the expectation that it will be rejected. Rejection then results in affirmation of the research hypothesis. Should significant differences appear, the

---

[19]Deobald B. Van Dalen, *Understanding Educational Research* (Enlarged and Revised Edition; New York: McGraw-Hill Book Co., Inc., 1966), p. 155. Used by permission of the McGraw-Hill Book Co., Inc.

null hypothesis would be accepted and the research hypothesis would be rejected. In utilizing a null hypothesis the investigator might indicate: "It is hypothesized that no significant difference exists between the musical achievement scores of beginning fifth grade trumpet and clarinet players in the Middle Valley Schools." Statistical measurement would then result in rejection of the research hypothesis and acceptance of the null hypothesis.

Barnes believes that the purpose of a hypothesis should be not only to indicate the nature of the problem but also to suggest the type of answers which must be found for it.[20] Furthermore, a hypothesis can specify the kinds of instruments to be used and indicate how the data are to be collected.

To reiterate, a hypothesis should be organized so that it may be not only tested easily but also stated in a clear and concise manner. When so formulated a hypothesis is more easily verifiable, thus fulfilling the purpose of the research more readily. To put it another way, a basic hypothesis is an *unbiased* statement of anticipated conclusions. It should be noted, however, that the term hypothesis is not synonymous with conclusion. It must be admitted that after data have been accumulated, a conclusion might be coincidental with a hypothesis formulated at the initiation of the research design. Any bias, of course, will tend to prevent not only the accumulation of valid data but also the deduction of sound conclusions.

The development of a testable hypothesis is frequently one of the most serious weaknesses of research designs, as will be noted later in this chapter. Yet it is "one of the most difficult and most crucial steps in the entire scientific process," according to McAshan.[21]

THE NEED FOR THE STUDY

The investigator should set forth in a direct manner the reasons why he feels his proposed study is needed and how the results may possibly be utilized. It is his task to convince the reader that this study will result in a significant contribution to the literature of the field. Sometimes this section of a research design is called "Significance of the Study," but, regardless of the designation, the investigator must avoid on the one hand the impression that here at last is research which will resolve the most vexing problems in music education and, on the other,

[20]Fred P. Barnes, *Research for the Practitioner in Education* (Washington: Department of Elementary School Principals, National Education Association, 1964), pp. 30-31.

[21]McAshan, *op. cit.*, p. 53. Used by permission of the McGraw-Hill Book Co., Inc.

an aura of apology. For instance, the use of such equivocal phraseology as "interest of the writer," "encouragement from the writer's peers," and "the writer's desire for musical growth" is hardly very persuasive. Such epithets are redundant, to say the least, and are an indication of intellectual immaturity. If one is hard-pressed to delineate objectively the significance of a proposed study, he may need to consider seriously the importance of it. To lend validity to his assertions, the researcher should cite statements from authorities in the field who share his conviction of the need for such a study. The absence of corroborating and supporting declarations, moreover, is not sufficient affirmation that the research is needed. To be significant, a proposal must rest on its own merits, with or without the substantiation of others.

INCIDENCE OF THE PROBLEM

Although not incorporated in all research designs, this section, when used, should contain a forthright and convincing account of what caused the investigator to select a particular topic. Frequently a problem encountered in teaching may be incident. As might be expected, this component of a research design is included more often in a prospectus for an Ed.D than for a Ph.D. degree, since the former basically is contingent upon locating and making practical applications of a problem, as will be recalled in Chapter 1. In other instances an examination of research reports and graduate projects, or correlative reading, may enable an individual to become cognizant of the incidence of a problem.

RELATED LITERATURE

One of the most consequential steps in the preparation of a research design is a review of related literature. Several reasons exist for this purview. They include: (1) avoiding possible duplication of efforts; (2) enabling an investigator to delimit his research problem; (3) determining what areas coincidental with one's interests need further investigation; and (4) discovering new approaches, methods, or insights into a problem.

In this section the investigator includes a brief historical resumé of his particular area of research, listing some of the most important sources of pertinent information. He should, in addition, include concise accounts of other concepts which may be relevant to his topic such as philosophical, psychological, sociological, or other implications.

In his reporting the researcher should indicate how the listed studies are related to his. This information needs to be presented from both a positive and a negative point of view. Certain materials, for instance, will have little or no pertinence to a researcher's problem and he should not hesitate to state this. On the other hand, some items may be omitted purposely which an uninformed reader might construe as an incomplete review of the literature.

It goes without saying that the researcher is expected to survey the literature of his field completely and carefully. This significant step will prove beneficial when he organizes his bibliography for the final report. Citations, whenever befitting, are included in this section, with appropriate corresponding footnotes since they help an investigator verify that he has familiarized himself with the literature. The onus is upon the researcher to determine which materials are pertinent and those which are irrelevant.

PROCEDURE IN COLLECTING DATA

In this section of the research design the investigator informs his readers of the way in which he proposes to collect and organize data to solve the problem (general statement) and the sub-problems (specific problems). He should employ as much detail as necessary to describe his procedures. Among the factors to be included are: (1) amounts of data needed; (2) kinds of data required; (3) where data may be procured; (4) when data should be obtained, if a time factor is significant; (5) instruments, equipment, or materials to be utilized for data collection purposes; (6) personnel involved with the accumulation of data; and (7) organization of data. Obviously, the nature of the research problem will determine how many of these steps are needed. Regardless of the number used, Cook emphasizes that the techniques utilized *"must be valid for the purpose of the study."*[22]

Once the procedure for collecting data has been established, the researcher has not only a clear and concise guide for conducting his own research but also a plan which may be followed by another investigator who might desire to replicate the study.

PROCEDURE IN TREATING DATA

The section of a research design relating to data treatment procedure is often the one which is the least satisfactory. It is reported in *Standards for Written Work* that the reason for this is because the researcher has not visualized the precise nature of his problem.[23] Once the data have

---

[22]Cook, *op. cit.*, p. 46. Used by permission of Allyn and Bacon, Inc.
[23]*Standards for Written Work*, p. 34.

been collected and organized, they need to be analyzed and interpreted properly if answers to the problem and sub-problems are to be forth-coming. The researcher needs to identify explicitly the methods and techniques he will use; generalizations alone will not suffice. This calls for a lucid and terse account of *how* the data will be treated. In an analytical study, for example, it is not enough to merely state that "the investigator will analyze the pianoforte sonatas of Muzio Clementi (1752-1832) to compare them with those of Wolfgang Mozart (1756-1791)." Definitive information relative to the factors of analysis should be in-cluded. A sample chart listing the items to be analyzed and compared such as key relationships, kinds of chords, and non-harmonic tones ought to be included here or in the Appendix. If presented in tabular form, the Appendix is the logical place for this information, with appropriate reference to it in the context. Other types of research designs should be correspondingly specific.

BIBLIOGRAPHY

Known also as "Preliminary" or "Tentative" Bibliography, this sec-tion contains references which the investigator considers to be the most important. No attempt should be made in the research design to incor-porate all reference materials. More to the point is an annotated account of the most significant ones. As the study progresses additional sources will undoubtedly be located. Actually the quest for data is an ongoing process, but for purposes of expediency the investigator needs to estab-lish some terminal limits. Then in the final report he includes not only the most current information but also the most recent bibliographical items relevant to his study.

It may prove beneficial in some designs to separate bibliographical items into primary and secondary sources. The former, of course, refer to original or firsthand accounts of information, such as personal letters or data reported as the result of an experiment. A secondary source contains items which are not original with the one reporting the informa-tion. For example, most books on the history of music would be con-sidered as secondary sources. Although the author presumably uses primary sources of data, his reporting of them results in an account which is secondary.

In this section of the proposal sources are presented in standard bibliographical form. The researcher must be careful to include the most recent edition of a publication. A second or third edition of a book, for instance, may be overlooked because a researcher does not realize the importance of using materials which are as up-to-date as possible. This is not to infer that older sources are less valuable, but rather to indicate that the investigator is obliged to keep informed of both the past and the present in his area of concentration.

PERSONAL QUALIFICATIONS

This section enumerates the investigator's education, degrees, courses taken, and professional and other experiences. In addition, writing and research are optional in some research designs. The import of these items is evident; their main purpose is to show that the researcher has adequate preparation and background to successfully pursue the proposed research.

APPENDIX

The Appendix normally contains information to be used in implementing or clarifying the proposed design. Reference to these items, as already observed, is made in the appropriate place in the context of the design. Preliminary questionnaires and proposed charts for musical analysis are typical of the specific kinds of material that are included.

DEFICIENCIES IN RESEARCH DESIGNS

The foregoing pages have stressed factors to be incorporated in a sound thesis proposal or research design. Yet, the fact remains realistically that knowledge of what should be included and the actual contents are not synonymous for the same reason that disparity will result among the reports of thirty music students who might be asked to write an essay on the topic "Music, a Necessity in the Life of Man."

Since this chapter has dealt largely with the research design plan in effect at New York University's School of Education, a reasonable postlude is an account of deficiencies which have been observed in designs organized according to this format. This is not to imply that proposals at New York University are any better or any worse than those of other comparable institutions. This writer's evaluation of research designs completed elsewhere shows a general consistency indicating that common areas of deficiency in any one institution will very likely also be found at another.

In one six-month period, eighty-eight research designs were examined by a committee appointed for that purpose by the Dean of New York University's School of Education. Subsequent evaluations have revealed a consistency in pattern of the weaknesses noted according to the following frequency:[24]

Area of Weakness	Percentage Containing Weakness
Methodology	85
Assumptions	35
Hypotheses	30
Suitability for Degree	27
Delimitations	26
Sub-problems	20
Definitions	20
Related Literature	18
Significance of Study	14
Format	14
Problem	5
Bibliography	4

Methodology, not unexpectedly, proved to be an overwhelmingly consistent area of deficiency. The term is analogous to data treatment procedure, which was discussed earlier in this chapter. Insufficiencies, as already noted, are largely due to the failure of a researcher to specify clearly what he proposes to investigate, how he intends to carry out his research, and his procedures for evaluating and interpreting the data when they are accumulated. Weaknesses under this category are such factors as: failure to list methodology for all sub-problems; failure to give procedures for testing hypotheses; use of general terms such as "analyze," "survey," "research," without indicating their specificity; lack of evidence regarding reliability of research instruments and techniques; no provision included for objectively evaluating data; criteria missing for selection of sources; and failure to list procedures for answering questions presented.

The most consequential inadequacies under the category of "Assumptions" resulted from the investigator's failure to defend or justify his assumptions. In other instances, items listed here should have been included elsewhere. For example, when an investigator "assumes" his project is significant, he should substantiate his assumption under "Significance of the Study," not under "Basic Assumptions."

Likewise, factors often listed as hypotheses should actually have been presented as assumptions or in some other appropriate area of the design. In addition, hypotheses were given which bore no relationship to the sub-problems or which subsequently were not developed in the

---

[24]Undated mimeographed report prepared by Office of Dean, School of Education, New York University.

design. A major weakness, however, appears to be the enumeration of hypotheses which are not testable.

When "Suitability for the Degree" was indicated as a deficiency, the implication was that an Ed.D. design was offered for a Ph.D. proposal, or vice versa. As noted earlier, the difference between the two usually is that the Ph.D. is regarded as pure research, with the reader expected to make his own applications of the research results, and the Ed.D. is construed as action research, with the investigator incorporating uses for the data into the study. Often the general topic chosen may be suitable for either degree, but the formulation and subsequent implementation of the design may well determine whether the study will be for the Ed.D. or Ph.D., when such options are available.

The investigator who presents delimitations convenient to manipulate may be guilty of altering the direction which the research would normally take because vital factors may have been excluded. Another common weakness is failing to give reasons for the specific delimitations presented. Invalidated statements naturally are suspect.

Failure to include all the sub-problems necessary to resolve the general problem of an investigation is, of course, dereliction in the organization of a design. This oversight may be due either to carelessness or to intellectual ineptitude. Another deficiency is that of confusing actual procedures with the formulation of sub-problems. Sub-problems actually are indications of an area to be investigated and as such require no designation at this point of "how" the research will proceed.

Definitions which lack delineation and specificity appear to be a common weakness in many designs. Occasionally a researcher, also, will fail to state how his definitions vary from generally accepted usage.

Inadequacies in the section entitled "Related Literature" essentially consist of failure to indicate how the materials relate to the study. Perhaps more consideration needs to be given to the possibility of disapproval when proposals contain a superficial or incomplete review of the literature. Reference has already been made to this, but such inadequacy is inexcusable if for no more compelling reason than the ethical and moral principles of scholarship involved.

One of the most recurrent deficiencies in the category "Significance of the Study" is the inability of a researcher to explain why his proposed study will be important. The assumption that the absence of research in a specific area is enough to justify it is fallacious.

Included under the area of "Format" are such miscellaneous items as misspellings, lack of pagination, disjunct presentation, and indifference to accepted procedures for conducting scholarly work. Although they may appear to be of minor import, any study in which these factors are treated with indifference can hardly be classified as good research. This writer is appalled at times by the apparent lack of concern on the part of some doctoral students in regard to correct format for footnotes, spelling, and conjunct presentation. A graduate student should not expect his adviser to remind him of all these details. If he is incapable of the particularity required for adequate proofreading, he should seek professional assistance from someone who is adept in this technique.

Although failure to precisely state a problem is seemingly an innocuous weakness, it is difficult to comprehend how any problem can be successfully pursued without a clear and concise formulation of the research. Another deficiency is presenting the problem in a manner which is prejudicial instead of formulating an unbiased proposition to be proven. The tendency to present a topic in hortatory manner may be anticipated when an individual is exuberant about his research but uninitiated in its techniques.

Finally, weaknesses in the bibliography category stem largely from the researcher's failure to present references in a form generally accepted for scholarly work and from the inclusion of many items relatively insignificant to the topic. The danger is that a research tyro may believe his cunning inclusion of a large number of references will suffice to indicate that he has acquainted himself with the literature of his field. The net result may be that he will neglect to include a few works which are essential to his study at the expense of numerous items of minor importance.

A research design, thesis proposal, or whatever else it may be called, serves a very important function. It is the researcher's plan or blueprint, as it were. A well-organized and carefully thought-out proposal can make the implementation of a research plan easier and the interpretation of data much more meaningful. A most important step in research planning is a review of literature in the field. Suggestions for obtaining bibliographic information follow in the next chapter.

QUESTIONS FOR REVIEW AND DISCUSSION

1. What is the function of a research proposal? What changes are permissible in a design as the actual research proceeds?
2. Compare the research design format recommended for use at your institution with the one discussed in this chapter. Note particularly elements which are common to both.
3. Why is the "Definition of Terms" section of a research design so consequential?
4. Differentiate between positive and negative delimitations and give an example of each one.

5. What is a basic assumption? How does it differ from a basic hypothesis?
6. Differentiate between a deductive and a negative hypothesis and give an example of each one.
7. Why is a review of related literature one of the most consequential steps in the preparation of a research design?
8. Compare the deficiencies in research designs listed in this chapter with those apparent in projects presented by members of your class.

SUPPLEMENTARY READINGS

BORG, WALTER R. *Educational Research: An Introduction.* New York: David McKay Co., Inc., 1963. Chapter 2.

BURKE, ARVID J., and BURKE, MARY A. *Documentation in Education.* Fourth Edition, Revised. New York: Teachers College Press, Teachers College, Columbia University, 1967. Chapters 1, 4, 14, and 15.

COOK, DAVID R. *A Guide to Educational Research.* Boston: Allyn and Bacon, Inc., 1965. Chapter VI.

GARRETT, ALLEN M. *An Introduction to Research in Music.* Washington: The Catholic University of America Press, 1958. Chapter XI.

HILLWAY, TYRUS. *Introduction to Research.* Second Edition. Boston: Houghton Mifflin Co., 1964. Chapters 9 and 10.

KERLINGER, FRED N. *Foundations of Behavioral Research.* New York: Holt, Rinehart and Winston, Inc., 1965. Chapter 2.

MCASHAN, HILDRETH H. *Elements of Educational Research.* New York: McGraw-Hill Book Co., Inc., 1963. Chapters 4 and 5.

MCGRATH, G. D., JELINEK, JAMES E., and WOCHNER, RAYMOND E. *Educational Research Methods.* New York: The Ronald Press Co., 1963. Chapters 5 and 7.

RUMMEL, J. FRANCIS. *An Introduction to Research Procedures in Education.* Second Edition. New York: Harper and Row, Publishers, 1964. Chapter III.

SAX, GILBERT. *Empirical Foundations of Educational Research.* Englewood Cliffs, N. J.: Prentice-Hall, Inc., 1968. Chapter 5.

TRAVERS, ROBERT M. W. *An Introduction to Educational Research.* Second Edition. New York: The Macmillan Co., 1964. Chapter 14.

VAN DALEN, DEOBALD B. *Understanding Educational Research.* Enlarged and Revised Edition. New York: McGraw-Hill Book Co., Inc., 1966. Chapter 8.

WHITNEY, FREDERICK L. *The Elements of Research.* Third Edition. Englewood Cliffs, N. J.: Prentice-Hall, Inc., 1950. Chapters V and VI.

WISE, JOHN E., NORDBERG, ROBERT B., and REITZ, DONALD J. *Methods of Research in Education.* Boston: D. C. Heath and Co., 1967. Chapter II.

• 4 •

Obtaining
Bibliographic Information

Any research depends on the utilization of bibliographic techniques to a certain degree. Some types of investigation obviously require more extensive bibliographic information than others. Historical, philosophical, or analytical research, for example, will more likely rely heavily on data to be found in libraries and archives than will experimental or descriptive research. It is in the library that a researcher normally receives preliminary information which corroborates the feasibility of pursuing or abandoning his proposed topic. It is also here that the investigator procures much of the information he eventually uses in his preliminary and final bibliographies. Yet it is paradoxical that many graduate students, embarking on the initial stages of thesis planning, are still unfamiliar with some of the most fundamental techniques of efficient library usage.

TECHNIQUES OF MORE EFFICIENT LIBRARY USAGE

It hardly seems necessary to suggest that the researcher should first acquaint himself with the general floor plan and holdings of the library. This is not to suggest that he will need to examine every listing in the card file prior to the selection of his topic. Instead he should acquaint himself with the library's card catalog, general and special collections, reference rooms, and facilities for the reproduction of materials. Since the card catalog will be discussed shortly, it will be bypassed for now. General collections include books, periodicals, government documents, and other publications, both recent and of older vintage. Special collections might consist of such items as writings, diaries, programs, letters, manuscripts, and other personal effects of an individual or a group. These would be especially pertinent for an investigator who wishes to become involved in intensive research relating to the life of one individual or group. For example, a researcher who is investigating the role music played in the life of Sidney Lanier (1842-1881) might examine holdings of the Lanier Room at Johns Hopkins University in Baltimore, Maryland.

The reference room contains standard sources of general information such as encyclopedias and dictionaries of all kinds. Specific attention will be directed to some of these later in this chapter. Finally, since an individual may wish to have an item reproduced by some photographic process rather than copy it by hand, especially if the material is extensive, it would be well for him to know what technical processes are available at the library, the cost for such duplications, and the approximate length of time each one takes. Further attention will be directed to these processes subsequently.

A general purview is necessary for an investigator to determine how many of his source materials are housed in the library which has been selected to initiate his quest for information. Also, he is able to learn, from a negative standpoint, whether he needs to look elsewhere for appropriate items. Should he decide this is necessary he still must find out where such materials may be found. Members of the library staff, the researcher's professional colleagues, and advisers are the most likely sources of such information. Any of these subsequently may lead him to another library to repeat the same procedures of acquainting himself with its holdings and facilities, examining the materials, and so on, until the needed information is found. *Subject Headings*[1] is a very useful tool before a researcher checks the card catalog in a library which utilizes the Library of Congress system. A comparable compilation also is available for libraries using the Dewey Decimal Classification.[2] These lists are useful to a researcher because they specify what subject headings are used in the card catalog.

CARD CATALOG

The card catalog undoubtedly is the most important single source of preliminary information for a researcher. Cards may be individually

---

[1]*Subject Headings*, Marguerite V. Quattlebaum (ed.), (Seventh Edition; Washington: The Library of Congress, 1966). Music entries, for example, listed between pages 862-869 of this edition, contain topics related to various phases of music. Additional notations may be found under more specialized music topics such as pianists, pages 982-986.

[2]Barbara M. Westby, *Sears List of Subject Headings* (Ninth Edition; New York: H. W. Wilson Co., 1965).

prepared and typed by the library or they may be commercially published by the Library of Congress or the H. W. Wilson Company. Each card contains a veritable wealth of information which sometimes is overlooked by the research tyro. Figure 1 is a reproduction of a catalog card for a recent publication in music. It is referred to as an author or main entry card. The identifying numbers correspond to the following: (1) library call number, which identifies where the book is shelved; (2) author's complete name; (3) date of author's birth (and death in the case of an author who was deceased at the time the card was prepared, or whose death subsequently has been recorded by a cataloger); (4) title of publication; (5) edition; (6) place of publication; (7) publisher; (8) date of publication; (9) number of pages in preface and in main body of book; (10) indication of illustrations; (11) height of book; (12) specific page references to bibliography; (13) notation of "tracings" or subject headings under which the book is listed in the catalog; (14) the Library of Congress call number; (15) Dewey classification number; (16) Library of Congress card number; (17) publisher of card; and (18) date of card code number.

The library call number (1) and the author's date of birth and death (3) are usually typed in by a member of the library staff. In

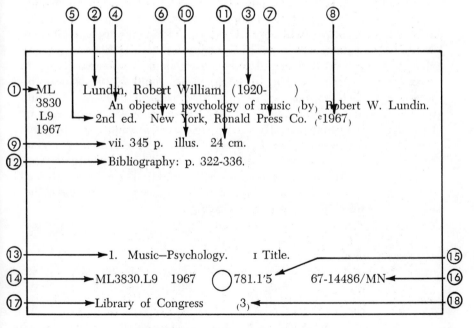

FIGURE 1.   Library Catalog Card

addition to a main entry card, illustrated in Figure 1, the card catalog contains additional entries for each publication. Cards containing identical information are filed in appropriate places of the card catalog but they include additional information typed at the top. The title card lists the title of the publication and the subject card identifies the subject which is printed at the bottom. Subject headings may either be in red or in capital letters, depending on local preference, to distinguish them from title designations. In addition, all libraries utilize a fourth entry, known as a shelflist card. It contains, in addition to call number, the number of copies of that publication in the library, even though they may be housed in different locations. The shelflist, normally used only by catalogers and others in technical services, is rarely available to researchers.

Returning to the main entry card, certain items have little or no significance for a researcher and are primarily of interest only to members of the library staff. These are height of the book (11), Library of Congress card number (16), publisher of the card (17), and date of card code number (18). To a librarian, height of a publication can be significant because many items in music and art are not uniform, being bound in a variety of sizes and shapes. To pose a very practical question, should the height of the adjustable shelves found in many libraries be altered just to accommodate one or two oversized musical anthologies, scores, or art portfolios, thus wasting much of the precious space which many libraries desperately need? Or, should those resources which are "oversize" be cataloged separately and housed together? These questions, of course, must be answered by the staff members of each library in accordance with the individual situation. It would be well for a researcher, however, to be aware that "oversize" materials exist should he be distressed because certain items he may be seeking appear to be housed in an unusual place. "Oversize" materials are indicated by some type of notation above the call number, frequently the symbol +. When separate shelving is indicated this factor should be added to the call card or slip submitted by a researcher. In addition, conventional-sized books may be shelved in a section of the library where they might not normally be expected to appear. For example, one large library classifies a collection of scholarly articles relating to emotional responses to music as RC489.M7M8, which places it with medical publications under the R category of the Library of Congress Classification system.[3] The main entry Library of Congress card, moreover, suggests ML3920.M896, which would indicate that it belongs under the "Literature of Music" or ML

---

[3]*Music and Your Emotions* (New York: Liveright Publishing Corp., [1952]).

classification, as will be noted subsequently. The suggested Dewey Decimal classification is 780.13, also under music.

In libraries which are decentralized the researcher should first examine the central or "public" catalog. The specific location as well as the number of copies of the material should then be noted at the top of the main entry card, such as Music Library, Education Library, Science Library, etc. A book on music education, for instance, might be in the education rather than in the music collection. An investigator who only examines the music card catalog might not find the desired publication listed there and thus assume that it was unobtainable in that library.

Returning again to items included on the main entry card, the author's complete name, the correct title of his publication, the edition, publisher, place and date of publication are all significant information to be included in a bibliography. The author's dates become significant when one is concerned with writings from a certain historical period, as would be true for many historical or philosophical research studies. Other headings under which the materials are found can be very helpful. These cross references, or "tracings" as they are sometimes known, can assist a researcher to locate additional sources relevant to his topic. For purposes of illustration, let it be assumed that an investigator knew that the name Lundin was associated with the psychology of music. By checking the subject heading of "Music—Psychology" he could find other sources in the same category.

Although the manner in which resource materials are classified in American libraries may vary in detail from one library to another, most items on the same subject will be cataloged in general to correspond to either the Dewey Decimal Classification or the Library of Congress system. Many smaller college and municipal libraries use the Dewey system whereas larger college, university, and city libraries find the Library of Congress schedule to be more utilitarian because the combination of letters and numbers and the larger number of classes makes it more flexible than Dewey.

First published in 1876 by Melvil Dewey (1851-1931), renowned progenitor of sound U. S. library science techniques, the Dewey Decimal Classification provides for the cataloging of published materials under ten major headings as follows:

000 General Works
100 Philosophy and Psychology
200 Religion
300 Social Sciences

400 Philology
500 Natural Sciences
600 Applied Sciences and Technology
700 Fine Arts and Recreation
800 Literature
900 History, Geography, Biography.

Music entries are assigned numbers from 780 through 789, with these representative examples:

780.01 Research
781   General Principles ("Theory of Music") and techniques
782   Dramatic music and production of musical drama
783   Sacred Music
783.026 Sacred Music—Christianity
784   Voice and vocal music
784.015 Appreciation (analytical and program notes)
785   Instrumental ensembles and their music
785.066 Orchestra
786   Keyboard instruments and their music
786.109 Historical and geographical treatment
787   String instruments and their music
787.1   Violin
788   Wind instruments and their music
788.7   Oboe and English horn
789   Percussion, mechanical, electrical instruments
789.1   Membranophones
789.913 Catalogs, lists, critical appraisal of recordings.[4]

The Dewey cataloging scheme has been replaced in many libraries by the Library of Congress system, devised by Herbert Putnam (1861-1955) and published in 1902. This is especially true in libraries where a greater diversification is desirable because of large holdings. The system of classification devised by the Library of Congress, one of the world's largest repositories of printed materials, is:

A	General Works—Poly-graphy	M	Music
		N	Fine Arts
B	Philosophy—Religion	O	Vacant; left for expansion

---

[4]*Dewey Decimal Classification and Relative Index* (Edition 17; Vol. 1; Lake Placid, N.Y.: Forest Press, Inc., 1965), pp. 1032-1071.

C	History—Auxiliary Sciences	P	Language and Literature
		Q	Science
D	History and Topography (except America)	R	Medicine
		S	Agriculture—Plant and Animal Industry
E-F	America		
G	Geography—Anthropology	T	Technology
		U	Military Science
H	Sociology	V	Naval Science
I	Vacant; left for expansion	W, X, Y	Vacant; left for expansion
J	Political Science	Z	Bibliography and Library Science.
K	Law		
L	Education		

Music entries are classified under three broad sub-headings of the M classification system of the Library of Congress as follows:

M Music
ML Literature of Music
MT Musical Instruction and Study.

Some representative entries within each of these areas are:

M Music
5-1459   Instrumental Music
1495-2199 Vocal Music

ML Literature of Music
159-3790   History and criticism
1100-1354 Chamber and orchestral music. Band (military music)
3800-3920 Philosophy, physics, psychology, esthetics, etc. of music

MT Musical Instruction and Study
40-67   Composition
               Rhythm, melody, harmony, counterpoint, etc.
170-810   Instrumental technics
               for organ, piano, string, wind, and plectral instruments
820-949   Singing and voice culture
855-883   Special technics
               Chanting, sight singing, choral singing, etc.[5]

---

[5]*Outline of Library of Congress Classifications* (Washington: U. S. Government Printing Office, 1965), p. 11.

From the extensive number identification system noted above it is easy to see why there might be discrepancies in the classification of publications. The classification systems, both of Dewey and the Library of Congress, are suggestive only. It is the prerogative of the library catalog department to assign a specific number to each item according to present holdings determined by the judgment of the individual cataloger. It should be noted, however, that the general classifications would fall within these basic patterns of headings. Thus, it would be unlikely to find materials relating to music instruction (MT classification) listed under ML (Music Literature). Some music libraries, moreover, utilize a scheme of classification for musical scores based on a decimal system devised by George S. Dickinson (1888-1964) though often modified by individual libraries to accommodate local conditions. The Dickinson-Columbia schedule includes these classifications for musical scores:

00-09 Collections, general and instrumental
10-69 Instrumental music (by medium)
70-99 Vocal music.[6]

Since the trend in library science today is toward open stacks or shelves, the student who is familiar with cataloging systems can go to the appropriate area of a library and examine materials firsthand. Another advantage of becoming familiar with these classification schemes is that an investigator may locate items appropriate to his musical topic which are cataloged under another area heading.

While most of the remarks above relate to published materials such as books, the researcher may have some occasion to examine various kinds of musical scores or disc or tape recordings. Unfortunately, less uniformity is usually found in regard to systems of cataloging musical scores. Often they are merely placed in portfolios and arranged alphabetically by title and by composer, conductor, or performer. In other instances they can be found cataloged according to some modified classification system such as that formulated by the Library of Congress. It is in the area of musical scores, especially, where confusion has been most prevalent. Notwithstanding, committees have been organized by the Music Library Association to clarify some of the indecision which frequently has resulted in libraries with large collections of musical scores. In 1963 the Classifications Committee of the Music Library Association published a recommended guide in which suggestions were proffered not only to reduce the number of distinctions in the M category but also to indicate

---

[6]Mary M. Ausman, "Classification of Music," mimeographed pamphlet, Queens College of the City University of New York, 1967), p. 1.

how the items listed under the MT (Musical Instruction and Study) may be reclassified under either M or ML.[7]

The appropriate classification of materials in a library is, of course, not the responsibility of the music researcher, but an understanding of the principles of classification can be useful to him in locating materials which are relevant to his research. To assist music library catalog departments, suggestions were made in 1951 by the Classifications Committee of the Music Library Association. These recommendations, which subsequently have been incorporated by many libraries, were provided for both the Dewey Decimal and the Library of Congress systems.[8]

As already indicated, some researchers may have occasion to use disc and tape recordings which are housed in special collections of a library. Library of Congress cards are available for many of the disc recordings, and this, of course, makes the search much easier. Card catalog numbers may be found in the discography section of each issue of *Notes,* official publication of the Music Library Association.[9]

In some libraries, especially those in which records circulate, the library maintains a separate card file for disc and tape recordings. Justification for this is the ease with which users may find the titles because they are conveniently listed under the name of each composer. Another reason is that records, as Shank and Englebrecht correctly state, wear out easily through continued handling and often will not be replaced, thus making it easier to maintain a separate catalog for them.[10]

It should be clear to the reader by now that the card catalog of a library can be a most valuable source of preliminary information and one which, regretfully, is not used as effectively and efficiently as it should be by many researchers.

SUGGESTIONS FOR NOTE TAKING

Even before determining which materials he wants to examine, a researcher should ascertain which system of note taking will best suit his needs. Actually, a uniformity in procedure is more important than the plan followed.

---

[7]"Condensation for the Library of Congress M Classification Schedule," *Notes: Supplement for Members,* No. 34 (June, 1963).

[8]See "Music Classification, Condensed L. C. Classification, Class M (first draft)," *Notes: Supplement for Members,* No. 15 (June, 1951), 9-15; and "An Alternate Music Classification for Use with Dewey 780 (preliminary edition)," *Notes: Supplement for Members,* No. 17 (December, 1951), 5-15.

[9]For additional suggestions regarding record cataloging see William Shank and Lloyd C. Englebrecht, "Records and Tapes," *Manual of Music Librarianship* (Ann Arbor, Mich.: Music Library Association, 1966), pp. 65-75.

[10]*Ibid.,* p. 71.

There are three common ways to record notes. Undoubtedly the most widely used involves making notations on blank or lined file cards, usually 3″ x 5″ or 4″ x 6″ because of the ease with which they may be handled and filed, preferably in a file box which the researcher can carry with him.

Other researchers prefer to place information on blank pieces of paper 8 1/2″ x 11″ or smaller, and then file them in a large manila envelope.[11] This system has the advantage of ease in keeping relevant material from a single source on one or two pages instead of on several filing cards, thus permitting facility of reference. If this procedure is utilized, manila envelopes containing a string loop fastener usually are more durable than those with flexible metal clasps.

Still a third way is to make notations in a looseleaf or spiral notebook, the size to be determined by the investigator. Although the looseleaf notebook provides for subsequent ease in arranging materials, it frequently proves to be less desirable because of inconvenience in handling. Pages may be detached easily from spiral notebooks; however, it would be well to carry a few paper clips to attach loose sheets to the notebook so they will not be misplaced before they have been inserted in an envelope or file box. Some researchers object to using spiral notebooks on the premise that pages which are detached have rough serrated edges which are difficult to clip together. There are esthetic objections also to the appearance of these irregular sheets which have been removed.

Regardless of which plan is used, the researcher must be methodical and consistent in his procedure and approach so he can obtain most of the information he needs the first time he examines the materials. This frequently is accomplished only with patience and practice. Smith is not alone in offering the advice that systematic note taking is accomplished only as a result of careful preparation, organized thinking, and resolute application.[12]

The data to be recorded on each card or sheet must be complete enough not only to be useful but also to save the researcher from re-examining the same item for information overlooked the first time. He should record first the library call number for the item in the upper left hand corner (also location if more than one library is used), and

---

[11]For ready reference, this writer has made it a practice to carry in his pocket a 4″ x 6″ note pad to which are attached one or two paper clips. Detached pages are then inserted between the backing and last page of the pad and clipped to it until they can be filed in a manila envelope. Sometimes it may advisable instead to carry several 3″ x 5″ or 4″ x 6″ file cards which are held together by a rubber band.

[12]Henry L. Smith, *Educational Research, Principles and Practices* (Bloomington, Ind.: Educational Publications, 1944), p. 74.

other pertinent information in case there is an occasion to refer to the material again. Next, every notation should list complete bibliographic information (author's full name, complete title, place, publisher and date of publication, and pages utilized). (How many times does a research tyro find it necessary to look up page numbers for quotations he has left out?) Notes should be placed on only one side of a card or sheet and may consist of: (1) direct quotations, (2) paraphrase of material, and (3) outline of important points.

In order to differentiate them from other types of commentary, direct quotations are enclosed between double quotation marks. Intellectual honesty demands that all items be quoted exactly as printed; this includes marks of punctuation as well. Mistakes in the original must not be corrected, but rather indicated with the Latin word [sic] in brackets. If extensive portions are to be quoted it would be advisable, in the interest of time and accuracy, to have them reproduced at a nominal cost by one of the photocopying processes now available in most libraries.

Paraphrasing of material should be done whenever possible to develop an investigator's facility in expressing what he reads in his own words. This will make it easier for him to resist the temptation to present a report which essentially consists of direct quotations held together by introductory statements in the author's own words. Studies written in this manner, unfortunately, are still being produced by graduate students in music education.

A mere outline of important points is rarely used by a beginning researcher. More experienced investigators often like to utilize this system because they can note subject headings and sub-headings along with page numbers and enough appropriate annotations to determine which items will be of greatest utility later on.

Regardless of which system of note taking a person employs, the notations must be gathered with a specific purpose in mind. Hillway reminds the research tyro that an experienced researcher continually anticipates how he can use the notes he accumulates.[13] Each day, when the researcher has finished his investigation, he should alphabetize, by author and title, the cards or sheets he has prepared and place them in a file box or envelope.

In the preliminary examination of a book it is well to examine the table of contents, noting carefully the chapter headings and sub-headings, the listings in the index, and then leaf through it, if necessary, to determine whether or not it is worth scrutinizing further. There ob-

---

[13]Tyrus Hillway, *Introduction to Research* (Second Edition; Boston: Houghton Mifflin Co., 1964), p. 96.

viously is no use in wasting time reading a publication which has few, if any, references listed in the table of contents or the index which are significant to the research. Time could be occupied more efficiently with materials containing beneficial information.

It may seem redundant to stress the importance of requisite reading skills since it generally is assumed that by the time one reaches graduate level he already has developed facility in reading rapidly and in distinguishing between what is relevant and unnecessary. Yet sometimes a research tyro does not realize that much valuable time can be saved if he will skim through an article or book to determine the most significant paragraphs, sentences, and key words. Notes may then be made of important items and paragraphs which are deemed essential to the study and can be reread before going on to new material. Burke and Burke, cognizant that note taking frequently is difficult and troublesome because the researcher is afraid that he will lose some consequential ideas as he reads, suggest that he have the material reproduced by some type of photocopying process whenever possible.[14]

Some research topics in music education may require using books and articles written in German, French, Italian, or another foreign language. A researcher who lacks sufficient foreign language skill to comprehend what he is reading would do well to consider another topic. To read an article or book almost exclusively with a lexicon is a slow, tedious, and frequently unrewarding procedure.

In addition to books, articles, and pamphlets, useful information is sometimes found in newspapers. It is helpful to clip articles of significance and place them in a manila envelope or folder. Since newspaper accounts do not always include the year and date of the article, the name of the newspaper, and specific month, day, and year should be noted on the margin or reverse of the clipping.

OBTAINING ITEMS FROM OTHER LIBRARIES

Sometimes source materials deemed important for a study are not available locally. It is necessary then to procure them by other means, either through inter-library loan or by some photocopying process.

Inter-library loan is a relatively easy way to obtain books and other materials from another library. The individual requesting items on inter-library loan must know where they may be obtained before he asks his local librarian to procure them. A nominal fee to cover postal charges

---

[14]Arvid J. Burke and Mary A. Burke, *Documentation in Education* (Fourth Edition, Revised; New York: Teachers College Press, Teachers College, Columbia University, 1967), p. 60.

both ways normally is the only charge. Materials obtained through inter-library loan often do not circulate and therefore must be used in the library requesting them. A two-week maximum period for using materials should be anticipated, with one renewal possible if there is no demand for them. Rare books and items regarded as irreplaceable if lost, rarely, if ever, are obtainable through inter-library loan. The researcher may then request a copy of non-circulating materials on microfilm or some other type of photocopying process. Microfilm, for instance, is a rela-tively inexpensive and practical way to procure copies of source materials which otherwise would be unobtainable. A microfilm reader has become standard equipment today even in the smallest libraries, private or public, so little difficulty should be experienced in locating equipment to read microfilms once they have been received.

PHOTOCOPYING MATERIALS

Various types of photocopying are available to reproduce items either in full-sized or in microtext versions. Full-sized copies, either positive or negative, are available through many processes. The photo-stat, one of the earliest to be used for music, is rather expensive for extensive copying and often takes considerable time to obtain. More recent processes such as Xerox, Verifax, Thermo-fax, and Diazo have the advantage of providing an individual with not only a rapid copy but also at a lower cost than the photostat.

Microtexts, both positive and negative, are of three kinds: micro-film, microcard, and microfiche. When a copy of an entire graduate project, rare book, or collection of musical manuscripts is needed, micro-film, either in 16 or 35 mm., provides a very practical and economical way to obtain it. Since microfilm has received such wide acceptance in this country, most libraries, as already observed, are equipped with at least one microfilm reader. In addition, portable readers are available for home use.

Microcards, of more recent origin than microfilm, require special equipment to enlarge the positive image contained on the 3" x 5" cards. The number of pages on a single card may vary from forty to sixty, depending on the size of the item reproduced. Microcards have begun to receive wide acceptance now and include not only an American thesis and dissertation publication series but also one containing reprints of many significant music books.[15]

---

[15]See *Microcard Publications in Music* (Rochester, N.Y.: University of Roches-ter Press, 1965).

Although widely used in Europe, the potentialities for microfiche still have not been realized to any extent in this country. The process, however, seems to be gaining in favor among librarians. For example, research studies available through the new Educational Resources Information Center of the U. S. Office of Education are obtainable either in hard copy or microfiche. Microfiche may be procured in either positive or negative but the latter seems to be better. A microfiche essentially is a piece of film (either 3" x 5" or 4" x 6") containing frames of microfilm. The 4" x 6" microfiche will accommodate up to sixty pages of textual material. Microfiche frames are easier to locate and store and for this reason the process has advantages over microfilm for both the researcher and the librarian. A microfiche reader is necessary, of course, for use with this process. Machines to read either microcards or microfiche, moreover, are now beginning to appear.

Even though a researcher may have a preference for one specific kind of microtext over another, the availability of items in that type of microtext and the accessibility of proper equipment to read the materials normally will determine whether microfilm, microcard, or microfiche will be used.

SPECIFIC REFERENCE MATERIALS FOR MUSIC

To present an inclusive listing of all references to which the researcher in music education might have recourse would be not only impractical but also beyond the purpose of this book. Sources most likely to prove beneficial are suggested in the sections which follow. The individual seeking specific information in a rather restricted area of music will find Duckles' annotated bibliography of research materials to be extremely helpful.[16]

DICTIONARIES AND ENCYCLOPEDIAS

Among the English language dictionaries and encyclopedias most likely to be used are *Baker's Biographical Dictionary of Musicians* (5th edition), revised by Nicolas Slonimsky, 1958; *Grove's Dictionary of Music and Musicians* (5th edition), 1954, with 1961 supplement, Eric Blom, editor; *The Harvard Brief Dictionary of Music*, by Willi Apel and Ralph T. Daniel, 1960; Willi Apel's *Harvard Dictionary of Music*, 1944; *The International Cyclopedia of Music and Musicians*, Oscar Thompson,

---

[16]Vincent Duckles, *Music Reference and Research Materials* (Second Edition; New York: The Free Press, 1967).

editor (8th edition, revised), Nicolas Slonimsky, editor, 1958; *The New Encyclopedia of Music and Musicians,* Waldo S. Pratt, editor, 1929.

In addition, foreign language dictionaries and encyclopedias for either general or specialized areas are available. Basic references are: Robert Eitner's *Biographisch-bibliographisches Quellen-Lexikon der Musiker und Musikgelehrten der christlichen Zeitrechnung bis zur Mitte 19. Jahrhunderts,* (reprint), 1947, 10 volumes; Hugo Riemann's *Musik-Lexikon* (12th edition), 1959; *Biographie universelle des musiciens et bibliographie générale de la musique* of François J. Fétis (2nd edition), 1866-70, 8 volumes, plus supplement, 1878-80, 2 volumes. The first two, obviously, require a comprehension of German and the third of French.

Reference materials in music relating to such diverse subjects as musical instruments, musical themes, band, and chamber music are also available. Respective examples of these are: Curt Sachs' *Real-Lexikon der Musikinstrumente, zugleich ein Polyglossar für gesamte Instrumentengebiet; mit 200 Abbildungen,* 1962; *A Dictionary of Musical Themes,* Harold Barlow and S. Morgenstern, compilers, 1948; Kenneth W. Berger's *Band Encyclopedia,* 1960; and *Cyclopedic Survey of Chamber Music,* Walter W. Cobbett, editor, (2nd edition), 1963, 3 volumes.

GENERAL REFERENCES

Often overlooked by musicians are such general references as *Dictionary of American Biography; Directory of American Scholars; Encyclopaedia Britannica; Encyclopedia of Educational Research,* Chester W. Harris, editor, 1960; *National Union Catalog,* with quarterly and annual cumulations; *Who's Who in America; Who's Who in American Education; Who's Who in the East* (with comparable volumes for the Midwest, West, and South and Southwest); and *Who Was Who in America.*

PERIODICALS

Periodicals in both music and other subject areas often prove to be one of the most valuable sources of information for researchers. An investigator can save himself considerable time by referring to such periodical guides as *Education Index, Music Index, Music Article Guide, Reader's Guide to Periodical Literature,* and *Social Sciences and Humanities Index,* which list title and author of article, name of periodical, and date and inclusive pages of the article. Most of these guides are up-to-date within a few months. In addition, many journals indicate on the title page in which sources they are indexed. An annual index, frequently in the last issue of a volume, also appears in most journals.

Many journals exist in music with varying objectives and contents. Some of the representative current American publications in music education are: *American Guild of Organists Quarterly, The American Music Teacher, American String Teacher, Brass Quarterly, Bulletin of Council for Research in Music Education* (Illinois), *Bulletin of the National Music Council, Bulletin on Research* (Pennsylvania), *Clavier, Colorado Journal of Research in Music Education, College Music Symposium, Current Musicology, Diapason, Electronic Music Review, Ethnomusicology, Folklore and Folk Music Archivist, Instrumentalist, Journal of the American Choral Foundation, Journal of the American Musicological Society, Journal of Band Research, Journal of Church Music, Journal of Music Theory, Journal of Research in Music Education, Missouri Journal of Research in Music Education, Music Educators Journal, Music Journal, Musical Quarterly, NACWPI Bulletin, Notes, Perspectives of New Music, Piano Quarterly,* and *Woodwind World.*[17]

Research reports also appear in many of the journals published by each of the state music educators' associations. In addition, trade journals such as *Connchord* and *Selmer Bandwagon* frequently contain articles relating to research of particular interest to instrumentalists. Another source of particular value for research of historical import is periodicals which no longer are being published. Such publications as *Educational Music Magazine* and *Woodwind Magazine* belong in this category.

Many colleges and universities prepare bibliographies of graduate research, either completed or in progress, which are available free or at nominal cost to the public. Some contain listings in several disciplines; others report only musical studies. Reports of sponsored research, both faculty and student, are distributed, in addition to the foregoing, by many colleges and universities.

Music educators engaged in research will often find useful data in periodicals and journals in other areas. Among those most likely to be useful are: *American Educational Research Journal, American Journal of Psychology, Education, Journal of the Acoustical Society of America, Journal of Aesthetics and Art Criticism, Educational Technology, Journal of Aesthetic Education, Journal of Applied Psychology, Journal of Educational Psychology, Journal of Educational Research, Journal of Experimental Education, NEA Research Bulletin, Phi Delta Kappan, Psychological Review, Review of Educational Research,*[18] and *Southern Journal of Educational Research.*

---

[17]For additional references see Chapter 17 in Ruth T. Watanabe, *Introduction to Music Research* (Englewood Cliffs, N. J.: Prentice-Hall, Inc., 1967).

[18]On a triennial basis the April issue of this publication devotes a section to research in music education. See Volumes XXV (1955), XXVIII (1958), XXXI (1961), XXXIV (1964), and XXXVII (1967).

Reports of research undertaken by staff members are sometimes printed by local school systems. For example, *Research Reports of Los Angeles City School Districts* include some projects in music education. Research in the field of music is also contained in publications from various state departments of education such as the *Minnesota National Laboratory News Bulletin.* The *ACLS Newsletter,* a publication of the American Council of Learned Societies, frequently contains information of interest to the researcher in music. *Computers and the Humanities,* a bimonthly newsletter, and *EDUCOM,* a ten-issue bulletin of the Inter-university Communications Council, are both computer-oriented and contain occasional articles of interest to music educators. The same is true of the *ICRH Newsletter,* a bimonthly publication of the Institute for Computer Research in the Humanities at New York University. *Educational Researcher,* official newsletter of the American Educational Research Association, which appears no more than eight times a year, includes many accounts of general interest to researchers in all disciplines of education.

YEARBOOKS AND PROCEEDINGS

Yearbooks of the Music Educators National Conference and its predecessor, the Music Supervisors National Conference, were published annually from 1910 to 1940, and are especially valuable for the researcher who is interested in philosophical and curricular trends in music education. *Music Education Source Book* [I], initially published in 1947, *Music in American Education: Source Book Number Two,* 1955, and *Perspectives in Music Education: Source Book III,* 1966, are successors to the yearbooks. *Proceedings of the Music Teachers National Association,* containing addresses and papers presented at the organization's annual conventions, was published from 1907-1949. Other items of import to the music researcher include *Proceedings of the National Association of Music Therapists* and *Yearbooks* of the National Society for Study in Education.[19] Additional potential sources of information are UNESCO publications on music education and periodic reports of the International Society for Music Education (ISME) and its semi-annual journal, the *International Music Educator.*

SPECIAL CATALOGS

Two important kinds of information, often overlooked by a music educator, are publications listing the holdings of music libraries and

---

[19]The Thirty-fifth *Yearbook,* Part II, 1936, and Fifty-seventh *Yearbook,* Part I, 1958, were devoted exclusively to music education.

thematic catalogs of incipits. These items are particularly beneficial to an individual who is interested in special collections. *Thematic Catalog of a Manuscript Collection of Eighteenth-Century Italian Instrumental Music in the University of California, Berkeley, Music Library,* by Vincent Duckles and Minnie Elmer, 1963, is an example of a publication by a university library. Representative of a municipal public library is the four-volume *Catalogue of the Allen A. Brown Collection of Music,* a very significant compilation of nineteenth-century opera and orchestral scores, published by the Boston Public Library from 1910-1916. Julia Gregory's *Catalog of Early Books of Music,* 1913, with the 1944 supplement, represents a valuable listing of books on music theory published before 1800 which are housed in the Library of Congress in Washington, D. C.[20]

In the past, catalogs of thematic incipits frequently have been marked by diversity of format from one library to another, with the result that an investigator sometimes finds the information contained in the card catalog less than satisfactory. The growing acceptance of electronic data processing (EDP) has opened up new potentialities for a more uniform system of cataloging thematic incipits according to LaRue and Logemann. They caution, however, that EDP is not inexpensive.[21]

DISSERTATIONS AND THESES

Since the vast majority of research in music education at present consists of reports which culminate in a graduate degree, the researcher should consider bibliographical compilations of these items to be a prime source. William S. Larson compiled two listings of completed master's and doctoral projects entitled *Bibliography of Research Studies in Music Education.* Covering the years 1932-1948, the first appeared in 1949. The second, published as Vol. V, No. 2, Fall, 1957 issue of the *Journal of Research in Music Education,* includes studies from 1949-1956. Roderick D. Gordon has continued the Larson bibliography of completed research but restricted the listing to doctoral studies. *Doctoral Dissertations in Music and Music Education (1957-1963),* compiled by Gordon, was published as Vol. XII, No. 1, Spring, 1964 issue of the *Journal of Research in Music Education,* and supplements have appeared in the first issue of 1965, 1966, and 1967 (Vols. XIII, XIV, and XV).

Doctoral Dissertations in Musicology, compiled by Helen Hewitt, lists studies both completed and in progress. This source should also be consulted by the researcher in music education. The fourth edition, pub-

---

[20]For additional references see Duckles, *op. cit.*
[21]Jan LaRue and George W. Logemann, "EDP for Thematic Catalogues," *Notes,* XXII (Summer, 1966), 1180.

lished in 1965, represents a cumulative listing of all items which had appeared in previous editions. Supplements to the fourth edition have appeared in the Fall 1966 and 1967 (Vols. XIX and XX respectively) issues of the *Journal of the American Musicological Society.*

Some master's theses in music are listed in *Master's Theses in Education,* Herbert M. Silvey, editor, which has appeared annually since 1953. The Larson bibliographies, however, constitute the best source for this information up to 1956. A regional compilation of master's degree projects in music education was completed by Borg and serves as a partial supplement to the Larson bibliographies.[22]

Research Studies in Education, an annual compilation undertaken by Phi Delta Kappa of doctoral dissertations, research reports, and field studies, includes many in music.

The foregoing compilations merely list titles of graduate research, whereas photographic copies of complete dissertations (either full-sized or microprint) and abstracts may be procured by the researcher who wishes to examine the research in detail.

University Microfilms, Inc.[23] began publishing doctoral dissertations on microfilm in 1938. An index to all doctoral dissertations accepted by institutions of higher learning in the United States and Canada is published annually by the same corporation. Over 150 colleges and universities participate in the program of the University Microfilms whereby monthly reports of doctoral research, numbering approximately 600 words each, are published in *Dissertation Abstracts.* Music projects are included under Section A (The Humanities). A recent catalog has been issued by University Microfilms entitled *Doctoral Dissertations Music: 1949-1964,* which lists the author, title, order number, and price of microfilm and Xerox copies of approximately 700 projects which have appeared in *Dissertation Abstracts* and its predecessor *Microfilm Abstracts.* DATRIX, a new computerized data retrieval system for doctoral studies operated by University Microfilms, will be discussed in the final chapter. As noted earlier in this chapter, some research reports may be obtained on microcard from the University of Rochester Press. Microcard Edition, Inc., Washington, D. C., also has a limited number of items of interest to the music researcher on microcard or microfiche.

GOVERNMENTAL PUBLICATIONS

A series of information booklets listing projects completed or underway, fortunately, is accompanying the current emphasis by the U. S.

---

[22]Earl E. Borg, "A Codified Bibliography of Music Education Research at the Master's Level in Selected Institutions of the North Central Association," (unpublished doctoral dissertation, Northwestern University, 1964).

[23]Now a subsidiary of the Xerox Corporation.

Office of Education in supporting educational research. In addition, research reports in music which have been printed by the U. S. Government Printing Office may be obtained from the Superintendent of Documents along with a brochure listing titles available. The pamphlets prepared at regular intervals by the Arts and Humanities Branch of the U. S. Office of Education are an even more lucrative source of music research projects. Included are research project number, the principal investigator and his institutional affiliation, title, and duration of projects which have been supported by federal funds.

Since November of 1966 *Research in Education* has been providing monthly accounts of research projects in various areas of education, including music, most of which have been supported by the U. S. Office of Education. Although the initial reports have been of research projects on deposit at the Educational Resources Information Center (ERIC) in Washington, D. C., others will be included once the backlog in ERIC has been eliminated.[24] *Office of Education Research Reports, 1956-65, Indexes and Resumés,* is a newly-issued two-volume directory of more than 1,200 significant educational research reports.

NECROLOGY

In order to make biographical information complete an investigator needs to discover sources of necrology. To examine all issues of newspapers and periodicals for several years to obtain this kind of information can be a very time consuming and frequently disappointing pursuit. Yet this undoubtedly is the best way to procure the needed information if it is not available elsewhere.

Fortunately for musicians and librarians Sirvart Poladian recently has made the task much easier by beginning a series entitled "Index to Music Necrology."[25] These accounts list name of the deceased, his nationality and musical distinction, date and place of death, and source of obituary.

This writer has made it a continuing practice to clip obituaries of musicians from newspapers, and then, after indicating date and publication, places them in a specially designated folder. From time to time the accounts are sorted and clippings appended to appropriate sources containing biographical sketches of these people. Such a system has

---

[24]Originally known as the Educational Research Information Center, the title of the acronym ERIC was changed in July, 1967 because the coverage of its publication, *Research in Education,* was expanded to include research in addition to that which was supported by federal funds.

[25]See *Notes,* XXII (Summer, 1966), 1193-1198 and *ibid.,* XXIII (June, 1967), 707-712.

advantages only if a person regularly pursues the policy over an extended period of time and has recourse to a newspaper which has extensive national and world-wide coverage.

Other publications such as the *Music Educators Journal* and *Time,* to mention only two with different coverage, also include necrology. Additional sources of necrological information include *Biography Index,* the *New York Times Index for Necrology,* and annual supplements to an encyclopedia, such as the *Britannica Book of the Year.* Maintaining a current chronography of every author listed in the card catalog, of course, is not the responsibility of the researcher. When data are not forthcoming, however, he must then obtain them in the best way he can.

ARCHIVES AND CENTRAL REPOSITORIES

Studies of a historical or analytical nature may make it necessary for a researcher to examine manuscripts, writings, and other artifacts in libraries or archives which are not open to the general public. An investigator interested in studying the compositions of New England composers, Charles C. Perkins (1823-1886) or James C. D. Parker (1828-1916), for example, almost certainly would need to plan a visit to the Harvard Musical Association in Boston, Massachusetts, to examine manuscripts, publications, and other materials of these composers housed there. For one interested in early Moravian music the collections of the Moravian Archives at Bethlehem, Pennsylvania, and Winston-Salem, North Carolina, contain prime source materials.

Unlike a public library, archives frequently are open only by invitation. A researcher, however, is usually granted the privilege to make visitations for research purposes if he follows the generally accepted pattern of protocol governing such matters. His procedure should be to: (1) ask permission to examine a certain collection or collections at a time convenient to the archivist, (2) state purposes and objectives for the visitation, and (3) obtain sponsorship from an institution of higher learning or recognized scholar in the field who is interested in the research. Authorities in the field and advisers usually can give excellent advice relative to the most likely repositories containing the information a researcher is seeking.

The Midwest Library Center, housing rarely used materials which normally circulate from the libraries of the Big Ten schools, and the New York State Library system are examples of central repositories which enable a researcher to procure materials that might otherwise be inaccessible to him. The new developments in information retrieval which are coming to the forefront in the future will make it possible for a scholar to receive within a matter of minutes an item which he may request. The material will be transmitted by a computer interchange system and can be reprinted on the spot, as it were, for the use of the one requesting it.

The Music Education Historical Research Center, which was established in 1965 at the University of Maryland in College Park, is envisioned to eventually become the most complete repository of music education materials in the United States. An investigator will soon be able to examine manuscripts, letters, papers, speeches, and other irreplaceable documents of leaders in music education both past and present. Also to be included are yearbooks, minutes from meetings of music educators, state music educators association publications, early instructional method books, and various other publications in the field of music education.

As noted earlier, the U. S. Office of Education recently established a documentation center known as ERIC to house and abstract research projects in education. These items are stored on magnetic tape and may be retrieved on demand by electronic computer. All projects in education which have been or currently are being supported by federal funds eventually will be included in this system of data storage, to be retrieved at a moment's notice. As already noted, research without federal subsidy will be included also.

The preparation of bibliographies of a composer's works or of articles in various areas of music is being undertaken by several individuals for use with information retrieval systems. The International Repertory of Music Literature (RILM), a computer-indexed international bibliography containing short abstracts of scholarly works about music published since January 1, 1967, is being directed by Barry S. Brook of Queens College, Flushing, New York. In addition, a special supplement to the *ACLS Newsletter* dated June, 1966, entitled "Computerized Research in the Humanities: A Survey," includes materials relating to bibliographical retrieval systems utilized in music.

One of the researcher's most important steps, it will be recalled, is that of examining literature in his field to determine the feasibility of his proposed study. The process seemingly is open-ended because new and significant information appears almost daily. It is important for the investigator to either possess or develop the proper techniques to efficiently utilize the many resources and processes of bibliographic information available to him. Some kinds of research are almost exclusively dependent on information obtained from various published and unpublished sources in libraries, archives, and private collections. Historical research, which best exemplifies this kind of investigation, will be discussed in the next chapter.

QUESTIONS FOR REVIEW AND DISCUSSION

1. What techniques can make use of the library more effective?
2. Why is the library card catalog an important source of preliminary information?
3. Compare methods of note taking. Give advantages and disadvantages of each one.
4. Consider the various photocopying processes and indicate which ones are accessible in your local library.
5. Think of a specific music topic and list categories under which reference materials may be found.

SUPPLEMENTARY READINGS

ALMACK, JOHN C. *Research and Thesis Writing*. Boston: Houghton Mifflin Co., 1930. Chapter IX.

BARZUN, JACQUES, and GRAFF, HENRY F. *The Modern Researcher*. New York: Harcourt, Brace and World, Inc., 1962. Chapters 4-6.

BEST, JOHN W. *Research in Education*. Englewood Cliffs, N. J.: Prentice-Hall, Inc., 1959. Chapter 3.

BORG, WALTER R. *Educational Research: An Introduction*. New York: David McKay Co., Inc., 1963. Chapter 3.

BRICKMAN, WILLIAM W. *Guide to Research in Educational History*. New York: New York University Bookstore, 1949. Chapters III and VI.

BURKE, ARVID J., and BURKE, MARY A. *Documentation in Education*. Fourth Edition, Revised. New York: Teachers College Press, Teachers College, Columbia University, 1967. Chapters 2, 3, 5, 10, and 15-22.

DUCKLES, VINCENT. *Music Reference and Research Materials*. Second Edition. New York: The Free Press, 1967.

GLENN, NEAL E., and TURRENTINE, EDGAR M. *Introduction to Advanced Study in Music Education*. Dubuque, Iowa: Wm. C. Brown Company Publishers, 1968. pp. 103-117.

GOOD, CARTER V. *Essentials of Educational Research*. New York: Appleton-Century-Crofts, 1966. Chapter 3.

———, and SCATES, DOUGLAS E. *Methods of Research*. New York: Appleton-Century-Crofts, 1954. Chapter 3.

Manual of Music Librarianship. Ann Arbor, Mich.: Music Library Association, Inc., 1966. Chapters V and X.

McGRATH, G. D., JELINEK, JAMES E., and WOCHNER, RAYMOND E. *Educational Research Methods*. New York: The Ronald Press Co., 1963. Chapter 8.

MORGAN, HAZEL B., and BURMEISTER, CLIFTON A. *Music Research Handbook*. Evanston, Ill.: The Instrumentalist Co., 1962. Chapter XI.

MOULY, GEORGE J. *The Science of Educational Research*. New York: American Book Co., 1963. Chapter 5.

SAX, GILBERT. *Empirical Foundations of Educational Research*. Englewood Cliffs, N. J.: Prentice-Hall, Inc., 1968. Chapter 4.

SCHNEIDER, ERWIN H., and CADY, HENRY L., "Evaluation and Synthesis of Research Studies Relating to Music Education," U. S. Office of Education Cooperative Research Project E-016, 1965. Item ED 010 298 in ERIC

Document Reproduction Service. Bethesda, Md.: National Cash Register Co., 4936 Fairmont Ave.

SMITH, HENRY L. *Educational Research, Principles and Practices.* Bloomington, Ind.: Educational Publications, 1944. Chapter IV.

VAN DALEN, DEOBALD B. *Understanding Educational Research.* Enlarged and Revised Edition. New York: McGraw-Hill Book Co., Inc., 1966. Chapters 5 and 6.

WATANABE, RUTH T. *Introduction to Music Research.* Englewood Cliffs, N. J.: Prentice-Hall, Inc., 1967. Chapters 2-7, 9-12, 16-17.

WHITNEY, FREDERICK L. *The Elements of Research.* Third Edition. Englewood Cliffs, N. J.: Prentice-Hall, Inc., 1950. Chapter IV and Appendix III.

WISE, JOHN E., NORDBERG, ROBERT B., and REITZ, DONALD J. *Methods of Research in Education.* Boston: D. C. Heath and Co., 1967. Chapter III.

CHAPTER

• 5 •

Historical Research:
A Chronicle of the Past

The collection of data pertaining to the past is known as history. Vincent notes that: "history is a narrative of the actions of human beings in connection with the topic of research, whether it be in politics, law, religion, music, or mechanical arts."[1] When data which have been assembled are interpreted the process is known as historiography, a procedure which is similar to the fourth of Dewey's steps of reflective thinking (accumulation and codification of data) discussed in Chapter 2 of this book. A researcher in music education who utilizes the historical method consequently is expected not only to obtain various kinds of information about the past related to his topic, but also to interpret them according to generally accepted techniques of historiography. Historical research also must employ the scientific method to adequately solve problems in history, as Best so appropriately remarks.[2]

PURPOSES OF HISTORICAL RESEARCH

Historical research is pursued for a variety of purposes. Results of the past may be used as the basis for a better understanding of the present or for predicting the future. Although this concept is not utilized as extensively in music education as it is in the social or political sciences, stylistic periods in music, for example, may be studied and better com-

---

[1]John M. Vincent, *Aids to Historical Research* (New York: Appleton-Century-Crofts, 1934), p. 139. Used by permission of Appleton-Century-Crofts.
[2]John W. Best, *Research in Education* (Englewood Cliffs, N. J.: Prentice-Hall, Inc., 1959), p. 86.

prehended with this objective in mind. The more formal, simple, and emotionally restrained Classical period in music may be better understood when contrasted with the highly chromatic, introspective, and less formal Romantic era. In the same manner, concepts of neoclassicism might become more evident when compared with classicism.

A desire to learn more about the life of a significant music educator, either contemporary or deceased, or the organization, development, and influence of a performing group or a professional organization presents many opportunities for a researcher who has an inclination in any of these directions. A historical study of the contributions to music and music education of Luther Whiting Mason (1828-1896) or Charles H. Farnsworth (1859-1947) would be examples of the former. Representative of the latter might be "The Chicago Symphony and Its Role in the Improvement of Musical Standards in Nineteenth Century United States" or "History of NIMAC and Its Influence on Music Education."

The quest for information to complete a missing link or bring solidarity to the figurative chain of knowledge about music is a third reason for the researcher in music education to undertake historical research. Intensive research to determine whether or not the composition which appeared about 1934 as Mozart's *Second Bassoon Concerto in B♭ Major* was actually written by the celebrated Austrian master is suggestive of the type of investigation appropriate for this kind of research. Doubts presently exist in the minds of many musicologists and instrumentalists regarding its authenticity. The possibility always exists, of course, that research in the future may either refute or verify these misgivings. The work, however, is not listed in the latest revision of the Mozart catalog of complete works.[3]

Undoubtedly the most significant reason for involvement in history today is the same one given by Thucydides (*c.* 460-*c.* 400 B.C.), generally acclaimed as the "father" of the modern historical method, who remarked that his purpose was "not to write for immediate applause but for posterity." This eminent Greek historian also explained very astutely that it was his duty to supplement, in a manner as accurate as possible, his own observations of the Peloponnesian War (431-404 B.C.) with the reports of others who were eyewitnesses to this famed ancient Greek conflict.

Although historical research in music is often regarded as the exclusive province of musicology, there really is little justification for this restrictiveness as an examination of historical studies in music education over the past twenty years readily reveals. Garrett, in defining the func-

---

[3]*Chronologisch-thematisches Verzeichnis sämtlicher Tonwerke Wolfgang Amadé Mozarts* (Weisbaden: Breitkopf and Härtel, 1964).

tion of the musicologist, indicates that he utilizes scholarly procedures to locate and organize data relating to the evolvement of all types of music.[4] These same conditions are incumbent upon the music educator engaged in historical research. There is no need for an investigator who uses the scientific method to be rigidly labeled, as is commonly done, according to some arbitrary distinction such as historian, musician, or educator. Rather, he should be regarded more properly as a "research scholar." This is in harmony with the views of Hockett who considers the utility of history as the "intellectual honesty which should be developed by the quest for truth in any field of knowledge, in defiance of all temptations to wander from the strait and narrow path which alone can lead to it."[5]

HISTORICAL RESEARCH PROCEDURES

Historical research is based on certain steps or procedures which, Hockett states, consist of "the gathering of data; the criticism of data; and the presentation of facts, interpretations, and conclusions in readable form."[6] The first point is, of course, closely related to sources and kinds of information needed for the study. External and internal criticism, to be discussed later in this chapter, are used respectively to determine the truthfulness and trustworthiness of the data. Hockett's final step, relating to exposition and interpretation of data, already has been referred to as historiography, but will recur throughout this chapter.

A slightly different emphasis is noted by Gottschalk, who asserts that "historical facts have to be (1) selected, (2) arranged, (3) emphasized or minimized, and (4) placed in some sort of causal sequence."[7] Gottschalk's first two steps relate to what Hockett calls "gathering of data." His third point bears a relationship to Hockett's "criticism of data" but with positive and negative implications. Finally, Gottschalk's sequence of data placement is closely allied to Hockett's "interpretations and conclusions."

The research of historians is sometimes criticized for being too subjective because the historiographer is not always in a position to exercise the rigid controls that are regarded as absolutely essential by the natural scientist. The historiographer, unlike the scientist, normally

---

[4]Allen M. Garrett, *An Introduction to Research in Music* (Washington: The Catholic University of America Press, 1958), pp. 2-3.

[5]Homer C. Hockett, *The Critical Method in Historical Research and Writing*, pp. 4-5. © 1955 by The Macmillan Co., New York. Used by permission of The Macmillan Co.

[6]*Ibid.*, p. 9. Used by permission of The Macmillan Co.

[7]Louis Gottschalk, *Understanding History* (New York: Alfred A. Knopf, Inc., 1958), p. 195.

concerns himself with more than an observation of the present. When a historiographer is involved in the preservation of today's chronology, which tomorrow will be history, he must be just as accurate and precise as the natural scientist in order that his objective of presenting and interpreting the truth be realized. A music critic, attending the world premiere of a composition by either a renowned or unknown composer, is on the threshold of history, as it were. His responsibility to the musical world in accurately reporting the performance of this new work is essentially no different from that of the reporter who writes the proceedings of a conference of the world's leaders for dissemination to the general public. Both have an obligation to provide information which is as objective, truthful, and unbiased as is humanly possible.

SOURCE MATERIALS

Source materials used by the historiographer normally are of two kinds, primary and secondary. A primary source of data, as noted in the third chapter, is "firsthand" information. When data are not original to the one reporting them they become "secondhand" or secondary sources. It also is possible to obtain information from a "tertiary" or other source even further removed from the original. Every effort should be made, though, to obtain original data because the fundamental basis of historical research is primary sources. Since this is deferentially recognized by a historiographer, avers Van Dalen, his energies are directed to obtaining this kind of information.[8]

An investigator who is involved in preparing the biography of a living person might use primary source materials such as correspondence with the individual; publications and manuscripts by the subject; legal and personal documents such as contracts, wills, and diaries; newspaper items; photographs and photocopies; concert programs; oral and written reports by contemporaries; and tape recordings of personal interviews with the subject.

Secondary sources often have value but should be utilized only when primary sources are difficult to procure or are untrustworthy. Brickman asserts, however, that reliable secondary sources are preferable to primary sources which are questionable or incomplete.[9] Secondary sources worthy of merit will be adequately documented since they should be based on primary materials. Accounts of a concert other than by a

---

[8]Deobald B. Van Dalen, *Understanding Educational Research* (Enlarged and Revised Edition; New York: McGraw-Hill Book Co., Inc., 1966), p. 179.

[9]William W. Brickman, *Guide to Research in Educational History* (New York: New York University Bookstore, 1949), p. 108.

person actually present are secondary as are specially prepared summary accounts of the minutes of official meetings. History books and many encyclopedia articles are secondary even though the author may have had recourse to primary materials. Likewise, publications by an individual may be primary sources, but when excerpts from them are quoted by another they become secondary.

The biographical account of a composer frequently includes an analysis of his music to indicate how events in his life may have influenced his creativity. For example, Doyle, in a doctoral study, combined historical with analytical research to identify the melodic and rhythmic characteristics of Louisiana Creole and Latin American folk music found in the compositions of Louis Moreau Gottschalk (1829-1869).[10] Doyle concluded that Gottschalk was not only the first American composer-pianist to achieve international recognition, but also the initial American to use folk songs and rhythms of the Americas in his compositions.

SELECTION OF TOPIC

Although factors in the selection of a topic already have been discussed at considerable length in Chapter 2, five that Brickman considers to be significant before the subject of the historical research has been determined are: (1) interest, (2) source materials, (3) the time factor, (4) relevance to course, and (5) specialized knowledge.[11] The reader will recognize immediately that these steps differ only slightly in emphasis from those listed in Chapter 2.

The energies of the researcher in music education should be directed specifically toward a topic in which he has an intense interest. A high school choral director, for instance, might be desirous of writing a history of the high school choral contest-festival movement in the United States. After preliminary investigation, however, he may find that source materials are so limited that it would be impractical for him to continue with his original idea without expansion. To expand the topic obviously would require additional time, a factor which might not be feasible in a course in research methodology such as that taught by this writer, where a deadline becomes an external factor imposed only by the duration of the instructional period.

Relevance to the course is an aspect which has not been mentioned previously. Brickman, in this connection, states emphatically that the topic of a research report should bear relevance to the objectives of

---

[10]John C. Doyle, "The Piano Music of Louis Moreau Gottschalk (1829-1869)," (unpublished doctoral dissertation, New York University, 1960).

[11]Brickman, *op. cit.*, pp. 3-5.

the research class.[12] While there may be exceptions, it is only logical that a researcher in music education would be expected to select a topic which he could develop in relationship to music education. This assumes that one of the principal objectives of a music education research course is to give a student experience in making practical application of the precepts he learns there. More diligent attention to Brickman's enjoinder could result in fewer music education research proposals being questioned on the basis of suitability.

In the realm of specialized knowledge, the reader hardly needs to be reminded that the researcher who is contemplating a study of the history of music education in Germany, to cite a possibility, should possess both an adequate reading comprehension of German, since most primary sources likely would be in German, and of the history of music education in general. It would be very impractical for such an investigator, as noted earlier in this book, to attempt logical translations exclusively with the use of a German-English lexicon, especially if he were unfamiliar with music education terminology and philosophical principles.

KINDS OF DATA

The musician involved in historical research will most likely find that his data fall into one or more of the following categories: (1) discovering heretofore unknown information about an individual, group, object, or era; (2) locating heretofore unknown creativity of an individual; (3) uncovering more complete or an authentic copy of an individual's works; (4) finding an individual's creative efforts which were known to have been written but which previously were not believed to be extant; (5) collecting, codifying, or analyzing information of historical import from diverse sources; (6) proving that reputed documents, statements, or creative works are spurious; and (7) rectifying incorrect statements, dates, or information that previously had been accepted as true or unchallenged.

One of the most gratifying by-products of historical research is the discovery of heretofore unknown information about an individual, group, object, or era. Although such data often result from serendipity, opportunities for revelations of this kind are all too infrequent in music education. The most likely sources of such information are newly discovered manuscripts, personal letters, or documents which previously were unavailable to the general public. Barzun and Graff give an interesting

---

[12]*Ibid.*, p. 4.

account of the former's discovery of a previously suppressed letter of Berlioz that appeared shortly after the first appearance of his Rákóczy March in 1846. The original was not only misdated but also distorted from a letter basically musical in content to one with "political" implications.[13]

Reports announcing the discovery of heretofore unknown creativity normally are of two kinds: items which have been identified positively as authentic and those about which some question remains regarding authenticity. Periodicals such as the *Journal of the American Musicological Society* and the *Musical Quarterly* frequently contain accounts of the discovery of lost items. Pauly, for example, reports on some newly discovered manuscripts of Michael Haydn (1737-1806), a composer of sacred music and younger brother of Franz Joseph Haydn (1732-1809). He indicated that as the result of several months of research in libraries in Austria, France, Germany, and Italy, he located extensive holdings, previously unknown, of the younger Haydn's manuscripts in the Bavarian State Library in Munich and in monasteries throughout Austria.[14] The credibility of Pauly's findings remains unchallenged at this writing.

The discovery a few years ago of a *Violin Concerto in C Major,* reputedly by Beethoven, is an example of a composition whose authenticity still is uncertain. Another is the Mozart bassoon concerto to which reference was made earlier in this chapter. In both instances further investigation is necessary before it can be stated with conviction that they belong to the respective catalog of works by these composers.

In addition to locating previously unknown works, another source of personal satisfaction to a researcher is to uncover a more complete or authentic copy of a musical composition or other creative work of an individual. This writer, for example, while examining stacks of uncataloged instrumental music at the Moravian Archives in Winston-Salem, North Carolina, in 1949, located a complete set of the *Three Trios,* Opus 3, of John Antes (1740-1811), minus the last page of the violoncello part. John Bland of London published these undated trios, apparently about 1785, because Antes was known to have been in England then. Prior to this writer's discovery in 1949 the only known set in existence consisted of a second violin and a violoncello part owned by the Sibley Musical Library at the Eastman School of Music in Rochester, New York. A comparison of the Eastman and Winston-Salem copies disclosed exact duplication. Thus by using the Winston-

---

[13]Jacques Barzun and Henry F. Graff, *The Modern Researcher* (New York: Harcourt, Brace and World, Inc., 1957), p. 101.

[14]Reinhard G. Pauly, "Some Recently Discovered Michael Haydn Manuscripts," *Journal of the American Musicological Society,* X (Summer, 1957), 97-103.

Salem first and second violin parts and the Eastman violoncello part it was possible to present the first modern performance of *Trio in D Minor,* Opus 3, No. 2, the second of these charming Haydnesque trios, at the University of Iowa, Iowa City, on May 19, 1950, with violinists Stella Hopper and Joanne Dempsey, and Charles Becker, violoncellist, as performing artists.

Antes, whose surname is the Greek equivalent of von Blume, was born at Frederick-trop, Montgomery County, Pennsylvania, on March 24, 1740. In accord with prevailing educational philosophy of the Moravians at that time, Antes intensively pursued musical instruction in his youth in addition to his other studies. In 1769, after being ordained at Marienborn, Germany, he went to Egypt as a missionary. While recuperating from physical inflictions suffered there, Antes composed some quartets and other compositions after which he returned to Europe in 1782. In Vienna, according to Grider, Antes met Haydn who assisted other musicians in the performance of some of his compositions.[15] It was during this period of convalescence in Cairo that the trios were written, as indicated by the inscription on the title page which states in part "Composti a Grand Cairo dal Sigre Giovanni A-T-S. Dillettante Americano. Op. 3." [Composed at Grand Cairo by Mr. John A-T-S. American Dilettante. Op. 3.] Quite in keeping with a custom of the time, Antes perplexingly listed himself as A-T-S, as just noted, a factor which resulted in his anonymity until 1940, when Carleton Sprague Smith, then chief of the Music Division of the New York Public Library, revealed the identity of this important Moravian composer.[16]

When any work is unearthed its importance ultimately may rest on its value when viewed in light of historical perspective. Under ordinary circumstances, the discovery of works by someone such as Antes, who is relatively unknown to music educators, probably would go unheralded. In terms of historical perspective, however, the Antes *Trios* assume a new dimension. They represent, as far as this writer has been able to discern, the earliest extant chamber music written by a native-born American.[17]

---

[15]Rufus A. Grider, *Historical Notes on Music in Bethlehem, Pennsylvania from 1741 to 1871* (Philadelphia: John L. Pile, 1873), p. 56.

[16]These trios have been reissued by Boosey and Hawkes, Oceanside, N.Y. and recorded in the Society for the Preservation of the American Music Heritage Series, Karl Krueger, editor, on Record MIA 99, "Instrumental Music in Colonial America," and on Columbia ML-6141 by members of the Fine Arts Quartet.

[17]For additional information see the microcard version of this writer's doctoral dissertation *The History and Practice of Chamber Music in the United States from Earliest Times up to 1875* (Rochester, N.Y.: The University of Rochester Press, 1958), pp. 241-247, 579-580, 654-726.

Another phase of historical research in music education which is bound to bring personal gratification is ferreting out an individual's creative efforts which were known to have been written but which previously were not believed to be extant. At the Moravian Archives in Winston-Salem, in the same pile of uncataloged instrumental compositions which contained the Antes *Trios*, this writer discovered the manuscript of "Parthia IX" by David Moritz Michael (1751-1825), generally regarded as the most important nineteenth-century Moravian instrumental composer. Rau and David, in their catalog of American Moravian music, report that "Parthia IX" was to be found neither at Bethlehem nor Lititz.[18] Previous to this they had indicated that the collections at Lititz and Bethlehem contained thirteen wind *partien*.[19] With the finding of "Parthia IX" it may safely be stated that Michael composed at least fourteen *partien*, all of which exist in manuscript in the Moravian Archives either at Bethlehem, which now contains the former Lititz holdings, or at Winston-Salem.[20] Since Bethlehem and Winston-Salem served as ecclesiastical headquarters for the northern and southern divisions of the Moravian Church, respectively, the duplication in manuscript of some compositions in the Archives of these two cities may be explained by the constant interchange of personnel. Michael, however, confined his activities to Bethlehem and Nazareth, Pennsylvania.

These *partien*, in accordance with the meaning of the word, were meant to be performed out-of-doors. Grider notes that they usually were performed from a balustraded balcony of the home of the Moravian Brethren on Wednesday evenings during the summer for the benefit of the citizens of the community.[21]

In four short technically easy movements, "Parthia IX," except for the second movement, is scored for two clarinets in B♭, two French horns in B♭, and bassoon. The first (Allegro), third (Minuet), and fourth (Allegro) are in the key of B♭ Major. The second (Andante), in the key of F Major, is scored only for two B♭ clarinets and bassoon.

Collecting, codifying, or analyzing information of historical import from diverse sources, sometimes known as "documentary research," represents another very important aspect of historical research in music education. In a doctoral study exemplifying this type of research, Warren traced the origins of the Music Education Research Council and the

---

[18]Albert G. Rau and Hans T. David, *A Catalogue of Music by American Moravians (1742-1842)* (Bethlehem, Pa.: The Moravian Seminary and College for Women, 1938), p. 102.

[19]*Ibid.*, p. 98.

[20]Regarding these Michael *partien* see this writer's doctoral dissertation, *op. cit.*, pp. 377-381, 820-851.

[21]Grider, *op. cit.*, p. 9.

Journal of Research in Music Education.[22] In research of this type the investigator assembles data from all available sources, codifies them, and presents his interpretations. The values of this type of study for the musical layman as well as the professional music educator are obvious. Someone who has neither the time nor the inclination to ferret out answers to his questions usually welcomes the opportunity to obtain detailed and comprehensive information from one codified source. It is for this reason that dictionaries and encyclopedias of musical biography, terminology, and other kinds of information are so widely used by music educators and others who are seeking ready references.

The annals of historiography are replete with examples of documents, statements, compositions, or items which, although they may have been accepted at one time as authentic, subsequently have been proven to be spurious. An often quoted example is the account of the fantastic and fanciful Cardiff Giant, unearthed in upstate New York in the late nineteenth century. Good tells of a different and more contemporary type of chicanery involving an individual who had received a baccalaureate degree from a music school in 1950 and who, by 1963, through extensive forgery, had been able to fabricate a transcript, complete with official registrar's seal, equivalent to two graduate degrees.[23] This writer's evaluation of the authenticity of a string quartet allegedly by Benjamin Franklin (1706-1790) and of a copy of a composition supposedly by Sidney Lanier (1842-1881) will be discussed later in this chapter under External Criticism.

Numerous examples exist in music as well as in history in general of the rectification of statements, dates, or beliefs that previously have been accepted as correct. Brickman, Gottschalk, and Hockett present several accounts to show that many anecdotes and statements attributed to George Washington, Thomas Jefferson, and Abraham Lincoln, among many other distinguished Americans, have proven to be illusory.

The correction of an improperly dated musical example which is well known to students of music history is cited. Hockett, in reporting on the English round *Sumer is icumen in,* says: "A recent example of misdating due to unskillful use of evidence concerns an old musical piece known from its opening words as *Sumer is icumen.* Nineteenth-century historians thought it was written about 1240 because that was the date of another piece in the same manuscript. Not until the 1940's was the

---

[22]Fred A. Warren, "A History of the Music Education Research Council and the *Journal of Research in Music Education* of the Music Educators National Conference," (unpublished doctoral dissertation, University of Michigan, 1966).
[23]Carter V. Good, *Essentials of Educational Research* (New York: Appleton-Century-Crofts, 1966), p. 166.

error discovered when a professor from an American university pointed out that the handwriting of the two pieces was not the same, and that the musical notation of the *Sumer* did not come into use until long after 1240, making the probable date of *Sumer* about 1310."[24] This rectification of date, of course, was made by the late Manfred Bukofzer (1910-1955).

Another example of pertinence to musicians will illustrate this point. Boston University generally has been acclaimed as the institution which, in 1876, granted the first Bachelor of Music degree in the United States. Eells, on the other hand, relates that a report of the U. S. Commissioner of Education for 1873 confirms that the distinction properly belongs to Adrian College in Michigan. He notes that Trustees Minutes of Adrian College, dated June, 1873, list Mrs. Mattie B. Pease Lowrie as the recipient of a Bachelor of Music degree in 1873.[25]

The evaluation of results of information has been discussed to some extent in conjunction with the foregoing seven kinds of data. The historical method, however, is more explicitly concerned with external and internal criticism, or the "how" techniques.

EXTERNAL CRITICISM OR AUTHENTICITY

Through the process of external (or lower) criticism the investigator learns whether or not the subject of scrutiny is authentic. Many aspects constitute the over-all meaning of external criticism, but the prime objective is to determine whether or not the item of concern is genuine. Hockett, in defining external criticism, states: "It examines *documents*—a comprehensive term which . . . includes not only manuscripts but books, pamphlets, maps, and even ancient inscriptions and monuments."[26]

Some of the questions which might be asked by a researcher in music education who is involved in external criticism are: (1) Where was the item originally located? Where is it now? (2) Is this document an original version or a copy? If a copy, where is the original? (3) What is the estimated age of the item? Does it appear to be as old as it should be to be authentic? (4) Are there autographs or other identifications which will make the process of verification easier? (5) Is the handwriting (in the case of manuscripts) consistent with other items by the reputed writer? (6) Are there any indications (diaries, news-

---

[24]Hockett, *op. cit.*, p. 26. Used by permission of The Macmillan Co.

[25]Walter C. Eells, "First American Degrees in Music," *History of Education Quarterly,* I (March, 1961), 36.

[26]Hockett, *op. cit.*, p. 14. Used by permission of The Macmillan Co.

paper accounts, programs, etc.) that such an item may have existed? (7) Is there any reason to suspect that this item may be a hoax?

The process of external criticism frequently necessitates involvement in auxiliary areas. Some of those most useful to a musician might be photography, paleography, semantics, chronology, geneology, and cartography. In addition he may find himself trying to determine the watermark of a document as well as the age and kind of paper used.

To answer the specific questions posed above by making an application of the principles of external criticism, attention is directed to an intriguing and beguiling flute and piano composition by Sidney Lanier (1842-1881) entitled "Danse des Moucherons." This writer has in his possession a negative photostat of this short, rhapsodic, chromatic work. In an attempt to locate the original manuscript the holdings of the Lanier Room at Johns Hopkins University in Baltimore, Maryland, Oglethorpe University in Georgia, and other likely sources were checked without success. In addition, personal correspondence with Lanier's children, each of whom courteously replied, failed to shed any light on manuscripts other than those at Johns Hopkins which, as just noted, does not possess the original to "Danse des Moucherons." Henry W. Lanier, who indicated that his manuscripts had been given to the Lanier collection at Johns Hopkins University, wrote the following regarding his father, a self-taught flutist and poet: "He once said to his wife what I believe to be literally true—that the difficulty with him was *not* to write down music. The moment he had time and strength, there were songs ready to be born."[27]

Lending validity to this statement it should be noted that several brief sketches may be found in the Lanier Room at Johns Hopkins University including his projected "Quartette," "Tuno Religioso" (for two flutes or violas), "La Reve," (three flutes and bass flute), and "Trio for flute, pianoforte and violoncello."

Inconclusive answers thus must be given to the first two queries when the principles of external criticism are applied. To the third, this writer was informed that his copy was reproduced directly from the original manuscript. The date 1873 appears after Lanier's name, yet the style of handwriting with regard to tempo and dynamics is inconsistent. The tempo markings, in particular, appear to be in a more contemporary hand, especially on the last two pages of the six-page composition. In addition, the twelve-line manuscript paper on which the composition was written bears this inscription: "Carl Fischer, New York. Monarch Brand Warranted." It is true that Sidney Lanier spent some time in

---

[27]Henry W. Lanier, personal letter, March 17, 1949.

New York from 1870 to 1872, the year in which Carl Fischer arrived in the city. Fischer's first business venture, however, was in musical instruments. It was not until considerably later that the publishing phase of the company began.

There are no autographs or other identifications on this writer's copy which would suggest a negative answer to the fourth question. The composer's name is indicated by a combination of upper and lower case hand lettering. The tempo and dynamic terms, as just noted, appear to be in two different kinds of handwriting, thus making them difficult to compare with the notation of the composer's name and identification of the composition. Starke, in his biographical and critical account of Lanier's life, includes a photostatic copy of the flute part of the second and concluding page of this "Gnat Symphony" which consists of only three and one-half lines.[28] The page does contain Lanier's account, in a very neat and unhurried handwriting, of the composition, which the composer describes as a "translation of the sound." As already related, this writer's copy contains six pages, including the piano part, but the last twelve measures of the flute part of the two versions do not agree.

In response to the fifth query, a comparison was made of the item just cited and another one by Lanier, his unaccompanied flute solo "Wind Song," which Starke indicates was performed in October of 1874, but apparently written earlier.[29] A strong similarity is evident in handwriting; both appear in a style which shows a lighter, more delicate and less hurried stroke than that in the copy of "Danse des Moucherons" possessed by this writer.

An indication that such an item by this Georgia poet-musician may have existed, the object of the sixth query, has already been cited in conjunction with the previous discussion and included in the bibliography under "Music by Lanier."[30] It also is listed in *Centennial Edition of the Works and Letters of Sidney Lanier.*[31]

To answer the seventh query, although the composition is listed by both Starke and Graham, because of the discrepancies which exist, it would appear that the authenticity of the copy of "Danse des Moucherons" in this writer's possession must be open to serious question. Perhaps additional research in the future will result in more convincing data to suggest otherwise. The universal dilemma faced by all historians who must pass judgment on a document, especially if there are some

---

[28]Aubrey H. Starke, *Sidney Lanier* (Chapel Hill, N.C.: University of North Carolina Press, 1933), opposite p. 174.
[29]*Ibid.*, opposite p. 184.
[30]*Ibid.*, p. 462.
[31]Philip Graham (ed.), *Centennial Edition of the Works and Letters of Sidney Lanier* (Vol. VI; Baltimore, Md.: Johns Hopkins Press, 1945), p. 389.

questions about its veracity, is pinpointed by Hockett, who prudently notes that additional evidence eventually may appear to alter previously accepted ideas.[32]

To cite another example of the utilization of principles of external criticism, this writer became intrigued by an item which appeared in a now defunct New York City newspaper a few years ago. The article, a dispatch from Lynchburg, Virginia, indicated in part that a previously unknown quartet for strings by Benjamin Franklin was soon to have its initial performance in Philadelphia, largely through the efforts of a woman who was an Associate Professor of French at a local woman's college. The professor's attention was called to this composition by the owner of a Parisian bookstore in which she was browsing. The article stated that the quartet was discovered by an eminent musicologist in a pile of forgotten works, although their location was not disclosed.[33]

Several factors should be noted relative to this quartet. The original manuscript, in tablature, was reputed by the transcriber to be housed in the Bibliothèque Nationale in Paris. Music librarian E. Lebeau, however, in correspondence with this writer, indicated: "la Bibliothèque nationale, et la Bibliothèque du Conservatoire qui en fait partie, ne possèdent ni quatuor ni aucune oeuvre musicale de Banjamin Franklin."[34] [The national library and the library of the Conservatory which is a part of it, possess neither the quartet nor any other musical composition of Benjamin Franklin.]

The real motive behind the use of tablature would be interesting to learn. In the preface to his transcription, which was published in 1945, the transcriber indicates that the original, in the Bibliothèque, as just related, is in the handwriting of a professional copyist of the late eighteenth century, who otherwise remains unidentified. Benjamin Franklin (1706-1790), served as United States Ambassador to France from 1776 to 1785, and it is known that he attended concerts while in Paris, including performances of chamber music at the salon of Madame Helvetius d'Auteuil. It does seem rather strange, though, that tablature would be used for a string quartet so late in the eighteenth century, since this type of writing, except for guitar and other fretted instruments, had largely been replaced by the conventional system of notation currently in use. Also unexplained is the rationale for placing each of the four instruments (three violins and violoncello) in scordatura. The utilization of this system of mistuning by Heinrich Biber (1644-1704) is well known, but the simple, uninteresting, single melody line employed for each instrument in the alleged Franklin quartet suggests no need

[32]Hockett, op. cit., p. 8.
[33]New York Herald Tribune, November 10, 1946.
[34]E. Lebeau, personal letter, April 7, 1949.

for scordatura, which normally was used with multiple stops. By using scordatura, however, each instrumentalist can play his part in this quartet entirely on open strings, another curious circumstance.

Each of the five movements is short. The first bears no subtitle, but appears to be in a march tempo. Other movements respectively are: menuetto, capriccio, menuetto, and siciliano. The *capriccio* and *siciliano* basically are tripartite while the others are in two parts structurally. Unusual, too, is the inclusion of five movements in a quartet of this period in musical history; also, the use of three violins and violoncello.

Information from the Franklin Institute of Philadelphia, where the first contemporary performance of the quartet was scheduled, was to the effect that the work had not yet been presented. Furthermore, all attempts to establish communication with the discoverer and the transcriber of the work proved to be fruitless. These repeated efforts continued for approximately two years, until the death of the transcriber.

Finally, no definite proof has yet been advanced to show that Franklin actually knew enough about the techniques of musical composition to enable him to compose a quartet or any other musical work for that matter. True, he often is credited with the invention of the armonica, or musical glasses, a distinction which he denied. Franklin, however, admittedly did make many improvements on the instrument, whose sweet and pleasant tinkling sounds were recognized in compositions by Mozart and Beethoven.

In view of the rather consistent pattern of negative evidence, it must be concluded that this work unquestionably is spurious. The Franklin quartet appears to be a musical joke, the product of an anonymous jester. It always is possible, though, that more positive data may be forthcoming in the future which could result in a more exact evaluation.

INTERNAL CRITICISM OR CREDIBILITY

Had the evidence regarding the Lanier and Franklin compositions been more positive, investigation of other factors, known as internal (or higher) criticism would have proceeded. Fortunately, there are many occasions when this additional step is necessary. Although it may be established through external criticism that a document, item, or statement is authentic, there may be inaccuracies or inconsistencies within. The purpose of internal criticism, according to Gottschalk, is to establish whether data are "at all credible, and if so, to what extent."[35] The more experienced researcher will frequently engage in external and

---

[35]Gottschalk, *op. cit.*, p. 138.

internal criticism simultaneously, in which he will use information from one to assist in the implementation of the other.

Internal criticism is divided into positive and negative phases by some historiographers. In making a distinction between them, Brickman states that positive criticism endeavors to ascertain the true meaning of statements, whereas negative criticism concerns a researcher's rationale for discrediting them as evidenced by the partiality or inefficiency displayed by a writer.[36]

Among the queries which must be answered by an investigator in music education when he is concerned with internal criticism are: (1) Stylistically is the document consistent with others by the writer? Are there major inconsistencies? (2) Are there any indications that the writer was inaccurate in his reporting? (3) Does the writer actually mean what he says? (4) Could this work have been written by someone else in the style of this individual? and (5) Is there any evidence that the writer is biased or prejudiced?

It generally is conceded that an artist does change his manner of expressing himself stylistically due to the natural process of artistic growth and development. For example, students of music literature are regularly concerned with comparing the various characteristics of a composer's stylistic periods. One of the most obvious examples is the three distinctive epochs in the creative life of Ludwig van Beethoven (1770-1827); the first ending about 1802, the second approximately in 1815, and the third in 1827.

Although a composer may show stylistic changes during his lifetime, the musical idioms which he uses usually persist throughout his creative life. Characteristic idioms serve as guides for the researcher when attempting to ascertain whether or not the composition in question is consistent with others by the same composer. When major inconsistencies are observed it is always possible that the composer has deliberately altered his style by using different idioms. On the other hand, the features which are incongruent also suggest that these works are indeed by two different individuals. In the instance of a composer such as Arnold Schoenberg (1874-1951), a change in both stylistic characteristics and musical idioms is apparent in the transition from the post-romantic style of the *Verklärte Nacht* to dodecaphonic *Pierrot Lunaire*.

Occasionally inaccuracies will be suspected in a document. The incorrect dating of a letter by Berlioz to his publisher indicating that he was forwarding the Table of Contents to a book is described by Barzun and Graff. Berlioz dated his communication "Thursday June 23"

---

[36]Brickman, *op. cit.*, p. 95.

and Barzun and Graff point out that the year must have been 1852, in which case June 23 fell on Wednesday. They also remind their readers that it was not unusual for Berlioz to mistake the day of the week.[37]

A third question which might be raised in regard to internal criticism is whether or not the individual actually meant what he said. Although some confusion understandably could come from a writer's assumption that his readers comprehend and agree with his definition and use of certain terminology, a misunderstanding often is more than merely a problem of semantics. Witness persons who use the word "cornett" when "cornet" is intended. Despite the difference of only a final "t" between the two words, the instruments are vastly dissimilar in nature. The former refers to an obsolete fifteenth- and sixteenth-century instrument, normally made of wood, containing six finger holes and played with a cup-shaped mouthpiece. A three-valved instrument constructed of metal, the contemporary cornet is similar to the trumpet, but shorter in length. Furthermore, the cup-shaped mouthpiece of the cornet is larger and deeper than the one used on the cornett.

The next query, more applicable to music than other disciplines, is concerned with compositions which may have been written by an imposter in the style of another. Especially suspect are "newly discovered" works by such well-known composers as Haydn and Mozart. Reasons for this type of deception vary, but one of the most common is to enable someone who is unheralded to capitalize on the name of an esteemed composer. On the other hand, there are numerous examples in which a musician, in good faith and with no attempt at deception, has completed works left unfinished by a composer at the time of his death. A representative example is Mozart's *Requiem*, which was finished by his protégé and intimate friend Franz X. Sussmayer (1766-1803).

Despite the best of intentions, it is difficult to be completely unbiased or unprejudiced. Some writers, of course, deliberately present a unilateral point of view, as may be evinced in some early textbooks on the history of music in the United States. The treatise by Frédéric L. Ritter, *Music in America*, for instance, is generally regarded as strongly oriented and prejudiced in the direction of German Romanticism.

In a general sense the realm of esthetic judgment is characterized by personal predilection and preference just as is the choice of an automobile or other personal utilitarian or luxury commodity. When reviewing a concert it likely would be more difficult for a critic who prefers the piano music of Liszt to that of Chopin to present an unbiased account when the works of both composers are being reviewed than it

---

[37]Barzun and Graff, *op. cit.*, p. 100.

would be for one who has no preference between them. Likewise, two different concert artists do not render performances of the same composition in precisely an identical manner. Gottschalk, aware of these differences in interpretation, comments: "perhaps it is desirable that they should. Musicians are, after a fashion, merely historians interpreting past achievements of a specialized nature."[38]

Historical research can provide many challenging and gratifying opportunities for a music educator to make significant contributions to man's knowledge. Through the application of principles of historiography the researcher in music can employ the scientific method to objectively obtain and evaluate data. Experimental research, which undoubtedly uses the scientific method more consistently and effectively than any other type, will be the subject of examination in the next chapter.

QUESTIONS FOR REVIEW AND DISCUSSION

1. For what reasons does a music education researcher pursue historical research?
2. Differentiate between primary and secondary sources and give some specific examples of each. How do you determine whether primary or secondary sources should be used?
3. Into what categories might data for historical research in music education fall? Substantiate your answer with specific examples.
4. Discuss the place of external criticism in historical research. What specific questions might a music education researcher ask when involved in external criticism?
5. What function does internal criticism serve in historical research? Differentiate between the negative and positive phases of internal criticism. What specific questions might be asked by the music education researcher engaged in applying the principles of internal criticism?

SUPPLEMENTARY READINGS

ALMACK, JOHN C. *Research and Thesis Writing*. Boston: Houghton Mifflin Co., 1930. Chapter VII.
BARZUN, JACQUES, and GRAFF, HENRY F. *The Modern Researcher*. New York: Harcourt, Brace and World, Inc., 1962. Chapters 7-10.
BEST, JOHN W. *Research in Education*. Englewood Cliffs, N. J.: Prentice-Hall, Inc., 1959. Chapter 4.
BORG, WALTER R. *Educational Research: An Introduction*. New York: David McKay Co., Inc., 1963. Chapter 9.
BRICKMAN, WILLIAM W. *Guide to Research in Educational History*. New York: New York University Bookstore, 1949. Chapters II, IV, and V.

[38]Gottschalk, *op. cit.*, pp. 207-208.

COOK, DAVID R. *A Guide to Educational Research*. Boston: Allyn and Bacon, Inc., 1965. Chapter II.

GARRETT, ALLEN M. *An Introduction to Research in Music*. Washington: The Catholic University of America Press, 1958. Chapters IX and X.

GOOD, CARTER V. *Essentials of Educational Research*. New York: Appleton-Century-Crofts, 1966. Chapter 4.

———, and SCATES, DOUGLAS E. *Methods of Research*. New York: Appleton-Century-Crofts, 1954. Chapter 4.

GOTTSCHALK, LOUIS. *Understanding History*. New York: Alfred A. Knopf, Inc., 1958. Chapters III, V-VII.

HILLWAY, TYRUS. *Introduction to Research*. Second Edition. Boston: Houghton Mifflin Co., 1964. Chapter 11.

HOCKETT, HOMER C. *The Critical Method in Historical Research and Writing*. New York: The Macmillan Co., 1955. pp. 13-70.

JOHNSON, H. EARLE. "The Need for Research in the History of American Music," *Journal of Research in Music Education*," VI (Spring, 1958), 43-61.

MOULY, GEORGE J. *The Science of Educational Research*. New York: American Book Co., 1963. Chapter 9.

PHELPS, ROGER P. "The Mendelssohn Quintet Club: A Milestone in American Music Education," *Journal of Research in Music Education*, VIII (Spring, 1960), 39-44.

SMITH, HENRY L. *Educational Research, Principles and Practices*. Bloomington, Ind.: Educational Publications, 1944. Chapter VII.

TRAVERS, ROBERT M. W. *An Introduction to Educational Research*. Second Edition. New York: The Macmillan Co., 1964. Chapter 4.

VAN DALEN, DEOBALD B. *Understanding Educational Research*. Enlarged and Revised Edition. New York: McGraw-Hill Book Co., Inc., 1966. Chapter 9.

VINCENT, JOHN M. *Aids to Historical Research*. New York: Appleton-Century-Crofts, 1934. Chapters II, V, and XII.

WHITNEY, FREDERICK L. *The Elements of Research*. Third Edition. Englewood Cliffs, N. J.: Prentice-Hall, Inc., 1950. Chapter VIII.

WISE, JOHN E., NORDBERG, ROBERT B., and REITZ, DONALD J. *Methods of Research in Education*. Boston: D. C. Heath and Co., 1967. Chapter IV.

· 6 ·

Experimental Research:
Purview of the Future

Experimental research usually is regarded as the most objective of the five methods of obtaining data discussed in this book. Because of the rigid controls exercised in experimental research it is possible to duplicate this kind of study and receive virtually the same results, something which is not as easy to accomplish in historical, descriptive, philosophical, or analytical research. Experimental, laboratory, or empirical research is sometimes regarded as "a glimpse into the future" because it can indicate what is possible under carefully controlled situations. Even though the investigator often has an idea of the outcomes of his study, with better controls possible in experimental studies, the results usually are more definitive than in other kinds of research. Research conducted in the laboratory has long been regarded as the "method of science." It is from the laboratory that scientific concepts were adapted and applied to educational research. Experimental research in education, however, usually attempts to empirically simulate these laboratory conditions in the classroom with groups rather than with individuals.

Research conducted by the experimental method essentially is of two kinds: basic or fundamental and industrial. Basic research, most often pursued without regard for material advantage, is perhaps best exemplified in music education by doctoral or postgraduate experimental projects which are concerned directly with finding realistic solutions to problems and only indirectly with financial benefits. Doctoral studies by Hammer[1] and Woelflin[2] and postdoctoral research by Petzold[3] and Spohn[4] are representative examples of basic experimental research in music education.

In contrast, industrial research is usually conducted primarily for economic or some other advantage. A music educator rarely is involved in this financially lucrative kind of activity although he may benefit indirectly when new products are marketed thereby improving his effectiveness as a teacher.

Many illustrious individuals have distinguished themselves in various areas of experimental research. Some of these are: Herbart and Pestalozzi (education), Binet, Terman, and Otis (psychology), Harvey (blood circulation), Faraday (electricity), and Seashore, Kwalwasser, and Wing (psychology of music). Recently music therapy has begun to achieve acceptance by both musicians and physicians so studies in this area, largely of an experimental nature, may be expected to increase. To cite a few examples, about fifty years ago Hyde studied the influence of music on pulse rate, systolic and diastolic blood pressure, and velocity of blood flow.[5] More recently Dreher, in a doctoral study, investigated the relationship between the verbal reports of subjects and galvanic skin responses to different kinds of music.[6] Another doctoral study, by Sears, was concerned with some of the effects of music upon muscle tension.[7]

PURPOSE OF EXPERIMENTAL RESEARCH

The purpose of experimental research is to show what can result under carefully controlled conditions. Observation of these precisely

[1]Harry Hammer, "An Experimental Study of the Use of the Tachistoscope in the Teaching of Melodic Sight Singing," (unpublished doctoral dissertation, University of Colorado, 1961).

[2]Leslie E. Woelflin, "An Experimental Study on the Teaching of Clarinet Fingerings with Teaching Machines," (unpublished doctoral dissertation, Southern Illinois University, 1961).

[3]Robert G. Petzold, "Auditory Perception of Musical Sounds by Children in the First Six Grades," (U. S. Office of Education Cooperative Research Project 1051, 1966).

[4]Charles L. Spohn, "A Diagnostic Testing Program with Appropriate Auto-Instructional Treatments to Meet Individual Differences in Learning," (U. S. Office of Education Cooperative Research Project 5-0262, 1966).

[5]I. M. Hyde, "Effects of Music Upon Electrocardiograms and Blood Pressure," The Effects of Music, Max Schoen (ed.), (New York: Harcourt, Brace and World, Inc., 1927).

[6]R. E. Dreher, "The Relationship Between Verbal Reports and Galvanic Skin Responses to Music," (unpublished doctoral dissertation, Indiana University, 1947).

[7]William W. Sears, "A Study of Some Effects of Music upon Muscle Tension as Evidenced by Electromyographic Recordings," (unpublished doctoral dissertation, University of Kansas, 1960).

regulated factors will enable a researcher to discern what commonly is referred to as a "cause and effect relationship." Also known as "causation," this concept, which is widely used in experimental research, is based on a canon formulated by the nineteenth-century English philosopher, John Stuart Mill (1806-1873). According to Mill, in a given situation, if all factors are constant except one, that variable is the "cause" for the particular "effect" which is observed. In reality, of course, it is not always a simple matter to rigorously regulate all elements in a classroom situation to the point where it is possible to isolate and manipulate only one. Regulation and control of variables will be treated in greater detail later in this chapter.

In educational research, including music, solutions to some of the perplexities which appear to be most pressing do not lend themselves to the experimental method because of the rigid controls imposed by this type of research. For instance, perhaps one of the most vexatious problems confronting many music teachers is that of scheduling adequate rehearsal time for performing groups. The descriptive method might be selected to survey policies regarding rehearsal schedules in effect in other schools. On the other hand, if a music educator were concerned with *how* he could make his rehearsals more effective he might experimentally contrast two procedural methods and compare the results statistically to determine which one appears to be more effective.

KINDS OF EXPERIMENTAL RESEARCH

Two types of research characterize the experimental method; namely, the laboratory and the classroom or field study. The laboratory study, which usually centers on the observation of one person or of a small group of persons, may be in a laboratory setting, in a location familiar to the subject or subjects, or in an especially arranged situation outside the laboratory but simulating laboratory conditions. The element of artificiality often associated with laboratory research is objectionable to some educators because the inflexibility often is unrealistic and those being tested do not respond normally because they sense the synthetic surroundings in which they find themselves. On the positive side, the laboratory usually provides a setting where more exact controls may be exercised than in the classroom. One of the best examples of laboratory research relating to the behavior of an individual is the extended study by Révész of the Hungarian child prodigy Erwin Nyiregyházy, which is discussed in the next chapter. Also of interest to musicians is the ongoing experimentation related to improving musical instruments conducted by highly specialized personnel in laboratories of the Conn Corporation and other instrument manufacturers.

Classroom or group research sometimes is referred to as field experimentation. In classroom research the behavior of individuals is observed under conditions involving certain predefined controls which, like laboratory research, are regulated as strictly as possible. This type of experimentation is useful where evaluation is needed for a new teaching method, curriculum innovation, or teaching procedure. As a rule it is more difficult to control all variables or experimental factors when observing the behavior of individuals than it is in a laboratory experiment involving musical instruments or other inanimate objects. Frequently discounted, moreover, because of the difficulty of adequate control, are such conditions as teacher attitude, interest, and bias, pupil motivation, and absence of pupils at the time of experimentation. Yet these uncontrollable factors can influence the results of a study considerably. Even the most diligent and meticulous investigator will find that these items become intangibles which fluctuate from one testing situation to the next despite all precautions to the contrary.

Strengths of the classroom method include the opportunity to observe a larger number of individuals simultaneously in a setting more natural than the laboratory. Experimentation in the room where the class usually meets suggests that there will be less student distraction than would be true in a laboratory environment because the classroom surroundings are part of the daily routine. The incidence of what is commonly called the "Hawthorne Effect" may be expected to be less prominent. When a subject is aware that he is participating in an experiment or recognizes that he is receiving special attention, some of the improvement in his performance may be attributed to the Hawthorne Effect, which derives its name from the Western Electric Corporation's Hawthorne plant where it was first observed by industrial psychologists. Measurement of the Hawthorne Effect, moreover, is precarious and uncertain at best.

Another advantage of the classroom method is that the observation of a larger number of subjects will produce a greater amount of data, hence more validity. To observe results obtained by 300 out of 500 violinists in a school system who are employing a new fingering concept is more valid than to rely on the experiences of twenty-five in only one school. Examples of experimental projects conducted by music educators using the classroom method are postdoctoral and doctoral research of Petzold[8] and Swanson,[9] respectively. Petzold was interested in determining differences and delineating skills apparent in each of the first six grades relating to rhythm, timbre, and harmony. The utilization of an experimental methodology in assisting the adolescent boy to acquire better singing skills as well as knowledge about and attitudes toward music was the objective of Swanson's study.

CONCEPTS OF EXPERIMENTAL RESEARCH

The precise regulations required in experimental research naturally necessitate a different approach to drawing comparisons from those used in the other kinds of research discussed in this textbook. Experimental research generally makes use of quantitative procedures employing mathematical or statistical methods, something which apparently frightened most music educators in the past. However, it has been noted by Petzold[10] and by this writer[11] that music educators have become increasingly interested in this type of research in recent years.

Rigid control has been mentioned as a *prima facie* requisite for successful experimental research. Two kinds of controls are central to experimental research; namely, holding certain factors constant and manipulating, changing, or varying others. The component which is used without any kind of alteration is known as the constant. When a condition is changed deliberately by the investigator, or subject to alteration, it is known as a variable. The various kinds of variables used in educational research are discussed throughout this chapter.

In order to establish a standard to serve as a basis for making comparisons a pretest may be given to all subjects participating in an experiment. The purpose of a pretest is simply to determine the status of each individual or group prior to conducting the experiment. A pretest may consist of either an appropriate standardized test or a measure devised by the investigator. McGarry used Form A of the *Watkins-Farnum Performance Scale* to find out the pretest scores for groups with which he subsequently experimented.[12] He then administered Form

---

[8]Petzold, *loc. cit.*

[9]Frederick J. Swanson, "Voice Mutation in the Adolescent Male: An Experiment in Guiding the Voice Development of Adolescent Boys in General Music Classes," (unpublished doctoral dissertation, University of Wisconsin, 1959).

[10]Robert G. Petzold, "Directions for Research in Music Education," *Music Educators Journal*, L (January, 1964), 39.

[11]Roger F. [P.] Phelps, "Current Status of Research in Musical Education," *School Music News*, XXV (April, 1962), 30.

[12]Robert J. McGarry, "A Teaching Experiment to Measure the Extent to Which Vocalization Contributes to the Improvement of Selected Instrumental Music Performance Skills," (unpublished doctoral dissertation, New York University, 1967).

B of the same test to ascertain posttest scores. A posttest, which consists of an equivalent form of the measure used for the pretest, is given as soon as possible after experimentation is completed to all subjects still remaining in the study. For various reasons, not all persons who are given a pretest are available for the posttest. The purpose of a posttest is to learn the status of each individual at conclusion of the experimentation. When data of the pretest and posttest are compared, evaluated, and analyzed statistically the investigator has a valid basis upon which to draw conclusions inductively.

One of the most widely used methods for experimental study in music education involves making comparisons between a control and an experimental group, which will be discussed subsequently under parallel-group research design. By this procedure classroom research can more closely approximate, than would be possible otherwise, the rigorous type of control and evaluation commonplace in the laboratory of the scientist. The control group may be regarded as the one which maintains a "status quo" situation because the investigator continues his usual procedure in working with it. Any changes or alterations of method or content take place in the experimental group, or the one in which changes or variables are effected.

In medical research some new drug may be given to the experimental group while a placebo, which looks identical to the drug being tested, may be administered to the control group. The purpose of the placebo, a harmless substance, is to achieve more uniform controls for the investigator. This is possible because the subject does not usually know whether he is receiving the ingredient being tested or the placebo. Thus he has no reason for reacting abnormally to the experiment, which he might do if he were aware of the contents of the treatment administered to him. Application of the principle of the placebo sometimes is possible in music education research, but its use generally is quite limited.

The concept of the single variable is applicable in almost all situations in experimental research to test the hypothesis which has been formulated. Implicit in the use of the single variable principle is that all other factors in the experiment remain constant. On the other hand, manipulation of this variable results in observable changed conditions, or what is often termed a "cause and effect" relationship. Frequently the terms "independent and dependent variable" are used, respectively, to delineate cause and effect. The independent variable, also known as "experimental variable," is the one that is manipulated or changed, while the dependent or "criterion variable" is the result of this manipulation. Here is an oversimplified example. In an experimental study where the objective is to learn what effect drill on a certain rhythmic pattern will have on a student's ability to recognize it in musical context, the drill is the independent variable and the reading skill which results is the dependent variable. Another experiment might be conducted to determine what effect listening to dodecaphonic music has on a theory student writing conventional four-part harmony exercises. It should be evident in this example that dodecaphonic music is the independent variable and the dependent variable is the student's harmony achievement.

Not all differences observable in the dependent variable may be attributed to the experimental factor or the independent variable. Some dissimilarities will result from errors due to conditions which cannot be regulated. These kinds of errors have been labeled by Lindquist as Type S, G, and R.[13] Type S, or sampling, errors are due to changes that may take place as a result of random sampling. Those under Type G relate to extrinsic factors which may affect one group, but not another, hence are known as group errors. When an experiment is replicated Type R, or replication, errors may be expected because of uncontrollable variations such as changes in mood of the groups being tested which are present in one administration of the experiment but not in others. The investigator, aware that such errors may occur, should take this into consideration and organize his study to include procedures that measure these deviations statistically.

A hypothesis, as observed in Chapter 3, is what an investigator believes will be the probable outcome of his study. In order for a study to be completely valid a researcher must test his hypotheses. Hypotheses, it will be recalled, may be stated in either positive or negative form. When listed negatively the hypothesis is called "null." In positive or declarative form the hypothesis indicates the relationship that is believed to exist between variables of the experiment. An investigator, for instance, might declaratively state: "It is hypothesized that a significant difference exists between the retention rate of individuals who learn bassoon fingerings by a teaching machine as contrasted with those who learn them by a conventional teaching method." A null hypothesis states that no difference will be apparent between the factors being compared. When stating the aforementioned example as a null hypothesis, it would read: "It is hypothesized that no significant difference exists between the retention rate of individuals who learn bassoon fingerings by a teaching machine as contrasted with those who learn them by a conventional teaching method." Confusion is to be expected on

---

[13]Everet F. Lindquist, *Design and Analysis of Experiments in Psychology and Education* (Boston: Houghton Mifflin Co., 1953), pp. 9-11.

the part of students who are unfamiliar with the concept of the null hypothesis because it seems redundant to state a hypothesis negatively when positive results are expected. Because of statistical techniques, however, it is easier to express a hypothesis negatively. The reason for this apparent contradiction is that statistically deviations are measured from zero. Dissimilarities statistically in accord with the way a hypothesis is advanced mean that it will be accepted; when not in agreement statistically it will be rejected. Statistical differences are discussed in greater detail in a subsequent chapter of this book.

The term "ex post facto" research frequently is encountered in studies by sociologists or behavioral scientists. Literally meaning "after the fact," this procedure is quasi-experimental in scope, because experimental procedures are simulated to determine cause and effect after they actually have taken place, therefore introducing a certain amount of subjectivity into the study.[14] A serious weakness of ex post facto research persists in the difficulty of controlling the independent variable since it must be reconstructed after the circumstance has occurred. An investigator who desires to determine the consequence of music instruction in reducing juvenile delinquency, to use a rather obvious illustration, might employ the ex post facto research concept. In this example the dependent variable is juvenile delinquency and music instruction represents the independent variable. The independent variable, or music instruction, however, may have transpired several years before an attempt was made to collate it with juvenile delinquency, or the dependent variable. Ex post facto research also might be used in experimental studies which differentiate the relationship between musical achievement and such factors as social status, aptitude, and intelligence.

VALIDITY OF DESIGNS

One of the most crucial steps in experimental research is determining the validity of the design being formulated. Campbell and Stanley[15] were among the first educational researchers to delineate two types of validity in experimental designs; namely, internal and external. Internal validity is concerned with learning whether or not an independent variable actually effects a change on the dependent variable. It is always possible that extraneous factors between the first and second observa-

---

[14]Kerlinger regards ex post facto as a separate type of research. See pp. 359-374 in his *Foundations of Behavioral Research* (New York: Holt, Rinehart and Winston, Inc., 1965).

[15]Donald T. Campbell and Julian C. Stanley, *Experimental and Quasi-Experimental Designs for Research* (Chicago: Rand McNally and Co., 1966), pp. 5 ff.

tions may have influenced the results subsequently obtained. A researcher must find out which results actually are due to *ipso facto* manipulation of the independent variable and those which are the product of a "confounding" or mixing up of effects of the variables. Seven of the factors listed by Campbell and Stanley, which may effect internal validity, have pertinence for experimental research designs in music education. They are historical events, the process of maturation, retesting procedure, changes in techniques for measurements or observations, statistical regression, biases or other factors of selection, and attrition of subjects.

In an experiment to measure degree of like or dislike for classical music, the subjects may have attended a live performance of Beethoven's *Symphony No. 6 in F Major* between the pretest and application of the independent variable or treatment. Although it may not have been related to the experiment, the Beethoven performance could have contributed to internal invalidity in at least two ways. First, if the subjects had never previously attended a symphony concert it could have been historically significant for them. Second, hearing this composition may have resulted in a more mature attitude toward classical music.

Practice effects of a pretest often influence the treatment, which is the third source of internal invalidity. Although the observer for both pretest and application of the independent variable may be the same, his method, techniques, or instruments used for observation may differ slightly, resulting in another kind of internal invalidity. Statistical regression, a fifth source, sometimes is referred to as a "regression toward the mean." This phenomenon may be observed when those, who previously received either extremely high or low scores, tend to regress toward the mean after the treatment.

Sometimes, despite all precautions to the contrary, an experimenter demonstrates a preference for one method over another, resulting in a sixth kind of internal invalidity. In other instances differences between the groups which were not apparent at the time of pretest become evident when the independent variable is applied. Students may drop out of the experiment before its completion for various reasons. This final indication of internal invalidity is sometimes referred to as "experimental mortality."

External validity attempts to determine the amount of generalization the results of the research have for other similar groups. For instance, a researcher should find out whether his data on the classical music preferences of unselected high school students apply only to his school or to a wider audience. Factors which most often affect external validity are reactions to the experimental procedures and the interaction between selection biases and the experimental variable. A pretest may result in either a favorable or unfavorable reaction by subjects toward the experimentation, although this might not be evident with a comparable group being tested elsewhere, hence would constitute a source of external invalidity.

Many times it is difficult to determine whether external invalidity is the result of inadequate selection procedures of the group being used for experimental purposes or to the treatment itself. Interaction implies that the group selected for treatment is not truly representative because the results obtained by a comparable group are different.

It usually is more difficult to control external than internal validity. Ideally a research design should make provision for both types of validity. However, when this is impossible, one which possesses internal validity only should not necessarily be regarded as weak.

EXPERIMENTAL RESEARCH DESIGNS

In the organization of a design to conduct experimental research an investigator must decide which method will enable him to best maintain the precise controls necessary to obtain the information he is seeking. Cook observes that experimental research designs may be categorized as either "equivalent group" or "factorial."[16] In designs which may be classified under the heading equivalent group, the components being contrasted are all equated as nearly as possible and the independent variable is the only factor which is not kept constant. The most common methods of equivalent research organization are single-group, parallel-group, and counterbalanced design.

Experimentation with the single-group method, as the name implies, is carried on with only one group or individual. Since the same individuals are used throughout the experiment this method has the advantage of causing minimal disruption to the regular class schedule of the group being utilized. The single-group method characteristically consists of three steps: pretest, experimentation, and posttest. When posttest and pretest scores are compared any differences attributable to the experimental treatment may be computed statistically by a "t" test.[17] A researcher in music education might organize a single-group study to measure attitudes toward atonal music. A pretest might be given to a group of college non-music majors to learn their attitude toward certain excerpts of selected atonal compositions. Following the pretest, the independent variable, which might consist of an intensive and detailed explanation of atonal compositional techniques, could be

---

[16]David R. Cook, *A Guide to Educational Research* (Boston: Allyn and Bacon, Inc., 1965), p. 106. Used by permission of Allyn and Bacon, Inc.
[17]See Chapter 10 for an explanation of this statistical tool.

presented. Results of the subsequent posttest would then be collated with pretest scores and treated statistically to ascertain differences attributable to the independent variable. A major weakness of the single-group method, due to the absence of a control group, is that it must be assumed that all differences between pretest and posttest scores are due solely to the experimental variable. Consequently it is difficult to take into account extraneous conditions such as weather, class mood, and unusual interruptions which could significantly affect the results.

A second type of experimental method is the parallel-group design, in which two or more groups, as nearly equivalent as possible, are employed at the same time. This procedure was mentioned earlier in this chapter in conjunction with the concept of control and experimental groups. As already observed, each group is presented with identical material, except that the experimental unit receives the experimental treatment or variable while the control group is held constant, hence is treated in the usual manner. If it seems desirable to include more than one experimental variable, then it will be necessary to use more than two parallel groups. Another alternative is to employ two experimental groups, each containing a different variable, which may be compared with one control group. Doctoral research projects by McGarry and Swanson, referred to earlier in this chapter, are examples of studies based on a conventional parallel-group design.

The assignment of individuals to each of the groups employed in parallel-group method research may be done by randomization, matching, or ranking after pretest scores have been obtained for each subject. Random selection, a technique used rather extensively in descriptive research, fundamentally means that each individual will be assigned to a group by some chance method such as flipping a coin. A disadvantage of random selection is that inadvertently one group may receive more persons with equivalent scores than the other.

In the process of matching the investigator attempts to pair individuals who have identical scores. For example, if two subjects receive a raw score of 49 on the pitch section of the revised *Seashore Measures of Musical Talents*, one would be placed at random in the control and the other in the experimental group. If only one person received a raw score of 48 on the same test and two attained 47, the one with the 48 might be dismissed from the experiment because there is no counterpart for him. Since two received 47, one would be put at random in the control and the other in the experimental group. This oversimplified example illustrates the most significant weakness of matching; namely, that an individual who has a pretest score for which there is no identical counterpart usually is excluded from the experiment.

In the ranking procedure all scores are arranged from the highest to the lowest and the two individuals with the highest scores, regardless of differences which may exist between them, are assigned to a group at random. The first chosen is placed in the experimental while the other is delegated to the control group. This random procedure of putting the first individual chosen in the experimental and the other in the control group continues until all subjects have been accommodated. Ranking technique, according to Borg, has advantages which make it superior to the others.[18]

The counterbalanced design, also known as "rotation-group method," or "crossover" or "switchover" design is a third type of equivalent research organization. This method frequently is used when there are several variables and groups involved. The variables are rotated in each replication so that all components eventually receive the experimental treatment. Counterbalanced design procedure is similar to that used with the parallel-group method except for the replications. The counterbalanced design has an advantage over the single- and parallel-group methods in that it can accommodate groups which are intact and have not been chosen by random assignment. The usual procedure, however, is to utilize control and experimental groups which have been selected according to criteria determined by the investigator when he organized his experiment. Since time lapses are necessary between replications, the difficulty in adapting the counterbalanced design to educational problems makes it of relatively limited utility, observes Borg.[19]

Figure 2 shows how three musical groups could be organized so that each one is exposed to the three experimental variables. In this

Replication	Ra	Rb	Rc
1	Group A	Group B	Group C
2	Group C	Group A	Group B
3	Group B	Group C	Group A
	Ra Mean	Rb Mean	Rc Mean

FIGURE 2. Counterbalanced Design Employing Three Groups

[18]Walter R. Borg, *Educational Research: An Introduction* (New York: David McKay Co., Inc., 1963), p. 301.
[19]*Ibid.*, p. 309.

instance Ra, Rb, and Rc each denote a different rhythmic pattern or variable, and the groups are identified by the letters A, B, and C. The purpose of such a study is to find out which of the three rhythmic patterns is the easiest to memorize. Following each replication the scores of the experimental variable for each group are compared with those of the corresponding dependent variable. The mean for each experimental treatment then is computed and recorded at the bottom of columns Ra, Rb, and Rc.

The designs discussed thus far have centered on maintaining precise controls throughout the experiment. Factorial design, on the other hand, enables an investigator to work with subjective and objective elements in the same experiment. In a factorial design it is possible to evaluate not only the effect of several diverse variables simultaneously, but also their interaction with one another. According to Mouly, factorial designs, which were developed by Ronald A. Fisher, have made the solution of some problems in educational research much easier.[20] The statistical analysis for factorial designs, however, is very involved and frequently serves as a deterrent to many investigators who might otherwise use this research device. By using a factorial design it would be possible to measure a musician's teaching competence by computing the interaction of factors such as his major applied performance skill, over-all musical knowledge, level of educational attainment, college course grades, musical and other experiences, pupil reaction to him, and his personality.

Experimental research, not used to any great extent by music educators, basically is the method of the scientist, and for this reason it sometimes is erroneously called "scientific research." The high degree of objectivity inherent in experimental research because of its system of precise controls is in contrast to the subjective nature of much descriptive research, where controls frequently are difficult to regulate accurately. Despite its shortcomings, some problems still are best resolved by descriptive research techniques, the subject of the next chapter.

QUESTIONS FOR REVIEW AND DISCUSSION

1. Why is the experimental research method generally regarded as more objective than the other types?
2. What is the purpose of experimental research?
3. The "causation" concept was derived from the writings of whom? What is meant by the term?

---

[20]George J. Mouly, *The Science of Educational Research* (New York: American Book Co., 1963), p. 346.

4. Contrast the laboratory and classroom types of experimental research, giving advantages and disadvantages of each.
5. What is meant by the terms "constant" and "variable"? Compare these with "control" and "experimental" groups.
6. What are the functions of dependent and independent variables in experimental research?
7. Why are pretest and posttest scores significant to experimental research?
8. What is the concept of the single variable? How is it used in experimental research?
9. Contrast the various kinds of experimental research designs presented in this chapter.
10. Differentiate between internal and external validity.

SUPPLEMENTARY READINGS

ALMACK, JOHN C. *Research and Thesis Writing*. Boston: Houghton Mifflin Co., 1930. Chapter VI.

BARNES, FRED P. *Research for the Practitioner in Education*. Washington: Department of Elementary School Principals, National Education Association, 1964. Chapters Two, Five, and Six.

BEST, JOHN W. *Research in Education*. Englewood Cliffs, N. J.: Prentice-Hall, Inc., 1959. Chapter 6.

BORG, WALTER R. *Educational Research: An Introduction*. New York: David McKay Co., Inc., 1963. Chapter 13.

CAMPBELL, DONALD T., and STANLEY, JULIAN C. *Experimental and Quasi-Experimental Designs for Research*. Chicago: Rand McNally and Co., 1966.

COOK, DAVID R. *A Guide to Educational Research*. Boston: Allyn and Bacon, Inc., 1965. Chapter IV.

CULBERTSON, JACK A., and HENCLEY, STEPHEN P. (eds.). *Educational Research: New Perspectives*. Danville, Ill.: The Interstate Printers and Publishers, Inc., 1963. Chapter 14.

GAGE, N. L. (ed.), *Handbook of Research on Teaching*. Chicago: Rand McNally and Co., 1963. Chapter 5.

GOOD, CARTER V. *Essentials of Educational Research*. New York: Appleton-Century-Crofts, 1966. Chapter 8.

———, and SCATES, DOUGLAS E. *Methods of Research*. New York: Appleton-Century-Crofts, 1954. Chapter 7.

HILLWAY, TYRUS. *Introduction to Research*. Second Edition. Boston: Houghton Mifflin Co., 1964. Chapter 12.

KERLINGER, FRED N. *Foundations of Behavioral Research*. New York: Holt, Rinehart and Winston, Inc., 1965. Chapters 2, 3, 12, 20, 21, and 36.

LINDQUIST, EVERET F. *Design and Analysis of Experiments in Psychology and Education*. Boston: Houghton Mifflin Co., 1953. Chapters 1 and 9.

MOULY, GEORGE J. *The Science of Educational Research*. New York: American Book Co., 1963. Chapter 12.

SAX, GILBERT. *Empirical Foundations of Educational Research.* Englewood Cliffs, N. J.: Prentice-Hall, Inc., 1968. Chapter 12.

SMITH, HENRY L. *Educational Research, Principles and Practices.* Bloomington, Ind: Educational Publications, 1944. Chapter VIII.

TRAVERS, ROBERT M. W. *An Introduction to Educational Research.* Second Edition. New York: The Macmillan Co., 1964. Chapters 5, 6, 13, and 14.

VAN DALEN, DEOBALD B. *Understanding Educational Research.* Enlarged and Revised Edition. New York: McGraw-Hill Book Co., Inc., 1966. Chapter 11.

WHITNEY, FREDERICK L. *The Elements of Research.* Third Edition. Englewood Cliffs, N. J.: Prentice-Hall, Inc., 1950. Chapter IX.

WISE, JOHN E., NORDBERG, ROBERT B., and REITZ, DONALD J. *Methods of Research in Education.* Boston: D. C. Heath and Co., 1967. Chapter VII.

• 7 •

Descriptive Research:
An Account of the Present

Descriptive research essentially is concerned with that which exists at the present time. It goes without saying that "the present" is here only for a fleeting moment, and then it becomes the past. For practical purposes of organizing descriptive research, however, the present will be construed in this book as an arbitrary unit of time span of relatively short duration which is defined by an investigator to circumscribe his study, although usually restricted to no more than a year in duration. In descriptive research emphasis is on the present at the time of observation, whereas in historical research emphasis is on the past. Descriptive research, then, may be considered as referring to the "status quo."

Research studies in the descriptive area, which have constituted the bulk of projects completed in music education and other subject areas in education until recently, have come under censure from many sources. Through an unfortunate misuse of this kind of research the descriptive method for solving problems has fallen into disuse in many institutions. This is unfortunate because descriptive research does not necessarily need to be shallow and subjective. Descriptive research which is organized and implemented appropriately can make important contributions to music education.

PURPOSES OF DESCRIPTIVE RESEARCH

In music education descriptive research usually is conducted for three purposes; namely, to: (1) obtain data on current conditions or procedures; (2) establish relationships among factors or conditions; and

(3) determine needs or trends. Frequently it is beneficial to know the current status of a subject area such as music. In several states, for example, the state music supervisor or consultant annually attempts through a survey to procure from each school district in the state information such as the following: number and kind of music teachers (vocal, instrumental, etc.); educational qualifications of each teacher; the number of students enrolled in each of the music courses or performance groups; kinds and number of district-owned instruments; and number and specific titles of textbooks and other instructional materials used for class instruction. These data, when assembled, can be used to show the relative status of music education in the state.

The mere accumulation of data, however, is not always the only purpose of descriptive research, as Van Dalen so appropriately notes in these words: "descriptive research is not confined to routine fact gathering. Predicting and identifying relationships among and between variables is the goal of the competent investigator."[1] Referring to the previous illustration, the state supervisor or consultant in music may, in addition to ascertaining the status of music education, make quantitative comparisons of music programs in various districts. This information can be especially useful when, for purposes of upgrading, the music program in one school district may be judged quantitatively to be inferior to others in terms of the items contained in the survey. Quantitatively it should be apparent that a descriptive study cannot indicate whether the musical performance standards in one school are superior to those in another, irrespective of quantity. Descriptive research can ascertain the presence of certain conditions but cannot adequately evaluate their effectiveness.

Returning to the example indicating kinds of data collected by state music supervisors, certain trends may become apparent as information is compared year after year. It may be evident, for instance, that music theory classes are becoming more prevalent in the high schools, which suggests that now more high school graduates enter college or university as music majors with a better theoretical background. Unmet needs for equipment and materials also may be apparent when the state music supervisor collates data acquired from the survey. These data can then be used to show a school administrator how his system compares to others of comparable size in regard to equipment and materials. Presumably the music director already 'knows, but he may be accused of promoting his vested interests if he persistently tries to convince his

---

[1]Deobald B. Van Dalen, *Understanding Educational Research* (Enlarged and Revised Edition; New York: McGraw-Hill Book Co., Inc., 1966), p. 203. Used by permission of the McGraw-Hill Book Co., Inc.

administrator of the situation. Sometimes the state supervisor of music can assist a teacher by providing comparative data on music programs in school districts similar to his own.

THE DISPARITY OF DESCRIPTIVE RESEARCH

A perusal of textbooks relating to educational research will reveal a lack not only of general consensus regarding what constitutes valid descriptive research but also of an acceptance of the terminology appropriate to it. The position taken here is that there is a rather large body of studies in music education, which, because of the methodology employed, may properly be categorized under a general grouping as descriptive research because they tell "what is" as the word "describe" implies.

Chapter headings in some textbooks which are indicative of areas used to classify descriptive research relate to: surveys, observations, growth and development studies, and documentary analysis. Even greater disparity is apparent in others where these specific items are included as subheadings in a chapter devoted to descriptive research.

There probably is more disagreement and confusion in the area of descriptive research than in any of the other four types discussed in this book. For this reason it may not be merely coincidental that descriptive research in music education has been looked upon frequently with disfavor by some who believe it to be too subjective and disorganized to enable an investigator to obtain valid data utilizing the scientific method.

On the other hand, until recently as already observed, the large bulk of research studies in music education fit categorically into the descriptive area. Petzold indicated the figure at 70 percent of all music education research completed during the ten-year period 1952-1962.[2] Conversely, it might be pointed out deductively that the greater the number of studies, the more reasonable it is to assume that there will be a higher proportion of inferior projects just on the basic principle that perfection is inversely related to the mass of items present. An oboist will not necessarily have a higher percentage of good reeds result when he makes 100 than when he produces only six.

The proliferation of descriptive research studies in music education (and education in general) is partially due to the inconsistencies just noted and also to a mistaken conception that this type of research is easy to organize and implement. This beguilement no doubt has con-

[2]Robert G. Petzold, "Directions for Research in Music Education," *Music Educators Journal,* L (January, 1964), 39.

tributed to much of the insignificant and superficial research which has resulted in a general discrediting of descriptive research by some educators.

Perhaps one of the most acrid indictments of descriptive research is given by Kerlinger, a behavioral scientist. In making reference to status surveys, a form of descriptive research, he says: "This type of study, so firmly entrenched in the educational mind, is not scientific. Except for sophisticated sampling designs, and the methods of the Census Bureau and of certain survey research agencies, it is more analogous to skilled clerical work. To ferret out pupil-teacher ratios, bonded indebtedness, curricular practices, and the like is basically routine fact-gathering and has little resemblance to scientific behavioral research."[3] In this indictment Kerlinger has put his finger on a valid criticism of much descriptive research of the past, namely the failure to employ the scientific method for planning, executing, and interpreting the research.

Considerably more sympathetic is Mouly, who observes that: "No category of educational research is more widely used than the type known variously as the *survey*, the *normative-survey*, *status* and *descriptive research*. This is a broad classification comprising a variety of specific techniques and procedures, all similar from the standpoint of purpose—that is, to establish the status of the phenomenon under investigation."[4]

KINDS OF DESCRIPTIVE RESEARCH

As already noted, considerable disagreement exists among researchers regarding types or kinds of descriptive research. One of the most concise identifications of types of descriptive research is given by Van Dalen who lists three kinds of studies: survey, interrelationship, and developmental.[5] Utilizing similar terminology is Cook who enumerates four types: analytical, developmental, predictive, and survey.[6] The designation "analytical" as used by Cook is concerned with relationships, thus is comparable to Van Dalen's categorization of interrelationship studies. Developmental and survey have the same connotation and title for both Cook and Van Dalen. Because Cook's designation of "predictive" studies

[3]Fred N. Kerlinger, *Foundations of Behavioral Research* (New York: Holt, Rinehart and Winston, Inc., 1965), p. 392. Used by permission of Holt, Rinehart and Winston, Inc.

[4]George J. Mouly, *The Science of Educational Research* (New York: American Book Co., 1963), p. 231. Used by permission of the American Book Co.

[5]Van Dalen, *op. cit.*, p. 206.

[6]David R. Cook, *A Guide to Educational Research* (Boston: Allyn and Bacon, Inc., 1965), p. 40.

to a considerable extent overlaps with experimental, perhaps it more appropriately should be included in this type of research rather than under descriptive.

It is this writer's premise that descriptive research studies in music education logically parallel the three major subheadings just noted by Van Dalen, but with slightly different nomenclature; namely, survey, correlation, and relationship. These categories, to be discussed separately, are not to be confused with descriptive research tools, which will be treated later in this chapter.

Survey studies include school, job analysis, content analysis, public opinion, and curriculum research. Case study and causal-comparative studies may be regarded as correlation research whereas progression includes growth and trend studies.

Survey Studies

The prime purpose of any kind of survey is to obtain objective data regarding the current status of a specific situation or activity. Data obtained from a survey may be used to make intelligent plans to meet future needs or to substantiate or refute the validity of a current practice. One of the most widely used types is the school survey which, according to Good, appeared around 1910.[7] Normally, surveys of this kind are conducted by local school officials or by research teams from a professional organization such as the National Education Association. Music can receive significant attention in this type of survey, moreover, as evidenced by the report resulting from research recently conducted by the Research Division of the National Education Association.[8] One section of this excellent report contains data on the status of music and art in the elementary schools and another on its relevance in the secondary schools of the United States. Included for the elementary schools are such pertinent items as time allotments for music by grade, personnel responsible for music instruction, instrumental music offerings, and equipment. Other aspects consist of trends in secondary school music enrollment, music courses added and dropped in secondary schools, music credits allowed for high school graduation, and public funds budgeted for music programs.

The local school survey is conducted primarily to obtain information about each family in the community on such factors as number of children, ages of children (both pre-school and currently enrolled

---

[7]Carter V. Good, *Essentials of Educational Research* (New York: Appleton-Century-Crofts, 1966), p. 206.

[8]*Music and Art in the Public Schools,* Research Monograph 1963-M3 (Washington: National Education Association, 1963).

in school), grades in which school children are enrolled, number of families owning their own homes, and occupation of each of the parents. Data from each of these items can be used to determine anticipated need for such things as additional classroom space, teaching personnel, and educational services. Fairly accurate predictions are possible in communities which have a relatively stable population. Data from a school survey even in localities having a highly mobile population can be useful when interpreted in light of the average of such factors as mobility rate, age of children enrolled in school, and occupation of the parents.

One of the ways in which a school survey can be of significance to the music education profession is in enabling a local board of education to plan for additional music personnel and equipment such as pianos, tubas, double basses and other items normally not purchased by the individual student. The music director establishes anticipated needs on the basis of proper balance in terms of enrollment figures for each of the instruments. Projected enrollments for required general music courses can be established quite accurately for a designated year by noting the number of students in each grade level who eventually will be enrolled. In addition, the number of families owning their own homes and occupation of each of the parents are significant not only in terms of helping to establish a tax base for budgetary purposes but also in indicating to a considerable extent the socio-economic and cultural status of families in a community. These kinds of data frequently are examined by school boards when school budgets are being prepared to ascertain the validity of requests for additional music personnel.

Job analysis is a term preempted from business and government by Van Dalen to study positions which involve administration, teaching, or noninstructional duties.[9] Information pertinent to this type of survey can be obtained by questionnaire, interview, personal observation, or examination of relevant documents and records. A survey recently conducted in the state of New York sought information including such job analysis items as administrative duties, scheduling, and teaching and non-teaching responsibilities.[10] More specifically, questions in this New York survey included assignment of the music teacher to cafeteria, bus, or study hall duty; time allotment for consultation responsibilities; scheduling procedures for music; audio-visual equipment utilized; and budgetary considerations.

---

[9]Van Dalen, op. cit., p. 210.
[10]"Survey of Music Practices in Nassau County, New York," (unpublished committee report prepared by Walter E. Matthews, West Hempstead, N.Y., 1966).

In another study Picerno was interested in learning the supply and demand for elementary school music teachers in New York State.[11] Citing a survey of 1957, and then followed up in 1964, Picerno noted that although the gap had been closed somewhat in the intervening years, the shortage of qualified music personnel is likely to persist for another ten years. The word "qualified" appears to be the key to this study as evidenced by the obvious trend away from the generalist toward the specialist, with its attendant manifestations for teacher training institutions.

A job analysis of instrumental teachers was undertaken by Sims who used a checklist to determine the teaching situation as well as general and specific duties relating to the teaching of instrumental music.[12]

Content analysis, also known as documentary analysis, or textbook analysis, is sometimes included as a phase of historical rather than descriptive research. Because of the techniques involved, however, it seems more logical to include it as a phase of descriptive research. In content analysis the investigator is concerned with utilizing existing materials in a given area to quantitatively determine their relationship or compatibility with certain concepts or philosophies. In a textbook analysis, for example, a comparison might be made of instrumental tutors printed in 1915 with comparable volumes published in 1965 to determine what pedagogical concepts have remained the same, what old ones have disappeared, and what new ones have appeared. Dominy examined books two, four, and six in each music series published since 1923 to determine how closely they followed the aims and purposes of elementary education.[13] She found that these textbooks largely utilized concepts which failed to employ the creative-appreciative approach to inquiry, evaluation, and judgment. In addition, she recommended that the materials should emphasize child growth and the possibilities which exist in music to enable each child to make choices of his own as the result of being exposed to many more kinds of music, including modern.

Although used rather extensively in business and politics, public opinion studies nevertheless do have some import for music education. Commercial public opinion surveys are very powerful and are used

[11]Vincent Picerno, "The Need for Elementary School Music Teachers in New York State," *Journal of Research in Music Education*, XIV (Fall, 1966), 213-219.

[12]William E. Sims, "A Job Analysis of Instrumental Music Teachers in Selected High Schools in Oklahoma with Implications for Teacher Education," (unpublished doctoral dissertation, Colorado State College, 1963).

[13]Elizabeth E. Dominy, "Music Textbooks in Elementary Education: The Appropriateness of Current Textbook Material in Elementary School Music in Relation to the Aims and Purposes of Modern Elementary Education," (unpublished doctoral dissertation, New York University, 1958).

widely to measure reaction of the public to a new product or procedure. Occasionally they are utilized by local governments and other organizations as a rather convenient way to obtain suggestions or to learn what improvements the general public feels need to be made. Public opinion polls generally reach the height of their popularity and are scrutinized closely just prior to state and national elections. Some defeated candidates even have gone so far as to accuse public opinion polls of influencing the public against them. Public opinion surveys obviously cater to biases or preferences, but this factor alone should not be sufficient to indict them as worthless. Because more scientific sampling procedures are being used now than formerly, public opinion polls usually are proving to be surprisingly accurate in predicting the outcome of state and national elections in the United States.

Research studies in music education occasionally make use of public opinion to obtain certain kinds of data that cannot be procured easily any other way. Pruitt, for example, used a public opinion survey to obtain from parents reasons why they thought their siblings withdrew from instrumental music programs.[14] Still another type of public opinion survey seeks to learn from music educators whether in their opinion there will be enough demand for certain projected publications or the contemplated manufacture of new products in music.

Curriculum survey or research, perhaps because it appears to overlap content analysis to some extent, is not regarded as a separate type of investigation by many writers on educational research. Travers, in noting the changing concepts and complexity of curriculum research, states: "the emerging concept of the curriculum held by research workers and others is that it consists of all the planned conditions and events to which the pupil is exposed for the purpose of promoting learning, plus the homework of theory that gives these conditions and events a certain coherence."[15]

Music education makes use of the following kinds of curriculum research: studying the curricular offerings in a local school district to determine whether they are adequate in terms of objectives and educational goals; comparing music curricula of various school districts to serve as a basis for organizing or revising an existing program; and determining the effect on the curriculum of educational television, teach-

---

[14]Jack S. Pruitt, "A Study of Withdrawals in the Beginning Instrumental Music Programs of Selected Schools in the School District of Greenville County, South Carolina," (unpublished doctoral dissertation, New York University, 1966).

[15]Robert M. W. Travers, *An Introduction to Educational Research*, pp. 62-63. (Second Edition; © 1964, The Macmillan Co., New York. Used by permission of The Macmillan Co.)

ing machines, and other items of educational technology. The aim in all of these types of research is to quantitatively make comparisons which are as free from subjective judgment as possible.

Grant examined the curricula of liberal arts colleges in California and surmised that increased enrollments will bear a direct relationship not only to upgrading performance standards but also to improving class instruction.[16] In another type of curriculum research, Alton evaluated the general music program in one school system and as a result recommended the appointment of a music supervisor, better articulation between various levels, the institution of a string program, and an in-service training program for music education teaching personnel.[17] Berg, in a doctoral study, described the scope and coverage of music instruction by educational television in the Metropolitan New York area.[18]

Correlation Studies

The various types of studies just noted have been concerned with means to "survey" the current status of a situation or prevalence of an idea. A second type of study, known as "correlation" or "interrelationship," shows relationships which exist for an individual, group, or agency. Emphasis here, as in the survey study, is still on the present, but with greater attention given to obtaining data which are more detailed and taken from fewer sources. The correlation area in music education comprises studies referred to as case, causal-comparative, and relationship.

One of the most widely used types of research in the correlation category is the case study, which also may be used in experimental research. A case study may portray the profile of a person at a specifically designated time or it may be a type which is much more commonly used; namely, a study continuing for an extended period. Although the medical and behavioral sciences traditionally have made extensive use of the case study technique there seems to be an increasing interest in applying this concept to the social sciences and humanities.

Because it is desirable to learn about the total interaction of a person not only with others around him but also with situations he encounters daily, case study research frequently is undertaken by a

---

[16]Donald P. Grant, "An Analysis of the Music Curricula of Selected Church-Related Colleges in California," (unpublished doctoral dissertation, University of Southern California, 1965).

[17]Louise M. Alton, "An Examination of the General Music Programs in the Junior High Schools of East Baton Rouge Parish, Louisiana, and Recommendations for Improvement," (unpublished doctoral dissertation, Columbia University, 1963).

[18]Richard C. Berg, "The Teaching of Music on a Series of Telecasts Sponsored by the Regents Educational Television Project," (unpublished doctoral dissertation, Columbia University, 1961).

team of qualified personnel, each a specialist in a certain area or discipline. For example, the investigator who is a musician might enlist the assistance of a physician, a psychologist, and a sociologist to cooperatively study in depth how the last chair player in the third clarinet section of a high school band reacts to the other members seated ahead of him in the clarinet section. This team might individually and/or collectively, through interviews, observation, testing, and the examination of personal written reports (such as diaries and letters) render a comprehensive account, offering recommendations for any advisable remedial action to assist the subject in making whatever adjustments are necessary. In most school systems the personnel in the guidance department are the key individuals in organizing and implementing studies involving the cooperation of subject matter specialists in various fields. The music teacher may find himself included on such teams, especially if the person being observed seems to do better in music than in other subjects. Case studies of this type, especially if they involve the cooperative effort of several competent people, are less likely to receive the criticism frequently leveled at them in the past, which, according to Mouly, often lacked an empirical basis.[19]

Révész's continuation study of the child prodigy Erwin Nyiregyházy, a protégé of Ernst von Dohnanyi (1877-1960), is one of the most extensive case studies dealing with a musician. A Hungarian music psychologist, Révész, in 1916, published the results of his eight-year intensive study and investigation of Erwin's development beginning at the age of five.[20] Révész shows that Erwin, even at a very young age, displayed unusual powers in the areas of tonal memory, absolute pitch, improvisation, and clarity in comprehension of harmonic, melodic, and formal structure, which are representative of the gifted creative mind.

Causal-comparative studies, as the name implies, compare the incidence of certain factors or conditions and then attempt to show the reasons why they occur. For instance, in a rather obvious example, an instrumental music director might be aware that thirty-eight girls and only two boys play flute and thirty-eight boys and only two girls play viola in his instrumental organizations. Then, if reasons for the imbalance between boys and girls on these instruments could be determined, steps might be taken to ensure a more equitable enrollment by sex, if the director felt this factor deserved attention.

In experimental research where this concept also is used, the investigator is able to rigidly control the dependent variables and then manipu-

---

[19]Mouly, op. cit., p. 356.
[20]Géza Révész, Analyse eine musikalisch hervorragenden Kindes (Leipzig, 1916). (The English version, The Psychology of a Musical Prodigy, was published in London in 1925.)

late the independent variable to determine the causal relationship. On the other hand, when behavioral scientists use the causal-comparative principle, they often are not able to control the comparative factors as easily as can the investigator in experimental research. As an example of a causal-comparative study in music education, Alford made a comparison of the emergence and development of musical responses of pre-school twins and singletons.[21] He found that responses to music are apparent in the pre-schooler, and suggests that music programs need to be initiated for them.

Relationship Studies

Relationship studies may be classified as either correlation or progression. It is in the area of correlation studies that most of those in music education research seem to have been concentrated. This is understandable when it is observed that a majority are in the general area of psychology of music. Relationship or correlation studies are conducted to show how two variables correspond to each other. Studies have been undertaken to determine the relationship between intelligence and musical aptitude, race and musical aptitude, and sex and musical aptitude, to mention a few. Some of the best relationship studies in music are reported by Kwalwasser.[22]

In a fairly recent relationship study Peterson developed a program to provide prognostic and diagnostic information about graduate music students on the basis of comparing musical aptitude and achievement test scores.[23]

Progression or developmental studies are concerned with changes or developments over a period of time. Two kinds of progression studies are normally found in music research, growth, and trend. Growth studies are usually classified as either longitudinal or cross-sectional. Longitudinal studies are time consuming and expensive but constitute the best way to study human development. Studies of this kind attempt to measure changes or developments in the same children at different age levels. Some of the best examples involve measurement of musical achievement over a period of years. The most recent research by Petzold, of the University of Wisconsin, is an example of a longitudinal study.[24]

[21]Delton L. Alford, "Emergence and Development of Music Responses in Pre-School Twins and Singletons: A Comparative Study," (unpublished doctoral dissertation, Florida State University, 1966).

[22]Jacob Kwalwasser, *Exploring the Musical Mind* (Boston: Coleman-Ross Co., 1955).

[23]Floyd H. Peterson, Jr., "A Study of the Relationships Between Music Aptitude and Academic Achievement of Graduate Music Students," (unpublished doctoral dissertation, Indiana University, 1963).

[24]Robert G. Petzold, "Auditory Perception of Musical Sounds by Children in the First Six Grades," (U. S. Office of Education Cooperative Research Project 1051, 1966).

It was conducted over a period of five years, although basically according to the experimental rather than the descriptive research method.

Stanton conducted a ten-year study of musical talent at the Eastman School of Music, in which she followed the students through their undergraduate career. She also compared each entering freshman class. Her investigation is an example of both longitudinal and cross-sectional use in experimental research procedure.[25]

Cross-sectional studies are more widely used than longitudinal, undoubtedly because they are less expensive and time consuming. They compare different individuals at the same age level or stage of development; for example, measuring the musical achievement of all fifth grade students in a school system each year. Cross-sectional studies frequently involve more individuals than longitudinal and also employ fewer variables. Franks, in his doctoral research project, concluded that useful high school differential grade predictions can be made for a student on the basis of his junior high school record.[26]

Trend studies identify trends or predict what is likely to take place in the future. One of the best known types of trend studies is the school census, conducted annually in many school districts. When not incorporated in a survey, the objective of a school census is merely to obtain the name, age, and educational status of each child in a family. Trend studies also have been used quite extensively in music education. Grumley, for instance, predicted that there will be an increase not only in the number of earned doctorates in music but also in the number of new doctorates sought for college level positions. He also forecast that despite a decrease in the over-all number of new faculty needed, there still will not be an oversupply by 1970.[27]

Trends in the teaching concepts of student teachers of music were investigated by Gray, who discovered that both high- and low-rated student teachers tend to adopt concepts and techniques which they have observed from teachers who are regarded as "effective."[28]

[25]Hazel M. Stanton, *Measurement of Musical Talent: The Eastman Experiment* (University of Iowa Studies in the Psychology of Music, No. 2; Iowa City, Iowa: University of Iowa, 1935).

[26]Dean K. Franks, "A Study of the Success of West Seattle High School Students in Language Arts, Foreign Language, Social Studies, and Music and Art," (unpublished doctoral dissertation, University of Washington, 1958).

[27]Fred K. Grumley, "A Study of the Supply and Demand for College Level Music Teachers with Doctoral Degrees, 1964-1970," (unpublished doctoral dissertation, Florida State University, 1964).

[28]Thomas L. Gray, "An Investigation of the Changes in Teaching Concepts of Student Teachers of Music," (unpublished doctoral dissertation, University of Iowa, 1962).

A less formal type of trend study is conducted by many teachers or music administrators to determine the direction of enrollment in specific music classes over a period of years. As a result an increasing or decreasing demand for certain courses may become evident. The popularity of the instructor, state requirements, or other indirect factors, however, may be the actual reasons for a trend which becomes apparent.

TOOLS OF DESCRIPTIVE RESEARCH

The collection of data for the various kinds of descriptive research discussed in the foregoing pages is predicated on the use singly, or in combination, of certain tools. Those most frequently utilized are questionnaire, opinionnaire, interview, rating scale, observation, checklist, and standardized tests.

Questionnaire

One of the most useful and widely used tools of descriptive research is the questionnaire. Unfortunately it also has been abused and misused with the result that there is a tendency today for a questionnaire to be regarded with anathema by the recipient. Borg has pinpointed one of the most serious weaknesses of the questionnaire when he observes that many of them "appear to have been thrown together by the graduate student during the short break between lunch and his two o'clock class."[29] When an investigator takes the time and thought necessary to construct a sound questionnaire, there is no reason why it cannot be used to acquire information that is unobtainable in any other manner.

Questionnaires basically are of two forms, closed and open-ended. The closed, also known as "structured" or "restricted" questionnaire, is objective, easy to administer, facile in response, and fairly simple to score and analyze. Because of its rigid construction, however, the respondent may not be able to express his answer exactly in the manner he wishes. This weakness can be overcome to some extent by providing opportunity for an alternative response.

Answers for the closed questionnaire may be in the form of (1) checking a "yes" or "no" answer, (2) underlining or circling the correct response, (3) ranking items (1, 2, 3, 4) according to their correctness or validity, or (4) inserting specific data in a blank or space provided.

---

[29]Walter R. Borg, *Educational Research: An Introduction* (New York: David McKay Co., Inc., 1963), p. 206. Used by permission of David McKay Co., Inc.

The four statements which follow correspond, respectively, to the closed questionnaire items just cited.

1. *Directions.* Check the correct answer.

   The section leader in each of your senior high school major instrumental performing groups (orchestra, band, etc.,) is required to study his instrument privately. Yes .... No ....

2. *Directions.* Underline the correct response.

   Extra chorus rehearsals, when needed, are scheduled (a) before school (b) during lunch hours (c) after school (d) other ....

   ....
   (please specify)

3. *Directions.* Underline the correct answer.

   How would you rate the attitude of your principal toward music?

1	2	3	4	5
enthusiastic	sympathetic	impartial	tolerant	antagonistic

4. *Directions.* Insert the correct answer in the blanks provided.

   How many full-time instrumental music teachers are employed in your school system? ....

The open-ended questionnaire, also called "free response" or "unrestricted," enables the respondent to reply in his own words, thus permitting him not only to be more candid but also to give reasons for his responses. Negatively, however, the time necessary to carefully and critically formulate an answer can be discouraging and restraining to a very busy individual. The investigator will also find that data obtained from an open-ended questionnaire frequently are difficult to tabulate, categorize, and summarize.

Rephrasing the first example just given to make it conform to an open-ended question, the investigator might ask:

What is your policy regarding private instruction for the senior high school section leader of your major instrumental performing groups?

Several factors should be kept in mind in the construction of a questionnaire. Among the most significant are: (1) only seek information which cannot readily be obtained elsewhere. The researcher should not use a questionnaire as a quick way to procure data that may be acquired only through intensive and time-consuming investigation; (2) instructions for completing the questionnaire should be concise and readily understood. Certain terms which have a specific connotation should be carefully defined; (3) questions should be phrased clearly and in terms which are unambiguous. When the respondent has to spend unnecessary time trying to determine the intended meaning, validity of the responses is diminished; (4) the questionnaire should be brief and to the point, yet long enough to obtain desired information. Unduly long questionnaires, if returned at all, are likely to be completed rather hurriedly or with some information lacking. To reduce what may appear to be an excessive number of questions if strung out one after the other, several items which are similar in nature may be incorporated into one question. The psychological effect of observing fewer separate questions also is conducive to better response; (5) the order in which questions are placed should be logical, proceeding from those which are simple and general to ones which are more complex and specific; (6) controversial questions and those which might prove disconcerting to the respondent should be avoided; and (7) format of the questionnaire should be psychologically conducive to a response on the part of the recipient. A poorly reproduced questionnaire, one which contains print too small to read easily or one in which items are too close together, normally will not receive favorable attention.

Prior to sending out his questionnaire an investigator should pretest it on some peers or on groups similar to those from whom he hopes to elicit responses, requesting that they note questions which need improvement. Suggestions received from the pretest will be useful in preparing a final version which has fewer inconsistencies than might be apparent without this "dry run."

Represented in Figure 3 is a questionnaire received by this writer a few years ago. Not only is the instrument poorly worded but it contains several misspellings. These errors could have been eliminated either through a pretest or by careful proofreading on the part of the investigator. It is questionnaires of this kind which have contributed to the general dislike associated with this kind of instrument.

Accompanying the finalized version of the questionnaire should be a covering letter in which the investigator candidly states the purpose of his study, relevance of his research to music education, sponsorship of his project, and date by which questionnaire is to be returned. He also encloses a self-addressed, stamped envelope. Through this letter the researcher must impress upon the recipient the importance of his reply. If answers are to be treated anonymously the investigator must so inform his respondent and maintain his integrity in that regard when questionnaires are returned and data tabulated. Sponsorship may be indicated either in the body of the letter itself or in the form of an attachment to it. An investigator must not assume that his enrollment at a certain college or university automatically entitles him to *carte blanche* endorsement for anything he sends out.

QUESTIONNAIRE ON TROMBONE METHODS

Name (Title)_____ Date_____

School _____ No. of years taught _____

Instructor at Elementary ☐ Jr. High ☐ Sr. High ☐ level. Private ☐

Mehtod you are now using_____ (OPTIONAL)

Do you see room for improvements in this method?   Yes ☐ No ☐

If so, please check (or add to) the list below.

    Too few explanations ☐

    No systematic progression of keys ☐

    Position chart too complicated ☐

    Too much familiar material ☐

    Not enough familiar material ☐

    No "natural" key for use as a reference (i. e. C for trumpet) ☐

    Studies inconsistant with student's level of performance ☐

    Moves too rapidly ☐

    Moves too slowly ☐

    Insufficient explanations of musical terms ☐

    Other:

    I realize that trombone students have many problems with regard to per-formance on their particular instrument. Hovever, do you feel that your students have serious problems with any of the following?

    Playing in natural and sharp keys ☐

    Playing legato passages ☐

    Playing slurs ☐

    Playing and interpreting accidentals ☐

    Using accurate slide positions ☐

    An inadequate over-all range ☐

Do you attribute the student's weaknesses to any of the following?

    Inadequate time to practice ☐

    Inadequate preparation of the average instrumental teacher ☐

    Reasons checked above with respect to methods ☐

    Other:

FIGURE 3.   Ineffectual Questionnaire

Although the precise time for expecting a questionnaire to be returned is dependent upon such factors as distance of mailing, length of questionnaire, and time of year when it is sent, a period of two to three weeks is not unreasonable. At certain times of the year, notably during football season and at Christmas and spring festival time, music teachers find themselves unusually busy and thus normally not as responsive to questionnaires as they might be at other times. Neither can it be taken for granted that the recipient of a questionnaire is so dedicated to the advancement of knowledge in music education that he will return it at his own expense. It is important that the researcher exercise the courtesy of providing a stamped, addressed envelope for the recipient's convenience.

The letter recorded in Figure 4 was received by this writer, although not in conjunction with a questionnaire. It is indicative, however, of an omniparous or so-called "shotgun" approach which should be avoided in a covering letter. This general type of request is frequently sent out as an appeal for information in lieu of a formal questionnaire. In addition to some incorrect punctuation, the letter makes two unrelated requests for entirely different information.

Dear Dr. Phelps:

I should like a copy of your results of "National Conference to Improve the Effectiveness of State Supervision of Music", under Cooperative Research Act, project S-370. I am also interested in any information that I can obtain on the audio device to help school children learn solfege. Thank you for your kind attention.

Yours sincerely,

FIGURE 4. *Omniparous Request for Information*

As soon as questionnaires are returned the tabulation of information may begin. Data may be recorded on blank questionnaires, on separate sheets of paper, on file cards (3" x 5" or 4" x 6"), or punched on IBM cards. It is good practice to number and date each questionnaire as it is received for ease in rechecking later on. In determining percentages every questionnaire sent out must be accounted for in the totals, either as usable or void. For example, if an investigator wishes to obtain a minimum of 200 responses, he may not continue sending out questionnaires to reach this goal without accounting for all of them in his totals. This may mean his total mailing might be as high as 300 questionnaires.

Although there is no general agreement among educational researchers as to what constitutes an acceptable minimum percentage for questionnaire returns to represent a valid study, in the opinion of Good, the minimum of 90 now seems to be plausible.[30] Formerly a minimum percentage of 75 was considered acceptable to many researchers, but the American Educational Research Association and other professional groups have insisted on and been able to reach a figure above 95 percent in some instances. A response this high usually is obtained only by follow-up techniques. Obviously the higher the percentage of response, the more valid will be the data.

The first follow-up, in the form of a letter or postal card, is usually transmitted about three weeks after the original questionnaire has been sent. The purpose of this reminder is to encourage those who have been dilatory in giving it attention. Approximately one week later another copy of the questionnaire plus a new covering letter may be sent out to those who still have not replied. Thus persons who may have misplaced the first questionnaire have another opportunity to complete and return it. If additional follow-up is desirable the investigator may resort to more expensive means of obtaining data such as special delivery or registered mail, person-to-person telephone calls, or telegrams.

Opinionnaire

The opinionnaire, sometimes known as "attitude scale," which measures a person's opinions, attitudes, or beliefs, is not used to any great extent in music education. Obviously the researcher must accept the information reported without using any objective measures to verify the validity of the statements. The respondent, for example, may conceal his real attitude or provide an answer that he thinks will be most acceptable to the investigator. Regarding techniques used, the respondent may be asked to indicate his degree of agreement or disagreement with certain statements, as in this example:

Directions. Circle the number above the descriptor which indicates your opinion of the statement which follows.

Music instruction should be provided for every child in the elementary school up to the limit of his ability and interest.

1	2	3	4	5
Strongly Agree	Agree	Agree with Reservations	Disagree	Strongly Disagree

[30]Good, *op. cit.,* p. 226.

Doctoral studies in music education utilizing the principle of the attitude scale have been completed by Ray[31] and Fulbright.[32] Ray reported that attitudes toward high school music group experiences are evident in the behavior of students and that it is possible to construct a valid and reliable instrument to measure them. According to Fulbright a college student's attitudes toward classical music are related to sex, musical training, and interest in musical activities, but not to occupation or income of his father.

Interview

The interview technique is an oral procedure for collecting answers to questions by a direct person-to-person basis. Frequently an interviewer utilizes a questionnaire on which he fills in the responses given by the person being interviewed. When used in this manner the questionnaire sometimes is called a "schedule."

It usually is possible to obtain more detailed data through an interview than by an impersonal questionnaire sent through the mail. In addition, the interviewer is able to ask for clarification of any answer he may not understand, which is impossible when using a questionnaire without additional correspondence. A restatement of the question also is possible when it becomes apparent that the query has been misunderstood by the one being interviewed. On the other hand, questions which might be embarrassing for a subject to answer in a face to face situation will frequently receive better response through the impersonal mail questionnaire, especially if anonymity is assured by the investigator.

Interviews may be either structured or unstructured. In the former the interview procedure follows a fairly rigid pattern in regard to questions asked, answers expected, and techniques used to encourage the anticipated responses. Data obtained through the structured interview are usually easier to modify and evaluate than those procured through the unstructured interview.

Flexibility of procedure and questioning mark the unstructured interview. The casual manner characteristic of this type of interviewing frequently results in obtaining responses that might not be possible through any other means. However, comparison of data received from various subjects is more difficult.

---

[31]Thomas A. Ray, "The Construction of a Scale to Measure Attitudes of College Freshmen Toward Their High School Music Group Experiences," (unpublished doctoral dissertation, Indiana University, 1965).

[32]Ercy G. Fulbright, "An Investigation of Relationships Between Cultural Background and Attitudes Toward Classical Orchestral Music Among College Undergraduates," (unpublished doctoral dissertation, Indiana University, 1964).

For best results, the interview technique should not be used by a person who is inexperienced in such procedures. Training and experience in guidance and personnel work provide a good background for the musician who desires to procure extensive information by this method. According to Rummel, the researcher employing interview procedures should develop proficiency in "(1) creating a friendly atmosphere, (2) asking questions, and (3) obtaining responses."[33]

Should an interviewer desire to use a tape recorder to preserve the comments on magnetic tape he should first obtain permission to do so from the one being interviewed. He should not resort to subterfuge through the use of hidden microphones and camouflaged listening devices. An interview preserved on magnetic tape, of course, has the advantage of being readily accessible should the investigator wish to recheck direct verbatim statements, something which is not always possible when remarks are paraphrased or recorded on paper.

Rating Scale

Rating scales may be used to measure traits or attitudes. Student recommendation forms which instructors fill out for placement bureaus or which supervisors complete in conjunction with student teaching evaluation frequently involve qualitative judgments indicated on rating scales. A series of numbers, for example, might be used to rate a person's skill in teaching, with 5 representing superior and 1 indicating inferior achievement. In this instance the intervening descriptors and corresponding numbers might be: above average (4), average (3), and below average (2). The respondent might be instructed to underline the item or to circle the number which most closely corresponds to his evaluation of the person in question.

Another type of appraisal might utilize terminology which is indicative of a subject's behavior as follows: Always Trustworthy, Usually Trustworthy, Occasionally Trustworthy, Rarely Trustworthy, Never Trustworthy. Response to this type of evaluation might be made by underlining or circling the appropriate phrase.

Frequently a graphic rating scale is used for character assessment. Lines and bars indicate the continuum of the descriptive terms employed in this type of rating scale. The evaluator checks or marks a spot on the contour which comes closest to his evaluation. His assessment may be indicated right on one of the vertical bars or at any place along the horizontal contour. A music teacher might use the following

---

[33]J. Francis Rummel, *An Introduction to Research Procedures in Education* (Second Edition; New York: Harper and Row, Publishers, 1964), pp. 103-104. Used by permission of Harper and Row, Publishers.

rating scale to record the diligence of a student's practice habits as evidenced by his performance at a private lesson:

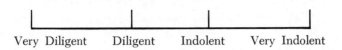

Very Diligent   Diligent   Indolent   Very Indolent

There are some hazards associated with the use of a rating scale. Frequently it is difficult to determine the specific trait or attitude to be measured. Another weakness is the so-called "halo" effect, in which judgments of one trait or attitude are influenced by others, resulting in unintentional bias. Thus, a person who displays a pleasing personality may be rightly or wrongly regarded as intelligent, or an individual who is artistic may be considered a liberal, which actually he may not be. The halo effect is difficult to control and usually is prevalent when uncertainty exists regarding the factors to be evaluated.

Observation

Direct observation obviously is the most objective way for a researcher to procure data for descriptive research. The method of observation has not been used very extensively in music education to evaluate behavior. This technique, however, has been employed widely by music supervisors for periodic evaluation of the performance of student teachers or regular instructional personnel. Various devices and instruments may be used in conjunction with this type of evaluation. A music director, for instance, can observe and evaluate the behavior and response of students "under pressure" who are auditioning for first chair positions in the school's instrumental organizations. He can use a checklist to record the student's reaction to sight reading and employ devices such as a stroboscope and a metronome, respectively, to measure accuracy in pitch and time or rhythmic pulse.

Checklist

A checklist is a relatively simple way to record information about an individual or a situation. It consists of a list of carefully defined items or statements which call for a check mark or a "yes" or "no" response. If, in the auditions noted above, the music director were to include on his checklist adjectives such as "calm," "steady," and "accurate," to indicate the manner in which each student approached the audition, he could readily record his reactions with a "yes" or "no" answer. When constructing a checklist, provision should be made for the evaluator to augment it with additional words or remarks which may seem appropriate at time of the observation. In supervising a teacher (student or otherwise) an evaluator might use a checklist containing items such as "poise," "self-confidence," "well modulated voice," "skill in questioning." The observation technique with accompanying checklist, although usually regarded as a tool of descriptive research, is occasionally included as a part of experimental research. An example is the checklist used by Swanson in a doctoral study on voice mutation in the adolescent male to note changes in attitude toward singing.[34]

Standardized Tests

Standardized tests in music and other subject areas are often employed in conjunction with experimental and descriptive research. Achievement tests in music, for instance, could be used to determine the present level of attainment. These data might then be used as the basis for growth studies, content analysis, or in conjunction with case studies.

There are approximately thirty music tests of various kinds on the market (aptitude, achievement, readiness, appreciation) which a researcher may use in conjunction with interest inventories, measures of mental aptitude, personality tests, and others. To discuss the purposes, kinds, and uses of tests is beyond the scope of this book. The reader is directed to Buros[35] for current data relating to tests in general, and to Whybrew[36] and Lehman[37] for specific information on music tests.

Concepts of validity and reliability, normally associated with tests and measurements, may also be used to evaluate data obtained by the various tools of descriptive research which have been described. Validity is an indication of whether or not an instrument or device measures what it is supposed to. For example, an investigator might ask himself "Does my trend study really determine trends?" On the other hand, reliability is an indication of whether or not an instrument or device will show the same results under identical or comparable conditions. When, for instance, similar findings are evident between two or more identical groups the instrument or device may be regarded as possessing reliability. Since these concepts basically are statistical, a more detailed

[34]Frederick J. Swanson, "Voice Mutation in the Adolescent Male: An Experiment in Guiding the Voice Development of Adolescent Boys in General Music Classes," (unpublished doctoral dissertation, University of Wisconsin, 1959).

[35]Oscar K. Buros, (ed.), Sixth Mental Measurements Yearbook (Highland Park, N. J.: Gryphon Press, 1965).

[36]William E. Whybrew, Measurement and Evaluation in Music (Dubuque, Iowa: Wm. C. Brown Company Publishers, 1962).

[37]Paul R. Lehman, Tests and Measurements in Music (Englewood Cliffs, N. J.: Prentice-Hall, Inc., 1968).

discussion of them is reserved for a subsequent chapter. In addition, the reader should consult any standard textbook on tests and measurements.[38]

SAMPLING

Although sampling commonly is referred to as a research tool, it actually is a statistical technique or procedure for drawing inferences about data obtained from a representative segment of the population being studied. The term "population" as used in connection with sampling is construed as the total group from which the sample is drawn. When data on all factors under consideration can be obtained for every individual in a population, it is unnecessary to use sampling. It might be both practical and possible to procure information from all living individuals who either have taught or currently are teaching harp in a state with a population of 5,000,000. To obtain responses from every living person who either has taught or currently is teaching any kind of instrumental music in that state, however, might be both impossible and impractical from the standpoint of time and money. A sampling of the instrumental music teachers then could be undertaken.

In determining the specific nature of a sample, three factors need to be kept in mind: (1) definition of the population to be studied, (2) determining where this population is located, and (3) delimitation of this representative sample. In defining the population an investigator might restrict his study to teachers of wind instruments. He would then need to determine who all of the wind teachers are and where they are located. To procure complete data might be not only time consuming but also impossible. Listings of music teachers could be obtained from such diverse sources as telephone books, city directories, membership lists of music educators, union membership lists, rosters of school personnel, and the services offered section of want ad columns in newspapers. It might then be decided to delimit the representative sample to private teachers of wind instruments. The group subsequently selected is representative of the entire population of wind instrument teachers. Any inferences drawn about wind instrument teachers would be based on information given by the sample group.

The two most commonly used types of samples are random and stratified. A random sample, as observed in the previous chapter, involves a chance selection, with each group or individual being given an

---

[38]For an especially concise and lucid account of these terms see Chapter 4 of Whybrew, *op. cit.* and Chapter 3 of Lehman, *op. cit.*

equal chance of being chosen. Most pre-election polls utilize the random sample principle. One of the most common methods of determining this kind of sample is through the use of tables of random numbers found in most statistics books. Representative elements of the population are assigned numbers. Then the size of the sample to be chosen is determined, for example, six. Starting anywhere on the table of random numbers and proceeding in any direction until the size of the sample has been reached, in this case the first six numbers, the digits which appear represent the ones which will constitute the sample.

A stratified sample employs random selection techniques but attempts to make specific subdivisions according to some predetermined plan. Thus, in a stratified sample, an investigator might be interested in obtaining a certain number of piano, string, woodwind, and brass teachers instead of assuming that his population would contain by chance selection a representative number of teachers in each of these areas.

After data from the samples have been procured, statistical techniques should be used which will permit the best tabulation and evaluation of results. The statistical treatment of data will be discussed in a subsequent chapter of this book.

Descriptive research, although one of the most widely used types in music education, especially at the master's degree level, probably has been misused and abused more than any other kind. Certain types of data, however, cannot be readily obtained by any other method. It is for this reason that descriptive research procedures undoubtedly will be used for some time yet in music education. By contrast, the philosophical research method has not been employed very much in music education. It is this type of research which will be treated in the next chapter.

QUESTIONS FOR REVIEW AND DISCUSSION

1. For what purposes is descriptive research undertaken?
2. Discuss the disparity surrounding descriptive research.
3. Contrast and compare the various kinds of studies included under the general heading of survey; namely, school survey, job analysis, content analysis, public opinion survey, and curriculum research. Give the purpose and indicate how each one may be implemented in music education.
4. What types of research are described as correlation studies in this chapter? Identify the purpose and tell how each one may be utilized in music education.

5. Discuss the types of relationship studies listed in this chapter and make an application of each one to music education.
6. What factors need to be kept in mind in the construction of a questionnaire? Distinguish between the kind of questions used in a closed and an open-ended questionnaire.
7. How does the opinionnaire differ from a questionnaire?
8. Discuss the interview technique as it relates to music education research. What are advantages and disadvantages of the interview as compared to the questionnaire?
9. What are the purposes in using a rating scale? Indicate precautions which must be considered when this research tool is used.
10. How may a checklist be used in music education research? What factors need to be considered in its construction?
11. Compare and contrast the techniques of random and stratified samples.

SUPPLEMENTARY READINGS

BEST, JOHN W. *Research in Education.* Englewood Cliffs, N. J.: Prentice-Hall, Inc., 1959. Chapters 5 and 7.

BORG, WALTER R. *Educational Research: An Introduction.* New York: David McKay Co., Inc., 1963. Chapters 10-12.

COOK, DAVID R. *A Guide to Educational Research.* Boston: Allyn and Bacon, Inc., 1965. Chapter III.

GAGE, N. L. (ed.). *Handbook of Research on Teaching.* Chicago: Rand McNally and Co., 1963. Chapters 6 and 7.

GOOD, CARTER V. *Essentials of Educational Research.* New York: Appleton-Century-Crofts, 1966. Chapters 5-7.

———, and SCATES, DOUGLAS E. *Methods of Research.* New York: Appleton-Century-Crofts, 1954. Chapters 5, 6, 8, and 9.

HILLWAY, TYRUS. *Introduction to Research.* Second Edition. Boston: Houghton Mifflin Co., 1964. Chapters 13 and 16.

KAPLAN, MAX. *Foundations and Frontiers of Music Education.* New York: Holt, Rinehart and Winston, Inc., 1966. Chapter 5.

KERLINGER, FRED N. *Foundations of Behavioral Research.* New York: Holt, Rinehart and Winston, Inc., 1965. Chapters 4, 18, 22, 24-28.

LEHMAN, PAUL R. *Tests and Measurements in Music.* Englewood Cliffs, N. J.: Prentice-Hall, Inc., 1968. Chapter 3.

MORGAN, HAZEL N., and BURMEISTER, CLIFTON A. *Music Research Handbook.* Evanston, Ill.: The Instrumentalist Co., 1962. Chapter VI.

MOULY, GEORGE J. *The Science of Educational Research.* New York: American Book Co., 1963. Chapters 10 and 11.

RUMMEL, J. FRANCIS. *An Introduction to Research Procedures in Education.* Second Edition. New York: Harper and Row, Publishers, 1964. Chapters IV-IX.

SAX, GILBERT. *Empirical Foundations of Educational Research.* Englewood
Cliffs, N. J.: Prentice-Hall, Inc., 1968. Chapters 8, 9, and 11.

SMITH, HENRY L. *Educational Research, Principles and Practices.* Bloomington, Ind.: Educational Publications, 1944. Chapter X.

TRAVERS, ROBERT M. W. *An Introduction to Educational Research.* Second
Edition. New York: The Macmillan Co., 1964. Chapters 8-12.

VAN DALEN, DEOBALD B. *Understanding Educational Research.* Enlarged and
Revised Edition. New York: McGraw-Hill Book Co., Inc., 1966. Chapters
10 and 12.

WHITNEY, FREDERICK L. *The Elements of Research.* Third Edition. Englewood
Cliffs, N. J.: Prentice-Hall, Inc., 1950. Chapter VII.

WHYBREW, WILLIAM E. *Measurement and Evaluation in Music.* Dubuque,
Iowa: Wm. C. Brown Company Publishers, 1962. Chapter 4.

WISE, JOHN E., NORDBERG, ROBERT B., and REITZ, DONALD J. *Methods of
Research in Education.* Boston: D. C. Heath and Co., 1967. Chapters V
and VI.

• 8 •

Philosophical Research: Rational Quest for Truth

Philosophical research is concerned with discerning truths or principles upon which knowledge in any field is based. Unlike experimental research, which is predicated on observing rigid controls to obtain data, the philosophical method of research fundamentally is based on reflective or critical thinking. Yet, these reflective or rational procedures are "disciplined" and "orderly," according to Wise, Nordberg, and Reitz, so valid results can be obtained from the philosophical method of research.[1] Rationalism, the concept upon which the philosophical method is based, employs *a priori* logic, wherein knowledge and truth are derived solely through reasoning rather than by the empirical method of science. *A priori* or metempirical reasoning establishes a cause and effect relationship which proceeds from assumptions regarded as self-evident to the deductive postulation of inferences or logical conclusions based on these assumptions. In a general sense all types of research use some of the procedures of reflection or rationalization, which is the keystone of philosophical research.

Philosophical inquiry and investigation are very old, stemming from the time of Aristotle and other Greek philosophers. As a specific method or type, however, philosophical research frequently is ignored by many who imply that it is of little value to educators because it commonly does not involve itself with problems which can be solved empirically. Admittedly, philosophical research is concerned largely with delineating

---

[1]John E. Wise, Robert B. Nordberg, and Donald J. Reitz, *Methods of Research in Education*, pp. 173-175. © 1967, D. C. Heath and Co., Boston. Reproduced by permission.

concepts and truths by reflective thinking, and therefore essentially is more subjective than experimental research, which is based on empirical observation. On the other hand, Brubacher reminds his readers that pragmatists view any type of thinking as research.[2]

Music education appears to be an area which can utilize the concepts of philosophical research even more than it has in the past. The potentialities in this discipline were noted as early as 1955 by Leonhard, who pointed out that the "areas of philosophy and esthetics have been neglected as areas of research by music educators."[3] Esthetics, a phase of music education which is a special field of inquiry in its own right, employs some techniques of inquiry different from those discussed in this chapter.

In descriptive research, it will be recalled from the previous chapter, an endeavor is made to find out what exists at the present time. Philosophical research, however, attempts to establish or determine concepts or truths which may be used to confirm or modify attitudes, beliefs, or principles.

SCIENCE VERSUS PHILOSOPHY

The methods of science, which depend largely upon empirical methods, make it easier to obtain quantitative data than is usually the case with philosophy. Yet, almost paradoxically, philosophy frequently evolves the theories which subsequently are subjected to scrutinizing experimentation and appraisal in the field of science. The more general "what" of philosophy is translated into the rather specific and objective "how" of science. Yet Smith notes that while facts can be discovered by science, their utility is determined by other means.[4] The basically subjective nature of philosophical inquiry, however, should not be sufficient justification of itself to rule out this concept all together as a method of research. Historical and descriptive research also utilize different principles from experimental research, yet they are accepted as valid methods in their respective areas. Philosophical, in common with historical, experimental, descriptive, and analytical research, by techniques different in some respects from those emphasized in other types of

---

[2]John S. Brubacher, *Eclectic Philosophy of Education* (Second Edition; Englewood Cliffs, N. J.: Prentice-Hall, Inc., 1962), p. 380.

[3]Charles Leonhard, "Research: Philosophy and Esthetics," *Journal of Research in Music Education*, III (Spring, 1955), p. 24. Used by permission of the *Journal of Research in Music Education*.

[4]Henry L. Smith, *Educational Research, Principles and Practices* (Bloomington, Ind.: Educational Publications, 1944), p. 101.

research, seeks to interpret truths evident in data which have been collected or are already on hand.

Those who maintain that science and philosophy are not compatible
frequently insist that science, because of its emphasis on the "how" and
rigid control of constants and variables, is able to obtain data in an
objective and valid manner not possible by any other method. Philosophy, by contrast, is concerned with the "what" or principles, ideals, or
concepts which are not always easy to quantify in a manner entirely
satisfactory to a scientist. Individual evaluation and interpretation play
conspicuous roles in philosophical research, and philosophers, when dealing with a general concept about which they agree in principle, are not
always in accord among themselves regarding how to best reflectively
arrive at inferences. For example, from a philosophical standpoint it
may be accepted universally by music educators that general music
is a desirable requirement for all junior high school students. Disagreement as to when it should be taught, by whom, for how long, and what
precisely should be included in general music, however, would not be
unusual. One group of music educators may insist that seventh grade
is the most desirable level to teach general music, while another may
feel that the eighth or ninth grade is more appropriate. Other specifics
also will vary accordingly. On the other hand, the music psychologist
might consider general music from the standpoint of objective measurement of the skills expected of each student. Such evaluation might take
the form of charting an oscilloscopic profile of the student as he sings
or, by means of a teaching machine, ascertaining his comprehension of
material covered in the course. In these examples science concentrates
on the "how" or the practical application of these theories or specifics,
whereas philosophy essentially is related to the "what" or ideas and
theory. Does this not suggest then that philosophy can be as important
as science, because each serves a different but equally significant purpose? To look at it another way, experimental and philosophical research
may be said to represent the two extremes in research objectivity, the
former generally the most objective and the latter the most subjective,
yet each is important in its own right.

It seems redundant to point out again that interpretation of data
is a most important step in all types of research; however, it should be
reiterated that when making an explication of data the investigator
utilizes the scientific method to arrive at the generalizations which result.
The scientific method, with its emphasis upon logical organization, objective implementation, and precise interpretation may be considered
to be a *prima facie* application of the philosophical concept of investi-

gation. For this reason some researchers aver that there is no distinct philosophical method of research. As already must be apparent, this book supports the premise that there is a distinct philosophical method of research. There is no reason why research which is philosophical in scope cannot be conducted just as competently and skillfully as any other type. Likewise the inferences derived deductively need not be any less valid than conclusions reached by other types of research methodology.

PURPOSES OF PHILOSOPHICAL RESEARCH

Music education can utilize findings of philosophical research for many purposes. One of the most important is to evaluate metempirically current practices in music education to determine which ones should be retained, abandoned, or modified. The curriculum is in a constant state of flux with innovations instituted periodically in order to keep pace with a rapidly changing world. This is apparent in the seemingly endless testing and evaluation of new concepts and procedures in the classroom. Music education fortunately has been involved in some of these innovative practices. Recall that about sixty years ago a revolutionary English concept of instrumental music teaching was brought to the attention of music educators in the United States. One of them, Albert G. Mitchell, was so intrigued with the possibilities of this promising method of teaching that he obtained a leave of absence from his position as a supervisor of music in the Boston Public Schools to travel to England to study firsthand this system of teaching violin in classes, commonly referred to as the Maidstone Movement. From this concept of violin class teaching has come the phenomenal development which subsequently has resulted in teaching all kinds of instruments to unprecedented numbers of students in classes in the United States. This idea has been adapted also to piano, voice, and organ instruction. The original Maidstone philosophical concept of class teaching has been implemented in the form of specific skills and techniques peculiar to each performing medium, with the result that many individuals have made contributions to this idea since then.

Although the value of class teaching in the development of sound music education programs rarely is challenged today, there still are many diverse ideas relating to specific and effective ways in which to implement this philosophical concept. The Suzuki, Kodaly, and Orff approaches are in the forefront at the time of this writing and, although there are similarities, each one has a different philosophical approach to methodology. These concepts eventually may result in the changing

of certain practices in the teaching of music. This will not come, ho..
ever, until it has been demonstrated that appropriation of the specific
techniques under consideration will result in more effective and meaningful learning by students. It is too early yet to determine whether
the Suzuki, Kodaly, and Orff approaches, as well as others, will result
in the retention, abandonment, or modification of some current practices in music education.

A second purpose of using philosophical research in music education is to define or clarify principles or concepts which may be used
to help the music educator solve some of his problems. As such, philosophical research is, of course, more concerned with determining *what*
needs to be done rather than *how* this is to be accomplished. For instance, through the application of techniques of philosophical research,
it may be decided that the values of a comprehensive and well-coordi-
nated program of music instruction for every child to the extent of
his interests and abilities is of such import that it is imperative for
every school to provide such instruction. Music educators frequently
have bemoaned the lack of specific information to present to super-
intendents and boards of education when they try to convince them
that music programs should be expanded or instituted, as the case may be.
Results of philosophical research can be used to lend validity to a teacher's contentions of what needs to be included in the music program,
but not necessarily how it is to be implemented. To cite an example,
in the pamphlet *National Leaders Speak for Music*,[5] many national
figures outside the field of music affirm why they think it is important
for all students to receive music instruction while in school. Suggesting
the manner of putting these philosophical concepts into practice, however, is neither the purpose nor the province of this pamphlet any more
than it is of philosophical research in the usual meaning of the term.

The synthesis of theories is a third purpose of philosophical research. Such a procedure is concerned with codifying, analyzing, and
then interpreting inferences evolved from this synthesis. A typical synthesis might consist of a study of the changing philosophies of music
supervision. It might then be possible to ascertain the effects these
modifications have had on the curriculum and the relationship they
bear to changes in other disciplines. It should be apparent that other
areas in the curriculum have and will continue to influence what transpires in music to some extent. Conversely, it hardly seems necessary
to point out that music, to a limited extent, also has influenced other
disciplines. The current interest in humanities or related arts courses

---

[5]*National Leaders Speak for Music* (Washington: Music Educators National
Conference, 1967).

may be considered to be a manifestation of this concept. A by-product of this idea has been the change in the way music theory and literature are taught in some schools. Instead of being concerned merely with technical perfection of the compositions being rehearsed, the choir, band, or orchestra director now finds that he frequently incorporates more of the theoretical, historical, and other related aspects of a composition into his rehearsals than in former years. Consequently the student is learning in a coordinated setting about composer, formal structure, and theoretical facts pertinent to the music being rehearsed. His musical education should be meaningful and pragmatic rather than an abstract and fragmented performance-oriented experience.

PHILOSOPHICAL CONCEPTS

In music education there are three philosophical concepts which seem to be used more than others; namely, pragmatism, realism, and idealism. Since they influence everything a music educator believes, says, or does, they have more than an indirect bearing on the consequences of philosophical research. Since philosophical inquiry is based on metempirical inferences, a comprehension of various philosophical ideas can make this process much more readily understood.

Pragmatism is a doctrine which states that ideas have validity only as they have practical value for the one employing them. Originally conceived in a slightly different form by American mathematician Charles S. Peirce (1839-1914), pragmatism was modified to some extent by another American, the psychologist William James (1842-1910), to the concept which has just been delineated; namely, utilitarianism. Because of its emphasis on practical applications, music educators appear to subscribe to the idea of pragmatism more than to any other philosophical idea. Perhaps this tendency to be purposive results from the skill and performance phases of music. Through applied skills, theoretical knowledge about music is put into practice. The current emphasis on presenting general music in a more meaningful manner is an example of the application of pragmatism. The objective of general music, a term which many music educators dislike, is to enable the average person to develop an understanding of and respect for the art of music. When music becomes meaningful to a person it has practical or pragmatic significance for him.

The doctrine of realism as applied to art and music relates to the recognition and portrayal of individuals, events, or situations as they actually exist rather than as they are imagined to be. Word painting of the Baroque era and program music of the Romantic period—especially *Don Quixote* of Richard Strauss (1864-1949)—may be cited as instances where attempts have been made to portray events or situations realistically through music. Objectivity may be regarded as significant to the concept of realism. Although this doctrine originated with Plato (*c.* 427-*c.* 347 B.C.), it was refined by French philosopher René Descartes (1596-1650) and Baruch Spinoza (1632-1677), a Dutch pantheist. Realism has assumed special significance in the area of esthetics of music where it has been concerned with factors such as the basis for realistic listening skills. In music education this idea may take the form of an objective evaluation that a conductor makes of a performing group. He may detect wrong notes, incorrect rhythmic figures, or other musical errors, and be willing to accept their existence realistically. This is not to suggest that the conductor should passively accept what he hears as the best the group can do. Rather, he acknowledges the deficiencies and uses them as a basis for striving to attain whatever musical ideals he may have in mind; thus, the element of idealism also enters in. To give another example of realism, a music educator who accepts the body of sound from a twenty-five-piece high school orchestra chooses his music accordingly rather than trying to play compositions which sound well only with a much larger ensemble.

Idealism in art and music is construed to mean that the realm of reality may be attained only in a person's imagination. Subjectivity rather than objectivity prevails in idealism. An idealist sometimes is characterized as a "dreamer," or the person who experiences more difficulty than usual in facing reality. Many beginning music teachers, due to inexperience, are more inclined to be idealists than realists, although there is a marked tendency in the opposite direction as they gain in experience. The concept of idealism, developed by German philosophers Georg Hegel (1770-1831) and Immanuel Kant (1724-1804), is better fulfilled by a music educator when combined with another doctrine, such as realism, as noted in the example relating to a conductor's evaluation of his performing organization. One final illustration of a confirmed idealist, however, relates to the music educator who believes that the omnipresent problem of the non-singer in the classroom can be eliminated completely by the time every child reaches the sixth grade.

In reality most philosophies of music education are not exclusively one concept or the other but rather a combination of one or more. An investigator involved in philosophical inquiry must discern similarities and differences in these ideas in order that his evaluation, inferences, or synthesis will be rational. Illogical organization and procedures can be just as disastrous to the outcomes of philosophical research as to any other type.

METHODS OF PHILOSOPHICAL RESEARCH

Although philosophical research is predicated largely on the utilization of inductive and deductive reasoning to draw inferences, there are certain methods or types of inquiry which may be used by an investigator. One of the most lucid delineations of methods of philosophical research is presented by Villemain, who lists three: analytic, critical, and speculative.[6]

The analytic method of philosophical research may be used to lend clarity to concepts, ideas, or words. This approach is especially significant when ambiguity surrounds a certain word or concept. The delimitations section in a graduate thesis, although not philosophical research in the same sense as the term is considered in this chapter, may be regarded as a type of explication similar to the rationale employed in the analytic method. This procedure may also attempt to find consistency of pattern in the use of a term or phrase, if this is the investigator's intention. The analytic method, for example, might be used to reflectively arrive at an understanding of what is meant by the "alto-tenor" concept of the adolescent boy's voice. Music educators would welcome such a clarification of terminology. The analytical method of philosophical inquiry has not been employed much in music education. More attention has been given to the critical method, perhaps because it seems to have more pertinence to the profession.

When educational objectives, practices, or concepts are evaluated the critical method of philosophical research is often employed. The critical method is intended to determine whether these objectives, practices, or concepts as stated are adequate or desirable. In order to make normative determinations it is necessary to employ some predetermined standard or basis for comparison so that acceptance or rejection may be made. Villemain emphasizes that the critical function of philosophy should be emphatic and productive rather than necessarily negative.[7] In music education the process of critical inquiry might serve to point out the most desirable ideas in teaching music reading. Ross, in a doctoral study, used the critical method to examine writings since 1920 in the areas of general education, music education, educational philosophy,

[6]Francis T. Villemain, *Philosophic Research in Education* (New York: New York University Press, 1953), p. 3.
[7]*Ibid.*, p. 4.

and philosophy of art to synthesize the philosophical principles contained in them as a basis for esthetic experiences in the elementary school.[8]

The speculative, also known as the "synthetic" method, endeavors to ascertain objectives and experiences considered to be important for the future. Their formulation is based upon *a priori* reasoning, which normally has been preceded by analytic and critical approaches. Through the speculative method new horizons may be opened. Some music educators and musicologists, for instance, are already speculatively planning for the immediate future when a digital computer may be used to enable a teacher to evaluate students more objectively and also to make some of the time-consuming administrative tasks, such as record keeping, relatively simple and almost instantaneous.[9] In a doctoral study using the speculative method, Fowler not only determined desirable objectives for music education today but also projected worthy goals and purposes for the future.[10]

Regardless of whether the analytic, critical, or speculative method of philosophical research is employed, the procedures for obtaining data by metempirical reasoning are basically the same for all.

TECHNIQUES OF PHILOSOPHICAL RESEARCH

Although the method of obtaining data in philosophical research follows a pattern similar to that relating to selection of the problem, discussed in Chapter 2 of this book, Villemain notes that there are two separate, but interrelated, procedures which he labels "inquiry" and "argument," respectively.[11] Under the first heading are some of the steps usually associated with the logical organization of the problem; namely, initial statement of the problem, tentative formulation of hypotheses and methods for testing them, designation of ideas to be presented, and collection of data. Of these four categories, perhaps the second is the most important because, more than any other, it will enable the investigator, through reflective thinking, to adhere to and implement his research plan.

---

[8]Jerrold Ross, "The Development of a Comprehensive Philosophy for Music in Elementary Education," (unpublished doctoral dissertation, New York University, 1963).

[9]For additional information about computer applications to music see the remarks of Jan P. LaRue and George W. Logemann in this writer's report "Seminar in State Music Supervision," (U. S. Office of Education Cooperative Research Project 7-8124, 1967).

[10]Charles B. Fowler, "A Reconstructionist Philosophy of Music Education," (unpublished doctoral dissertation, Boston University, 1964).

[11]Villemain, *op. cit.,* pp. 9-10.

In the formulation of an argument the researcher develops the ideas initially presented in a logical and sequential manner. The major theme of the argument and its various sub-headings evolve systematically along with their relation and significance to the study. Then come the accumulation of data and pertinent theories, followed by formulation of basic assumptions, postulation of fundamental philosophical ideas, and development of conclusions with their implications. These procedures have already been developed in the third chapter of this book so will not be repeated here. Other subjects, conjectures, calculations, and assessments should be included when they are pertinent, according to Villemain.[12]

In actual practice, inquiry and argument are frequently fused either in part or completely, although the steps listed in each do not necessarily need to follow one another in the order presented above. When such a combination plan is followed, naturally, the original tentative outline is never really affirmed until all data have been obtained, evaluated, and interpreted. The reason for this is that alterations may be necessary as the *a priori* reasoning process progresses. When this procedure has been completed the investigator is able to either sustain or reject his initial plan.

Although philosophical research is based upon deliberation and rationalization, it nevertheless can be used to determine truths, concepts, or hidden assumptions significant to the music educator. Quantitative data are more difficult to obtain through the normative procedures used in philosophical research than they are in other types of investigation, especially experimental. Notwithstanding, through rationalization the logical analyzation and interpretation of philosophical concepts can result in valid contributions to man's knowledge.

Frequently it is the objective of a music researcher to examine and analyze the compositions of a composer. In this way the bases of his compositional techniques and other factors may be better understood. The method of analytical research is the object of the next chapter.

QUESTIONS FOR REVIEW AND DISCUSSION

1. For what purposes is philosophical research undertaken?
2. What is the relationship of science to philosophy?
3. Discuss pragmatism, realism, and idealism as they relate to music education. Give a specific musical application of each concept.
4. Compare and contrast the three methods of philosophical research presented in this chapter.

---

[12]*Ibid.*, p. 11.

5. How may the philosophical techniques of "inquiry" and "argument" be applied to music education?

SUPPLEMENTARY READINGS

BROUDY, HARRY S. "A Realistic Philosophy of Music Education," *Basic Concepts in Music Education,* Fifty-Seventh Yearbook of the National Society for the Study of Education. Chicago: University of Chicago Press, 1958. Chapter III.

FOWLER, CHARLES B. "Discovery Method Its Relevance for Music Education," *Journal of Research in Music Education,* XIV (Summer, 1966), 126-134.

LEONHARD, CHARLES. "Research: Philosophy and Esthetics," *Journal of Research in Music Education,* III (Spring, 1955), 23-26.

McMURRAY, FOSTER. "Pragmatism in Music Education," *Basic Concepts in Music Education,* Fifty-Seventh Yearbook of the National Society for the Study of Education. Chicago: University of Chicago Press, 1958. Chapter II.

MILLER, THOMAS W. "The Influence of Progressivism on Music Education, 1917-1947," *Journal of Research in Music Education,* XIV (Spring, 1966), 3-16.

SCHNEIDER, ERWIN H., and CADY, HENRY L. "Evaluation and Synthesis of Research Studies Relating to Music Education," U. S. Office of Education Cooperative Research Project E-016, 1965. Item ED 010 298 in ERIC Document Reproduction Service. Bethesda, Md.: National Cash Register Co., 4936 Fairmont Ave., pp. 237-240.

SCHWADRON, ABRAHAM A. "Aesthetic Values in Music Education," *Perspectives in Music Education.* Source Book III. Washington: Music Educators National Conference, 1966. pp. 185-194.

SMITH, HENRY L. *Educational Research, Principles and Practices.* Bloomington, Ind.: Educational Publications, 1944. Chapter VI.

VILLEMAIN, FRANCIS T. *Philosophic Research in Education.* New York: New York University Press, 1953.

WHITNEY, FREDERICK L. *The Elements of Research.* Third Edition. Englewood Cliffs, N. J.: Prentice-Hall, Inc., 1950. Chapter X.

WISE, JOHN E., NORDBERG, ROBERT B., and REITZ, DONALD J. *Methods of Research in Education.* Boston: D. C. Heath and Co., 1967. Chapter IX.

• 9 •

Analytical Research: Analysis of Musical Structure

Walter Kob

Although the analysis of musical structure as a basis for systematic style criticism is technically the province of musicology rather than of music education *per se*, the two disciplines are not independent or unrelated.[1] Studies concerned with the suitability of specific items or of collections of music literature for use in certain learning situations, for example, frequently require analysis of the music. Analysis may be necessary or desirable not only for the purpose of determining technical particulars but also to insure the cultural pertinence of the pedagogical aims. Some scholars in the field of music education are sufficiently concerned with the descriptive, critical, and historical aspects of musical materials that style criticism based on analytical techniques becomes the primary aim of their research.

THE PLACE OF ANALYTICAL RESEARCH IN STUDIES IN MUSIC EDUCATION

That research in music education often entails analysis of musical structure may be exemplified by citing the type of study which attempts to discover whether or not the musical growth of children is best fostered through emphasis on a specific musical concept—say, the penta-

---

[1]The premise that music education is an allied branch of systematic musicology is established by Glen Haydon in *Introduction to Musicology* (Englewood Cliffs, N. J.: Prentice-Hall, Inc., 1941), pp. 1, 9, and 186 ff.

tonic scale, or tonality as expressed by melodic skips, or form. In studies of this type, literature must be examined and accurately analyzed with respect to the pertinent structural elements. Consideration of categories or of grading may depend on the results of analysis. This is true not only in the development of a syllabus or course of study but also in developing teaching aids: textbooks, programed materials, musical achievement tests, and graded collections of materials for use in skill subjects such as sight reading and keyboard harmony. Most such investigations need not involve an elaborate analytical procedure, and it is possible that the location of suitable examples may be accomplished by simple visual and aural inspection.

If two or more collections of materials, such as song books or books of music intended for use in learning to play an instrument, are to be evaluated with respect to selected elements (melodic range, tessitura, meter, rhythmic patterns, mode, form, or what not), a more systematic analytical procedure may be called for. However, the primary purpose of the analysis will remain that of gathering data to support some pedagogical plan or hypothesis, and not of assessing musical style.

THE ANALYSIS OF STYLE: SCOPE
OF THE RESEARCH SUBJECT

Analytical research that is undertaken for the purpose of style criticism or of relating compositional techniques to theoretical or esthetic concepts is quite another thing. Here it is understood that the analysis and the presentation of the data is only the first step in the research. Sometimes aspiring candidates for graduate degrees naively think that the reporting of data collected—the bare statistics which result from the musical analysis—is all that is needed. This is a mistake, for, although the information revealed may be of some value, it is the interpretation of the data that earns the respect of other scholars. Analytical information on such a subject as "The Chamber Music of Brahms" must have relevance. It is not enough to know, for instance, that 35 percent of the chromaticism in Brahms' music involves the diminished seventh chord; it is necessary to demonstrate in what way this information is significant. Following are some ways in which such relevance or significance might be established:

1. The data can be compared with that on the music of another composer. This could point up those structural procedures which are used by both, as well as those which are peculiar to one or the other. In some studies it might also be pertinent to establish the possibility of influence. The problem here is that very few reported

studies based on a scientific method are available as sources for comparison. This is true particularly with respect to the "great" composers of the eighteenth and nineteenth centuries, certainly nothing comparable to the famous study of the style of Palestrina by Jeppesen.[2] In analyzing and characterizing the piano music of John Field (1782-1837), for instance, how can one validate (or refute) the assumption sometimes made that it is very similar to that of Chopin if the style of Chopin has never been scientifically investigated? Doyle, in his analysis of the music of Louis M. Gottschalk, faced this problem, though style definition was not the main purpose or contribution of his study.[3]

2. The data can be compared with similar data on music in a different medium by the same composer—chamber music versus piano music, for example. Here, again, the possibility that there may be a prior study with which to relate the findings is remote. Of course, a comparative study analyzing music from both sources can always be set up.

3. The stylistic aspects of music from one period of a composer's creative life can be compared with those from another—early works versus late works, for instance. The idea usually is to attempt to describe changes or "growth" in a composer's style. Landau, in investigating the chamber music of Hindemith, divided the composer's career into five-year periods.[4] Analyzing a sample from the works composed in each period, he was able to show the limited extent to which Hindemith appears to modify his style to conform to his harmonic theories as he developed them over a span of years.

4. The statistics can be interpreted in terms of the history of the medium or form, or of a technical device. Supposing it were the history of chamber music, the analysis might be confined to such matters as texture, sonority, instrumental techniques, and form.

5. The statistics can be interpreted in terms of certain esthetic concepts, such as "romanticism" or "symbolism," or with relation to a system of philosophy.[5]

6. The statistics can be used to support a hypothesis concerning the existence of a unique or particularly noteworthy compositional de-

---

[2]Knud Jeppesen, *The Style of Palestrina and the Dissonance* (Second Edition; London: Oxford University Press, 1946).

[3]John G. Doyle, "The Piano Music of Louis Moreau Gottschalk (1829-1869)," (unpublished doctoral dissertation, New York University, 1960).

[4]Victor Landau, "Paul Hindemith, a Case Study in Theory and Practice," *Music Review*, XXI (February, 1960), 45.

[5]Ira C. Singleton, "The Rationality of Eighteenth Century Classicism: a Study of the Relationships Between the Rationalistic Philosophies of Descartes, Spinoza, and Leibnitz and the Classicism of Haydn, Mozart, and Beethoven," (unpublished doctoral dissertation, New York University, 1954).

vice that has been overlooked in earlier critical analysis: hidden thematic relationships, for example, or atypical tonal schemes.

7. If the music exhibits national or ethnic traits, or actually quotes folk music, this point can be emphasized, and the relation to original folk sources can be established. Among numerous examples, one can cite Sternfeld's analysis of Stravinsky's treatment of Russian folk songs in *Petrouchka*.[6]

8. The relationship between style characteristics as determined by analysis and the pronouncements of music theorists can be the subject of research. The work of Landau on Hindemith as composer and theorist has been mentioned above. Additional examples of this approach are the studies by Vincent Jones in the area of harmony[7] and by this writer in the area of form.[8]

This list of approaches to the problem of interpretation does not exhaust the possibilities. Its purpose is to illustrate the principle that analytical research must go further than uncritical description of assembled data.

A study in which the final document merely presents a running narration of the analysis, measure by measure and phrase by phrase, or a series of graphs or diagrams that describe the sequence of happenings in a line from beginning to end is also inadequate. The reader of the report might just as well read through the score itself. It is probably unwise, certainly unnecessary, to include such narrative material in the final document even if it is accompanied by interpretive discussion and the drawing of conclusions.

PROBLEMS OF DELIMITATION AND SAMPLING

The practical need to delimit the scope of a projected study is as important in the field of style criticism as in other areas of research. The following list of hypothetical subjects illustrates how delimitation can be set both as to structural elements and as to the extent or amount of the literature analyzed:

Formal Structure in the Kreisleriana of Schumann
Canon and Fugue in the Music of Max Reger

---

[6]Frederick W. Sternfeld, "Some Russian Folk Songs in Stravinsky's Petrouchka," *Notes*, II (1945), 98-104; reprinted in *Norton Critical Score of Petrushka*, Charles Hamm (ed.) (New York: W. W. Norton and Co., Inc., 1967), pp. 203-215.

[7]Vincent Jones, "The Relationship of Harmonic Theory and Practice from Rameau to 1900," (unpublished doctoral dissertation, Harvard University, 1934).

[8]Walter Kob, "The Smaller Forms of Instrumental Music, 1740-1815, in Relation to Theories of Musical Form," (unpublished doctoral dissertation, University of Rochester, 1965).

Tonality in the Piano Preludes of Debussy
Harmonic Root-progression in Verdi's *Otello*
Texture in the Choral Works of Brahms
Melodic Structure in Selected Songs of Schubert
Dissonance Treatment in Two Symphonic Poems of Richard Strauss.[9]

It is not suggested that such delimitations are obligatory. Critical studies embracing all elements of style for the total output of a composer can and have been made, but this represents an enormous task. There may be a danger of superficiality if the scope is too large. At the same time, a study based on harmonic progression in only three piano sonatas of Haydn, for instance, is so limited in scope that its contribution would be small. Such a study would make a good term paper for a course in literature and materials.

In comparing the styles of two or more composers, there is a built-in delimitation in the fact that there is an assumption that they belong to a homogeneous group either with respect to geography (national origin), style period (they worked about the same time), direct association (a teacher-pupil relationship, for instance), or esthetic philosophy (impressionism). Mozart and Haydn are probably the most famous pair, but then there are Debussy and Ravel, J. C. Bach and Abel, Schoenberg and Berg, and countless other possibilities. The doctoral study by Dailey is an example of a comparison of the styles of two or more composers.[10]

An important type of study is limited to a specific compositional device as used over a period of time by selected or representative composers. This can be a form, a rhythmic technique (hemiola, for example, or syncopation), a harmonic technique (the Neapolitan Sixth, modulation, tonality schemes, etc.), or any other element that delineates structure. Examples of this type of study are Nelson's investigation of the history of the variation,[11] Haydon's work on the evolution of the six-four chord,[12] and the writer's study of the pavane as a musical form.[13]

---

[9]A further idea as to the numerous ways in which delimitation may be made can be obtained by reading through the lists of titles in *Doctoral Dissertations in Musicology*. See also Lincoln Spiess, *Historical Musicology* (New York: Institute of Mediaeval Music, 1963), pp. 14-15, 21-23, 27-35, and 40-41.

[10]William A. Dailey, "Techniques of Composition Used in Contemporary Works for Chorus and Orchestra on Religious Texts as Important Representative Works of the Period from 1952 through 1962 (*Canticum sacrum* of Stravinsky, *Prayers of Kierkegaard* by Barber, and *Magnificat* by Hovhaness," (unpublished doctoral dissertation, Catholic University of America, 1965).

[11]R. U. Nelson, "The Technique of Variation: A Study of the Instrumental Variation from Antonio de Cabezon to Max Reger," (unpublished doctoral dissertation, University of California, 1948).

[12]Glen Haydon, *The Evolution of the Six-Four Chord* (Berkeley, Calif.: University of California Press, 1933).

[13]Walter Kob, "The Pavan," (unpublished master's thesis, University of Rochester, 1943).

Allied to the problem of delimitation is that of sampling. In some studies the selection of representative pieces, or of pieces by representative composers, may be a methodological problem. Furthermore, it is not always necessary to analyze complete works in order to obtain adequate data. If over-all form is not under consideration, a sampling procedure can often be devised. It may be more fruitful to analyze samples of many works rather than to analyze a few complete works. Landau delimited his study to the initial period or phrase group, the period or phrase group containing the median measure or barline, and the smallest natural division including the last three chords in two movements (the first and the nearest subsequent movements in contrasting tempo) of each composition.[14] Since he was concerned only with harmonic theories and techniques as defined by Hindemith himself, this procedure resulted in what seems to be a valid sample. Nettl has pointed out that if a random sample is homogeneous, even though it is small it will be reliable, but that if it displays diversity its chances of being representative are not as great, so that a larger sample is required for reliability.[15]

Attention now is directed to the techniques and problems of analysis itself. These are grouped according to the traditional categories of harmony, melody, rhythm, and form, but it should be remembered that these areas are interrelated in many ways. In most styles, rhythm is an aspect of melody, while both are involved with certain aspects of harmony and form.

HARMONY

Since there are so many aspects of harmony that are subject to analytical research, it seems wise to precede the discussion with a list:

1. Types of chords (sometimes called "vertical sonorities" or "species")
   a. Inversions as a sub-category
2. Functions of chords
   a. Chromatic variants
   b. Essential and non-essential chords
3. Dissonance treatment (suspensions, etc.)
4. Harmonic progression
   a. Types of root movement
   b. Progressions of specific chords
   c. Harmony at cadences

---

[14]Landau, op. cit., p. 45.
[15]Bruno Nettl, Theory and Method in Ethnomusicology (New York: The Free Press of Glencoe, 1964), p. 136.

5. Tonality structure
   a. Modulation
   b. Over-all tonal coherence
6. Harmonic rhythm
7. Texture (homophonic, heterophonic, etc.)
   a. Doubling and spacing
   b. Instrumental color (orchestration)
8. Imitative devices.

It will be noted that the list includes techniques that are traditionally within the province of counterpoint. The dichotomy of harmony and counterpoint as separate entities is false, for in almost all styles they are so interwoven that they are part of the same cloth. Even the simplest of homophonic settings involves the existence of a fundamental bass line that adds counterpoint to the predominating tune. Hindemith calls this phenomenon the "Two-voice framework."[16] Counterpoint is certainly concerned with harmony; the term itself describes a phenomenon in which associated melodic lines come together at certain "points." The succession of these points may not delineate a harmonic progression in the classical sense (so-called "functional harmony"), but they are harmonies nevertheless, or "consonant combinations."[17] Some music, of course, emphasizes the individuality of melodic lines more than other music, in which case it may be stated that it is more polyphonic in texture or that it develops the linear element to a greater extent. It seems advisable, therefore, not to set up a category of "counterpoint" as distinct from "harmony."

Most items in the above list of analytical elements in harmonic structure lend themselves to a statistical approach. A research study may deal with only a limited number of aspects, but it is desirable to go beyond the first two items on the list; namely, the frequency of chord types and of chord functions. Although such basic information is important, it misses some of the most essential features that give a piece of music its stylistic individuality. It is like trying to delineate literary style by reporting word frequency or the frequency of various types of sentence structure. The fact that Debussy uses a significant number of chords of the ninth, or the thirteenth, or of whole-tone chords is of limited value if the process he uses to join them together is not

---

[16]Paul Hindemith, *The Craft of Musical Composition*, Vol. I (Revised Edition; New York: Associated Music Publishers, 1945), pp. 113-115.
[17]This assumes recognition of the fact that the concept of what constitutes an acceptable consonance varies among styles. Contrapuntal action defines what is sensed as a consonance (therefore a harmony).

known. It is more important to know how he achieves tonal coherence. This points to items 2b (Essential and non-essential chords), 4a (Types of root movement), and 5 (Tonality structure).

As to the distinction between essential and non-essential chords, older methods of harmonic analysis disregarded this factor. All consonant vertical sonorities in a phrase (or in a piece, for that matter) were valued on an equal basis regardless of rhythmic position or of whether they are primarily tonality defining (harmonic) or linear (contrapuntal) in function. To give an extremely simple example, the two-measure motive in Example 1 is analyzed using the traditional approach at *a*.

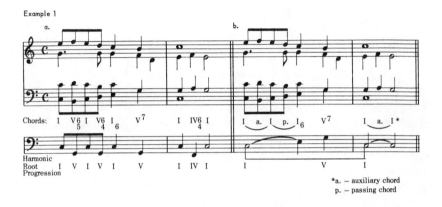

Example 1

In this case, data on frequency of chord function would include five instances of Tonic, three of Dominant, and one of Subdominant. This disregards the larger movement of Tonic with auxiliary and passing chords resulting from contrapuntal movement, moving to Dominant on the fourth beat, and back to Tonic with the auxiliary $\frac{6}{4}$ as sketched at *b*. The latter shows how this excerpt expresses an essential $I - V - I$ progression. This analysis is based on the assumption that there is an aural distinction between a chord used contrapuntally and one which more predominantly defines harmonic motion. It illustrates in an elementary way what is meant by the term "tonality structure." Represented on a larger scale, a modulation from C major to G major would be a progression from Tonic to Dominant.

It is due, no doubt, to growing dissatisfaction over the limitations of the traditional method of harmonic analysis that there has been so much recent interest in the analytical theories and procedures of Heinrich Schenker. Schenker was a pioneer in methods of describing tonality structure and meaning. All researchers who expect to make studies involving the analysis of harmony should be acquainted with the Schenker approach.[18] This does not mean that it is necessary to follow the system in all its terminological detail; however, most scholars will wish to seriously consider whether they should not make some adaptation of the basic idea. It may be particularly useful in analysis of tonal coherence in the music of the twentieth century as well as in that of the Middle Ages and Renaissance, music with which the traditional concepts and methods are almost completely inadequate. Strangely enough, Schenker himself was not sympathetic with the style changes in modern music because he believed that, since the basic over-all tonality schemes in most of the music by composers of the eighteenth and nineteenth centuries were I – V – I progressions, or variations thereof (I – II – V – I, I – III – V – I, etc.), there was some sacred truth behind this fact and that all good music should be based on such plans. It is not necessary, of course, to accept this judgment in order to apply the method. Salzer and others have demonstrated the adaptability of the system to contemporary music, and it should not be disturbing if the over-all tonal scheme of the first movement of Hindemith's *Second Piano Sonata,* or any other piece, does not follow a classical formula. In actual fact, the main tonality scheme of the Hindemith movement is G – F – G – C – G.[19]

A scholar in the field of analytical research is frequently faced with problems of terminology and classification. In the case of chord species, the classification of triads as major, minor, diminished, or augmented is quite universal, while that of seventh chords and other structures is debated. The writer favors the system of identifying types of seventh chords according to the method introduced by French theorists in the latter part of the last century. It recognizes four numbered species and several special types, as illustrated in Example 2.

Example 2   Seventh chord species

| first | second | third | fourth (major seventh) | diminished seventh | doubly-dissonant (also, whole-tone) |

[18]Adele Katz, *Challenge to Musical Tradition: A New Concept of Tonality* (New York: Alfred A. Knopf, Inc., 1946). See also Felix Salzer, *Structural Hearing: Tonal Coherence in Music,* 2 vols. (New York: Charles Boni, 1952).

[19]For a complete diagrammatic analysis of this work see Salzer, *ibid.,* Vol. II, pp. 298-305. For a good illustration of the application of the system to medieval music, see his article, "Tonality in Medieval Polyphony," *The Music Forum,* Vol. I (New York: Columbia University Press, 1967), pp. 35-98.

This terminology is specific, and it is as convenient as any. It seems less cumbersome than the system which calls the first species a "major-minor seventh." As to chords of the ninth, each of the numbered species of the seventh can be combined with either the major or the minor ninth, but some of these structures are extremely rare in most styles.[20] When it comes to chords of the eleventh and thirteenth, no systematic terms have been devised. Where such structures are found frequently (such as in music by Debussy and other impressionist composers) they are most commonly based on the first species seventh, such sonorities as the following being favorites: D–C–F♯–B (thirteenth), D–C–F♯–B–E (thirteenth with major ninth), D–F♯–C–E–G♯ (augmented eleventh—also whole-tone), D–F♯–C–E♭–G♯ (augmented eleventh with minor ninth).

Classification is also a problem with respect to chord function in chromatic harmony, since chromatic chords may be used in several ways:

1. As contrapuntal chords
2. As "Dominant-function" chords—the "Applied Dominant" concept.
3. As functional substitutes for standard diatonic chords in a harmonic progression. The Neapolitan sixth in place of Supertonic in cadences is a good example.
4. As one in a parallel series, usually all of the same species. In the classic and romantic periods it is commonly the diminished seventh that plays this role.[21]

"Harmonic rhythm" is a term which seems to have been created by Walter Piston, although the concept of the relationship of harmonic change to rhythm and form had been recognized by some earlier theorists. The term refers to the rhythm created by a succession of chord changes. Although harmonic rhythm is certainly an aspect of structure, no method has been published that systematically identifies the conditions and situations under which it relates to other aspects of structure. In the common style of the baroque-classic-romantic tradition, changes of harmony tend to coincide with metric accent, so that when they do not coincide a sense of syncopation is created. A fast harmonic rhythm (frequent change) is usually a concomitant of slow tempo and short phrases, such as in the *C minor Prelude* of Chopin, whereas a slow harmonic rhythm (infrequent change) often goes with fast tempo and

---

[20]For a brief discussion of the classification of ninths, see René Lenormand, *A Study of Modern Harmony* (London: Joseph Williams, 1915), p. 27.

[21]For some good examples, see Robert A. Melcher and Willard F. Warch, *Music for Advanced Study* (Englewood Cliffs, N. J.: Prentice-Hall, Inc., 1965), pp. 20-23.

longer phrases—longer, that is, in terms of the number of measures as seen in the score.

MELODY

In comparison with the area of harmony, less attention has been accorded the structural analysis of melody. Style criticism has tended to emphasize harmony and form and to avoid study of melodic line in depth. Outside of the field of ethnomusicology, almost no studies have been made that are devoted to melodic structure alone. Pennington's investigation of melody in the music of Fauré is exceptional.[22]

That most investigations limited to aspects of melody are in the field of ethnomusicology is not surprising since the source materials of primitive and folk music are often monophonic. The work of Bruno Nettl is important, not only as a contribution to the scholar's knowledge of ethnic music but also because of his development of method in melodic analysis.[23] The work of Béla Bartók in developing a system for analyzing and classifying the folk melodies that he collected is also important.[24]

What elements of melodic style can be described? Besides others, there are the obvious ones of range, mode, intervallic content, rhythmic features, and form. A systematic method for identifying characteristic melodic patterns needs to be developed. It is apparent that a research scholar must often create his own analytical techniques, especially in a neglected area such as melodic analysis. Armour, for example, devised a method of graphically showing melodic contour, another element of melodic structure.[25] Related to contour is the question of melodic climax, while direction tendencies at the beginning and ending of phrases is still another element of structure that can be studied.

In the case of melodic material in a tonal idiom it may be valuable to investigate the processes by which melodies suggest harmonic meaning. This is related to the question of melodic pitch patterns as well as

[22]Kenneth Pennington, "A History and Stylistic Study of the Melodies of Gabriel Fauré," (unpublished doctoral dissertation, Indiana University, 1961).

[23]Nettl, op. cit., Chapters V and VI.

[24]Béla Bartók, Hungarian Folk Music (London: Oxford University Press, 1931); Rumanian Folk Music, Benjamin Suchoff (ed.), 3 vols. to date (The Hague: Martinus Nijhoff, 1967). Suchoff is also preparing an edition of Bartók's Tabulation of Serbo-Croatian Material for publication by the New York Bartók Archives.

[25]Eugene Armour, "The Melodic and Rhythmic Characteristics of the Music of Traditional Ballad Variants Found in the Southern Appalachians," (unpublished doctoral dissertation, New York University, 1961), pp. 81-110. See also, Sirvart Poladian, "Melodic Contour in Traditional Music," Journal of the International Folk Music Council, III (1951), 30-35.

to the concept of tonality structure as discussed in the section on harmonic analysis. In the initial melodic theme of the first movement of Ravel's *Sonatine* for piano, quoted in Example 3, it is the F♯ — C♯

Example 3

skip that establishes the strong sense of an F♯ tonal center. The supporting harmonies are diatonic triads proceeding in parallel motion with the melody. A similar technique occurs in the second theme of this movement (Example 4), although in this case there is more counterpoint

Example 4

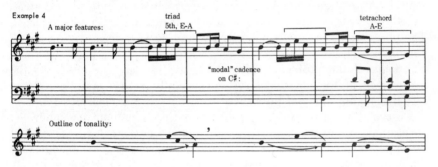

to the melody. The harmonies, which are not completely shown in the example, do not effect a clear tonal harmonic progression, but the melodic outline strongly projects the tonality of A major.

RHYTHM

Meter, rhythmic pattern, and accent are all aspects of rhythmic structure. They are sometimes referred to as "temporal elements." The main problem arises out of confusion over the definition of these terms. Sachs presents an excellent discussion of this problem.[26] As in the case of the other elements, it is most important that the researcher analyze and classify his data according to the true nature of the rhythmic experience. Frequently no recognition is given to the fact that most music which starts with an anacrusis involving at least one beat tends to engender an underlying sense of anacrusis persisting through a phrase,

[26]Curt Sachs, *Rhythm and Tempo* (New York: W. W. Norton and Co., Inc., 1953), Chapter 1.

then often on throughout a piece. This is a matter of meter as well as of rhythmic pattern. In the following phrase:

there are four measures—not five, or not three complete measures and two incomplete. If it is assumed that a basic meter, such as $\frac{3}{4}$ without anacrusis, may continue for a given number of measures regardless of the succession of rhythmic patterns that are superimposed on it, the same interpretation holds true for music which starts with an anacrusis. In other words, a category of anacrusic meter should be recognized. The phrase in the example just given would be in anacrusic triple meter (amphibrach).

Some of the problems in rhythmic analysis are the result of the inadequacy of the notational system currently in use and the related fact that composers and publishers have not always been consistent in the use of time signatures to represent specific rhythmic meanings. As an example, the notation of that peripatetic tune known in the United States as "Twinkle, Twinkle, Little Star" can be found in at least four different versions, as illustrated (for one phrase) in Example 5.

It is a fair assumption that these are all meant to convey the same expressive effect: simple duple meter with trochee rhythmic patterns. They would all have to be counted in one category when it comes to organizing data. This suggests that there is a danger in overclassification due to an unscientific notational system in the source material. To go a bit further, there is no point in distinguishing between $\frac{3}{4}$, $\frac{3}{8}$, and $\frac{3}{2}$ if it is obvious that they all express simple triple meter. There are, as well, instances where a piece written in $\frac{3}{8}$ has all of the characteristics of compound duple meter and could have been notated in $\frac{6}{8}$ or $\frac{6}{4}$. The motive, $\frac{3}{8}$ ♩ ♪| ♫ can, and often does, have the same rhythmic connotation as if it had been written $\frac{6}{4}$ ♩ ♩♩♩♩ . A good example is the second movement of Beethoven's *Sonata*, Opus 27, No. 1, for piano, which is written in $\frac{3}{4}$, as follows: $\frac{3}{4}$ ♩♩♩ |♩♩♩ |♩♩♩ |♩♩♩ | . It belongs in the same rhythmic category as another piece (or this one) notated: $\frac{6}{8}$ ♫♫ | ♫♫♫♫ | ♫♫ . Quite often this kind of "mis-barring" can be spotted by noting the number of measures in a phrase and where the cadences come, and usually by the way in which accent is produced by chord changes. Other cases may be more obscure.

The foregoing discussion illustrates the general principle that categories set up for classifying data must be realistic and based on the music as it is sensed.

FORM

The analysis of form leans heavily on terminology and classification developed in the nineteenth century and early in this century, a time when style criticism was not as scientifically oriented as it is today. Generally speaking, the theories were not based on a study of large samples of literature from a variety of sources, and it must be suspected that in many cases isolated examples were chosen to fit the theories.

As in the case of rhythm, the definition of terms and the relation of terms to meaningful units of structure are methodological problems. Consider, for example, the term "phrase."[27] It is used to identify a specific unit of form. But what one theorist identifies as a phrase, another calls a motive, still another a period. Some writers use the term to describe a variety of situations which are said by others to be in separate categories. A similar lack of exactness and uniformity exists with respect to the use of other terms.

Confusion is sometimes created over describing the two different situations where, on the one hand, a section of a piece is repeated and where, on the other hand, a theme or section returns to an earlier state-

---

[27]For a finely drawn definition, see Douglass M. Green, *Form in Tonal Music* (New York: Holt, Rinehart and Winston, Inc., 1965), pp. 6 ff.

ment following an intervening part. The term "repetition" is sometimes loosely applied to both ideas. It seems better to reserve "repetition" for the first situation and use "return," "restatement," or, if the return is to the beginning, "recapitulation" for the other. Similarly, the distinction between concepts generally known as "variation" and "development" are sometimes confused through indiscriminant use of the terms.

With reference to the form of complete compositions, most research has been on aspects of the sonata form. There is an increasing tendency to give greater emphasis to the subject of tonal design with relation to the placement of themes and the larger divisions of the form. There is the form that the tonality structure creates, a point which was touched on earlier in the section on harmonic analysis.

An important branch of form analysis is the study of thematic transformation and of thematic relationship. In this connection, attention is drawn to Reti's theory of "thematic process."[28] Even though it may be decided that Reti carries his theory too far, the idea merits some thought and may encourage the analyst to look for "hidden" relationships that exist in certain compositions.

ANALYSIS OF CONTEMPORARY MUSIC

Contemporary music requires its own battery of analytical techniques, since the traditional ones are no longer pertinent for the most part. This would be particularly so in the case of serial music, electronic music, and other experimental procedures of the *avant-garde*.

Hanson has devised a system of classification of vertical sonorities based on interval content.[29] Among several recent publications that include suggestions for the classification of compositional techniques, noteworthy is Ulehla's book on contemporary harmony.[30] The possible usefulness of the Schenker approach has already been pointed out. New analytical procedures are inherent in the twelve-tone row technique and serial composition in general as described by Rufer, Krenek, Perle, and others.[31]

---

[28]Rudolph Reti, *The Thematic Process in Music* (New York: The Macmillan Co., 1951).

[29]Howard Hanson, *Harmonic Materials of Modern Music* (New York: Appleton-Century-Crofts, 1960).

[30]Ludmila Ulehla, *Contemporary Harmony* (New York: The Free Press of Glencoe, 1966).

[31]Josef Rufer, *Composition with Twelve Notes Related Only to One Another* (New York: The Macmillan Co., 1954); Ernst Krenek, "Extents and Limits of Serial Techniques," *Musical Quarterly*, XLVI (April, 1960), 210-232; George Perle, *Serial Composition and Atonality* (Berkeley, Calif.: University of California Press, 1962).

Concerning the most recent techniques in experimental music, the best source of information is periodicals, particularly *Perspectives of New Music* and *The Journal of Music Theory*. Also recommended is a book by Hiller and Isaacson.[32]

USE OF COMPUTERS

Scholars in the field of analytical research are excited over the potentialities in the use of computers as an aid to processing analytical data.[33] Computers can deal with masses of data, and they can be programed to codify and correlate the statistical information. Following is a list of some advantages in using the computer in analytical studies:

1. The saving of time. Certain processes that might take weeks to accomplish when done by the individual can be completed in a few minutes by a computer.
2. The machine can store the information conveniently and recall the data as needed.
3. Types of information which might never have been sought without computer aid can be easily obtained with it. The identification of characteristic melodic patterns is an example of just one of many possibilities.
4. Statistical computations will be more accurate than when performed by most individuals.

A good example of computer-assisted studies that have been reported is one by Teitelbaum.[34] He developed a method of examining intervallic relations as compositional determinants in atonal music. As part of his report he examined the value of computer utilization in such an analytical endeavor.

Most information theory research to date has been based on analysis of atonal music. However, there is no reason to believe that computers cannot be used as an aid in describing other music, and there has been some experimentation along these lines. Selleck and Bakeman, for instance, made a study of certain aspects of form in Gregorian Chant,[35] and Youngblood analyzed a group of songs by Schubert, Mendelssohn,

[32]Lejaren A. Hiller and Leonard Isaacson, *Experimental Music* (New York: McGraw-Hill Book Co., 1959).

[33]The best single reference detailing applications of computer programing to musical analysis is Hiller and Isaacson, *ibid.*, especially pp. 165-170, and *passim.*

[34]Richard Teitelbaum, "Intervallic Relations in Atonal Music," *The Journal of Music Theory*, IX (1965), 72-127.

[35]John Selleck and Roger Bakeman, "Procedures for the Analysis of Form: Two Computer Applications," *The Journal of Music Theory*, IX (1965), 281-293.

and Schumann, as a result of which he was able to make objective conclusions concerning the differences and similarities among the three
composers.[36] Both of these studies involved computer programing.

Some of the reports have pointed out certain limitations in the
assistance that the computer can give.[37] It appears that the time saving
factor may not be as great as some people had anticipated. In the first
place, the music has to be pre-analyzed to the point where data to be
programed are identified. This would take more time for certain aspects
of structure than for others. Furthermore, the data must be coded and
punched on cards before they are fed to the machine, and this process
is still a tedious human operation. Then, too, a program of tasks for the
computer must be devised in order to obtain the information needed for
drawing significant conclusions. It is in the actual production of the
information where use of the computer saves a great deal of time. Perhaps the day is not far off when the machines will be developed to the
point where they can scrutinize the musical score and analyze it directly.
Of course, this would not eliminate the problem of the inadequacy of
the present notational system, nor would it eliminate the task of setting
up the program. Furthermore, it will no doubt still be necessary for
the scholar to prepare a written research report!

While statistical techniques provide useful tools for the objective
interpretation of data in analytical and descriptive research, they are
equally important in experimental research. Some of these procedures
will be discussed in the next chapter.

QUESTIONS FOR REVIEW AND DISCUSSION

1. For what purposes may analytical research be undertaken?
2. Discuss the approaches to stylistic interpretation which are listed in
   this chapter.
3. How may research studies of style criticism be delimited?
4. What aspects of harmony are pertinent for analytical research? Of
   melody? Of rhythm? Of form?

SUPPLEMENTARY READINGS

BABBITT, MILTON. "The Use of Computers in Musicological Research," *Perspectives of New Music*, III (Spring-Summer, 1965), 74-83.
BUDGE, HELEN. *A Study of Chord Frequencies Based on the Music of Representative Composers of the Eighteenth and Nineteenth Centuries.* Teachers College Contributions to Education. No. 882. New York: Teachers
College, Columbia University, 1943.

---

[36]J. E. Youngblood, "Style as Information," *The Journal of Music Theory*, II
(1958), 241-250.
[37]Teitelbaum, *op. cit.*, p. 77.

CONE, EDWARD T. "Analysis Today," *The Musical Quarterly,* XLVI (April, 1960), 172-188.

DALLIN, LEON. *Techniques of Twentieth Century Composition.* Second Edition. Dubuque, Iowa: Wm. C. Brown Company Publishers, 1964.

FORTE, ALLEN. "A Theory of Set Complexes for Music," *The Journal of Music Theory,* VIII (Winter, 1964), 136-183.

GARRETT, ALLEN M. *An Introduction to Research in Music.* Washington: The Catholic University of America Press, 1958. Chapters III-VI.

GREEN, DOUGLASS M. *Form in Tonal Music: An Introduction to Analysis.* New York: Holt, Rinehart and Winston, Inc., 1965.

HAYDON, GLEN. *Introduction to Musicology.* Englewood Cliffs, N. J.: Prentice-Hall, Inc., 1941. Chapter V.

HILLER, LEJAREN A., and ISAACSON, LEONARD. *Experimental Music.* New York: McGraw-Hill Book Co., Inc., 1959.

JEPPESEN, KNUD. *The Style of Palestrina and the Dissonance.* Second Edition. London: Oxford University Press, 1946.

KATZ, ADELE. *Challenge to Musical Tradition.* New York: Alfred A. Knopf, Inc., 1946.

KRENEK, ERNST. "Extents and Limits of Serial Techniques," *The Musical Quarterly,* XLVI (April, 1960), 210-232.

LARUE, JAN. "Symbols for Analysis: Some Revisions and Extensions," *Journal of the American Musicological Society,* XIX (Fall, 1966), 403-408.

McHOSE, ALLEN I. "Musical Research in the Definition of Bach's Contrapuntal Harmonic Style," *MTNA Proceedings for 1948.* Pittsburgh, Pa.: The Association, 1950. pp. 129-150.

NETTL, BRUNO. *Theory and Method in Ethnomusicology.* New York: The Free Press of Glencoe, 1964. Chapters V and VI.

SACHS, CURT. *Rhythm and Tempo.* New York: W. W. Norton and Co., Inc., 1953.

· 10 ·

Elementary
Statistical Concepts

Many times, as already noted, it is advisable to use statistical techniques to quantify and treat data obtained in experimental, descriptive, or analytical research. This is necessary because of the large number of comparisons usually involved in these three types of research. An understanding of the basic concepts of statistics is necessary in order for a researcher to interpret more objectively the data which he accumulates. Some of the fundamental precepts most likely to be used by a music education researcher are presented in the pages which follow. For more advanced techniques, the reader should consult the references listed at the end of the chapter among other sources.

REASONS FOR USING STATISTICS

There are several reasons for using statistical procedures in treating data. Through the use of statistics data may be: (1) codified, (2) analyzed, and (3) interpreted. Implicit in the first category is both the compilation and codification of data. Scores or results of testing or making comparisons are of little value unless they can be collected in one place and classified in a manner which is useful to the investigator. In an obvious example, when the scores attained on a test by fifty trumpet players are to be related to those of fifty clarinetists, it is important that two separate listings be maintained, one giving trumpet results and the other clarinet data. Then these findings can be compared more effectively.

Once data have been collected they need to be analyzed to determine relationships which exist, if any. Comparisons might be made between individuals within each group or between the two groups as a whole. The interpretation of data is concerned with an attempt to find out whether differences are due to the effects of the experimental treatment (or the independent variable) or may be accounted for by chance alone.

Statistical concepts to be discussed in this chapter include measures of central tendency, variability measures, criteria for evaluating test effectiveness, correlation, errors, and levels of significance.

KINDS OF STATISTICS

Statistics are normally differentiated as being either descriptive or inferential. Descriptive, sometimes called "parametric" statistics, relate to arithmetical comparisons of scores from the sample being used in the experiment. In descriptive statistics, the relationship existing among the scores obtained from comparison units of reasonably equal size may be seen graphically and objectively, thus may be usefully compared. Inferential, or "non-parametric" statistics, refer to inferences or generalizations about data obtained from a sample which are related to the population as a whole. Descriptive statistics numerically "describe" a particular group; inferential statistics "infer" what may be assumed to be representative of a large group or population. Inferential statistics also specify the degree of error which may be anticipated when these inferences are made.

MEASURES OF CENTRAL TENDENCY

Measures of central tendency, averages, or means, are used to show the relative position of an individual in comparison with others in a group. For statistical purposes it is assumed that the scores of all individuals may be plotted along a normal probability curve, also known as a "bell-shaped" or "Gaussian" curve, as illustrated in Figure 5.[1] In this hypothetical example, it is assumed that the mean or most common or critical value is 0. Deviations from this central point are listed either as positive or negative and the total for all components of the curve equals approximately 100 percent. It will be observed that there are as many scores to the right as there are to the left of 0 in Figure 5.

---

[1]The figures given in each category represent approximate percentages. They have been rounded off purposely to simplify the mathematical concepts used in this chapter.

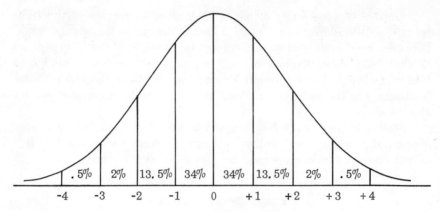

FIGURE 5. *Normal Probability Curve*

The tails of a normal curve are asymptotic, that is, they never touch the horizontal line or abscissa, but always approach it.

It will be recalled that the mean, or arithmetical average, of all the scores in Figure 5 is 0. The mean undoubtedly is the most useful of all measures of central tendency. It is obtained by adding together all the scores and dividing by the number of measurements used. The statistical formula for computing the mean is

$$M = \frac{\Sigma\, X}{N},$$

in which M = the mean or average of the scores
Σ = upper case Greek letter sigma, meaning "the sum of"
X = each score
N = number of measurements.

Assume that scores of 35, 37, 40, 43, and 45 are obtained on a music aptitude test. Then $\Sigma\, X = 200$, divided by N = 5, resulting in M = 40.

A second useful measure of central tendency is the median, identified by Md. The median represents the middle point of the scores. In other words, half of the scores occur above and half below the median. In the comparison of scores just given, 40 is both the median and the mean. In a normal or symmetrical curve both mean and median will coincide, as they do in Figure 5 at 0. When the scores are not distributed evenly, an asymmetrical curve or skew results, as may be observed in Figures 6 and 7. In Figure 6, where the tail is skewed positively to the right, the mean is to the right of the median. When a curve is skewed negatively to the left, as in Figure 7, the mean is to the left of the median.

The mode, a third measure of central tendency, is indicated by the symbol Mo. This term denotes the most prevalent interval in a distribution of scores. For example, in a tally of the scores 4, 8, 4, 6, 4, 1,

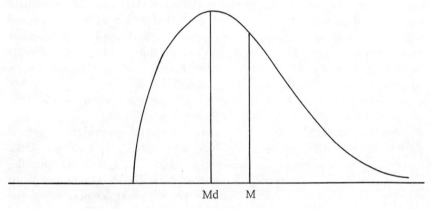

Md   M

FIGURE 6.   Positively Skewed Curve

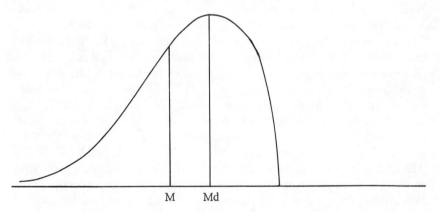

M   Md

FIGURE 7.   Negatively Skewed Curve

and 7, the mode is 4 because it occurs more frequently than any other number. A distribution containing two non-contiguous intervals where scores are concentrated is called bimodal as evidenced by these figures: 3, 6, 7, 4, 3, 2, 9, 7, 1, 3, 8, 5, and 7. In this instance 3 and 7 are the numbers that make this distribution bimodal. The mode usually is the least useful of the three measures of central tendency just discussed because it may fluctuate from one set of data to the next.

VARIABILITY MEASURES

Often it is desirable to learn how much variation or variability takes place within the sample or group being studied. Variability measures can be used to show the amount of deviation which may be expected when treatment or an experimental procedure is applied to another experimental group. The easiest method of determining variability is to compute the difference between the lowest and the highest scores. Known as the range, this technique usually is not too satisfactory because extreme scores tend to convey a false impression of the true range of variability.

Semi-interquartile range or quartile deviation provides a method by which variability can be determined with reasonable accuracy. One-quarter, or 25 percent, of the scores fall below Q_1, or the first quartile; three-quarters, or 75 percent, of the scores are below Q_3, or the third quartile. The semi-interquartile range contains about 50 percent of the scores and is considered to be the difference between 75 percent and 25 percent, or between Q_3 and Q_1, divided by two. Because scores of both the highest and lowest quarter are eliminated, there is less likelihood that extreme scores will influence the quartile deviation.

The average deviation, commonly referred to as AD, is the amount of deviation of each score from the mean when the algebraic signs are disregarded. Average deviation (AD), also known as mean deviation, is determined by the following steps: (1) add together all the scores and divide by N, or the number of scores. For example, 3, 15, 6, 10, 5, and 9 total 48, divided by 6 or N, resulting in M = 8; (2) subtract each score from M, resulting in 5, −7, 2, −2, 3, and −1. Disregarding the algebraic signs the scores total 20. When divided by N or 6, the AD = 3.3, which represents the average deviation between each score in the distribution. An inherent weakness in determining average deviation is that direction of variability from the mean (M) is disregarded, as evidenced by the failure to consider negative scores.

Standard deviation is a more precise measure of variability than average deviation because algebraic signs are taken into consideration. The deviation of each score from the mean is squared. The results are all positive because the algebraic product of both positive and negative scores is positive. These squared deviations are totaled and the square root of their mean is known as standard deviation, indicated by the lower case Greek letter sigma σ, or by lower case s. The formula for computing standard deviation is:

$$\sigma = \sqrt{\frac{\Sigma X^2}{N}} \, ,$$

in which σ = standard deviation
ΣX^2 = sum of squared deviations from the mean
N = number of measurements.

Squaring the deviations from the mean listed in step 2 above results in 25, 49, 4, 4, 9, and 1, which total 92. When divided by N (or 6) the variability is 15.33. The standard deviation, determined by taking the square root of 15.33, is 3.92.

CRITERIA FOR EVALUATING TEST EFFECTIVENESS

When tests, either standardized or otherwise, and other appraisal instruments are being considered for research purposes their reliability and validity must be scrutinized carefully. A test or an instrument which is reliable will show comparable results when administered under the same conditions. If a subject receives an extremely high score when tested initially and a very low one on the second measurement the reliability of the instrument is open to question, assuming the testing factors were comparable in both instances. Three methods commonly used to determine reliability are: (1) parallel or equivalent forms, (2) test-retest, and (3) split-half.

In the parallel or equivalent forms method, two tests containing items which are as equivalent as possible are used. This technique is used to reduce the incidence of recall or practice which might result between the initial and second testings. A test by Watkins and Farnum, containing Forms A and B, represents a good example of an equivalent forms instrument in music.[2]

The identical instrument is administered twice to the same individuals in the test-retest method and the scores are then correlated. The possibility always exists, of course, that results on the second test may have been affected by practice, recall, or other factors. The split-half technique is based on one test administration only. By random arrangement the score of each person on half of the test items is compared with his score on the other half. A correlation is then made between the two halves.

A test or instrument which measures what it purports to measure may be regarded as valid. For instance, if a test is designed to measure musical aptitude, its validity may be determined by the degree to which

---

[2]John G. Watkins and Stephen E. Farnum, *Watkins-Farnum Performance Scale* (Winona, Minn.: Hal Leonard Music Co., Inc., 1962).

it is successful in this regard. Tests may be validated by: (1) sampling and comparing items found in similar preexisting instruments; (2) studying instruments for which validity has already been established to note similarities and differences; (3) comparing class grades, teacher ratings, and marks received on similar tests with scores obtained on the instrument being validated; and (4) determining whether or not the philosophical or theoretical bases for the test actually are consistent with what they should be to measure what the test purports to do.

CORRELATION

Correlation, expressed by lower case r, indicates a coefficient of reliability, or the relationship between two sets of paired scores or variables. Relationships of correlation may vary from a positive one of $+1.00$ to the negative -1.00. The more two scores agree, the more positive the correlation; conversely, the more they disagree, the more negative the correlation.

The two most frequently used techniques for determining correlation are the Pearson product-moment coefficient correlation or r and the Spearman rank-difference or rho, designated by lower case Greek letter ρ. Product-moment correlation, which shows deviations from 0 in a frequency distribution, may be computed by the formula

$$r = \frac{\Sigma z_x \, z_y}{N} \, ,$$

in which r = product-moment correlation coefficient
Σ = sum of
Z_x = mean standard deviation of X variable scores
Z_y = mean standard deviation of Y variable scores
N = number of measurements.

Although not widely used, product-moment correlation can assist a researcher to pinpoint the variability evident between two observations for each individual. In other words, the two variables are compared.

When it is desired to show the correlation between individuals by ranks rather than by variables, the Spearman rank-difference correlation technique may be used, applying this formula:

$$\rho = 1 - \frac{6 \, \Sigma \, D^2}{N(N^2-1)},$$

in which ρ = rank-difference correlation coefficient
ΣD^2 = sum of differences between ranking of the two variables squared
N = number of measurements.

Figure 8 is an example of rank-order correlation scores obtained by a group of high school juniors on two music aptitude tests administered by this writer.[3] Raw scores and ranks are listed for each test, and the

Student	X_1	X_2	X_1 Rank	X_2 Rank	D	D^2
A	49	42	1.0	5.0	-4.0	16.00
B	42	39	7.0	8.5*	-1.5	2.25
C	48	45	2.0	2.0	0.0	0.00
D	40	43	10.0	4.0	6.0	36.00
E	46	39	4.0	8.5	-4.5	20.25
F	41	44	8.5	3.0	5.5	30.25
G	47	46	3.0	1.0	2.0	4.00
H	39	40	11.0	7.0	4.0	16.00
I	45	41	5.0	6.0	-1.0	1.00
J	41	37	8.5	11.0	-2.5	6.25
K	44	38	6.0	10.0	-4.0	16.00
						148.00

*Subjects F and J both attained a score of 41 on X_1, therefore share the mean of ranks 8 and 9. The same is true for subjects B and E under X_2.

FIGURE 8. *Rank-order Correlation of Scores Obtained on Music Tests*

differences between Ranks 1 and 2 are listed in D. Finally, D^2 gives the squares of the differences between each pair. Using data from Figure 8 the Spearman rank-order difference correlation for these scores is:

$$\rho = 1 - \frac{6\ (148)}{11\ (121-1)} =$$

$$1 - \frac{888}{1320} =$$

$$1 - 0.67 =$$
$$0.33.$$

MEASURES OF ERROR

Reference was made earlier in the chapter to errors which may result from making inferences from a sample to the general population. A difference between the population mean and the sample mean is

---

[3]X_1 signifies pitch scores on the *Seashore Measures of Musical Talents;* X_2 denotes scores on the *Kwalwasser Music Talent Test,* Form A.

known as a standard error. Expressed another way, standard error accounts for differences which may be observed between scores actually obtained and those expected in the normal population. The lower case Greek letter mu (μ) is used to indicate population means and σ denotes its standard error or standard deviation. It will be recalled from the normal probability curve (Figure 5) that approximately 68 percent of the scores occur between a deviation of ± 1. This means that the scores for these 68 percent will be no more than one standard error (σ) from their true scores. A deviation of no more than two standard errors ($\pm 2\sigma$) from the true scores may be anticipated for approximately 95 percent of those being evaluated, and so forth.

One of the most common measures of error is that of standard error of the mean, indicated by the formula

$$\sigma_m = \frac{\sigma}{\sqrt{N}},$$

in which σ_m = standard error of the mean (also indicated by S_m)
σ = standard deviation
N = size of the sample.

When inferences are made involving two variables it is necessary to use another formula. The standard error of the Pearson product-moment coefficient correlation is one of the most useful measures of this type. The Pearson product-moment measurement of deviation may be determined by the formula

$$\sigma_r = \frac{1 - r^2}{\sqrt{N - 1}},$$

in which σ_r = standard error of the product-moment correlation
r^2 = product-moment correlations squared
N = size of the sample.

LEVELS OF SIGNIFICANCE

Related to measures of error, notes Guilford, is determining what levels of significance need to be employed.[4] These significance levels enable a researcher to make a decision regarding whether to accept or reject the null hypothesis, a concept which was discussed in the third chapter.

If a null hypothesis is rejected when it should have been accepted a Type I error results. The probability of committing a Type I error,

---

[4]J. P. Guilford, *Fundamental Statistics in Psychology and Education* (Fourth Edition; New York: McGraw-Hill Book Co., Inc., 1965), p. 205.

called a level of significance, is indicated by lower case Greek letter alpha α . A null hypothesis which is accepted when it should be rejected is known as a Type II error. Lower case Greek letter beta β designates the level of significance for a possible Type II error.

Levels of significance are established by the researcher, most frequently at .01 or .05. When a significance level of .01 is adopted the chances of rejecting a null hypothesis when it should be accepted are one in one hundred. A significance level of .05 means that there are five chances in one hundred that the null hypothesis will be rejected when it should be accepted. The lower the level of significance the less likelihood there is that a null hypothesis which should be accepted will be rejected, and vice versa.

A t test may be employed to find out whether or not a hypothesis should be rejected. When measured by a t test the probability deviations occurring between the sample and population means may be confirmed by referring to a table of t distributions. Found in most statistics books, these t tables include computations for both .01 and .05 levels of significance. The formula for a t test is:

$$t = \frac{\mu - M}{\frac{s}{\sqrt{N}}},$$

in which $t = t$ test
$\mu =$ population mean
$M =$ sample mean
$s =$ standard deviation
$N =$ size of sample.

Degrees of freedom (df) need to be considered when using a table of t distributions. These indicate the number of independent observations considered in relation to the mean. Referring again to Figure 5, the normal probability curve, it will be recalled that the sum of algebraic deviations from the mean must be 0. Therefore, the total number of degrees of freedom will be one less than the number of scores being analyzed. For example, even when comparisons are being made with only two means, one degree of freedom will be lost. Then using a t table the computations under 1 df should be consulted to find out whether the null hypothesis is to be accepted or rejected.

The use of statistical techniques constitutes a type of data treatment and interpretation which is used only with certain kinds of research. All research data need to be reported, however, irrespective of the type of investigation involved in obtaining them. Preparation of a research report is discussed in the next chapter.

QUESTIONS FOR REVIEW AND DISCUSSION

1. When is it appropriate to use statistics in research in music education?
2. Make a specific application to music of each of the three measures of central tendency discussed in this chapter.
3. What variability measures are most likely to be applicable to music education research?
4. How may correlation be determined?
5. Discuss measures of error.
6. What is the purpose in determining levels of significance? How may this determination be accomplished?

SUPPLEMENTARY READINGS

BERNSTEIN, ALLEN L. *A Handbook of Statistics Solutions for the Behavioral Sciences.* New York: Holt, Rinehart and Winston, Inc., 1964. Chapters 2, 3, 6, and 7.

BEST, JOHN W. *Research in Education.* Englewood Cliffs, N. J.: Prentice-Hall, Inc., 1959. Chapters 8 and 9.

BORG, WALTER R. *Educational Research: An Introduction.* New York: David McKay Co., Inc., 1963. Chapters 6 and 7.

EDWARDS, ALLEN L. *Statistical Methods for the Behavioral Sciences.* New York: Holt, Rinehart and Winston, Inc., 1954. Chapters 2-6, 8, 12-13, 15-16.

FERGUSON, GEORGE A. *Statistical Analysis in Psychology and Education.* New York: McGraw-Hill Book Co., Inc., 1959. Chapters 1-3, 6-7, 10, 12, and 18.

GAGE, N. L. (ed.). *Handbook of Research on Teaching.* Chicago: Rand McNally and Co., 1963. Chapter 4.

GUILFORD, J. P. *Fundamental Statistics in Psychology and Education.* Fourth Edition. New York: McGraw-Hill Book Co., Inc., 1965. Chapters 3-6, 10, and 14.

HILLWAY, TYRUS. *Introduction to Research.* Second Edition. New York: Holt, Rinehart and Winston, Inc., 1965. Chapter 13.

KERLINGER, FRED N. *Foundations of Behavioral Research.* New York: Holt, Rinehart and Winston, Inc., 1965. Chapters 9, 10, and 14.

LEHMAN, PAUL R. *Tests and Measurements in Music.* Englewood Cliffs, N. J.: Prentice-Hall, Inc., 1968. Chapter 4.

LINDQUIST, EVERET F. *Design and Analysis of Experiments in Psychology and Education.* Boston: Houghton Mifflin Co., 1953. Chapters 2 and 3.

MORGAN, HAZEL B., and BURMEISTER, CLIFTON A. *Music Research Handbook.* Evanston, Ill.: The Instrumentalist Co., 1962. Chapter XI, Appendices A and B.

MOULY, GEORGE J. *The Science of Educational Research.* New York: American Book Co., 1963. Chapter 6.

RUMMEL, J. FRANCIS. *An Introduction to Research Procedures in Education.* Second Edition. New York: Harper and Row, Publishers, 1964. Appendix B.

SAX, GILBERT. *Empirical Foundations of Educational Research.* Englewood Cliffs, N. J.: Prentice-Hall, Inc., 1968. Chapters 6 and 7.

SCHOER, LOWELL A. *An Introduction to Statistics and Measurement: A Programmed Book.* Boston: Allyn and Bacon, Inc., 1966. Chapters 1-3, 5-6, 9-10.

VAN DALEN, DEOBALD B. *Understanding Educational Research.* Enlarged and Revised Edition. New York: McGraw-Hill Book Co., Inc., 1966. Chapters 13 and 14.

WALKER, HELEN M. *Mathematics Essential for Elementary Statistics.* Revised Edition. New York: Holt, Rinehart and Winston, Inc., 1951. Chapters 4, 7, 10, 15, and 17.

———, and LEV, JOSEPH. *Statistical Inference.* New York: Holt, Rinehart and Winston, Inc., 1953. Chapters 2, 5-10, 12, and 14.

WHYBREW, WILLIAM E. *Measurement and Evaluation in Music.* Dubuque, Iowa: Wm. C. Brown Company Publishers, 1962. Chapter 3.

WISE, JOHN E., NORDBERG, ROBERT B., and REITZ, DONALD J. *Methods of Research in Education.* Boston: D. C. Heath and Co., 1967. Chapter VIII.

· 11 ·

Writing
the Research Report

Data collection is a most important and significant step in implementing the research proposal. Yet the research process cannot be regarded as having been completed until findings of the study along with interpretations and implications have been made public, most often in the form of a written report of some type. Mention was made in the second chapter that this final phase of research is not handled as carefully as it should be sometimes. Unfortunately this is a syndrome which affects some graduate students who, after all data are obtained, seem to adopt the attitude, "Well, I'm glad that tiresome chore is done," and consequently just put together some kind of perfunctory report with which they hope to satisfy degree requirements. Fortunately for the music education profession this approach usually is not successful. Rather disturbing, nevertheless, is the number of graduate students who continue to put together large amounts of incongruous material. A research report without direction and purpose is as useless as an interstate highway without points of egress properly marked. It is in the research report that the investigator is able not only to display his scholarship but also to demonstrate his understanding of sound principles of reflective thinking.

FORMAT OF THE RESEARCH REPORT

A graduate research report is composed essentially of three complementary parts, which for purposes of the ensuing discussion will be called preface, the main body, and epilog. The prefatory section contains the title page, acknowledgements, table of contents, list of tables, and list of figures. Some institutions require the inclusion of an approval sheet with signatures of the candidate's sponsoring committee. This page, when required, immediately follows the title page. Because of minor deviations from one institution to another, a student should obtain the style sheet adopted for his institution before beginning work on the final report, so that he may organize his study accordingly. Likewise, in reporting federally-supported research projects the appropriate manual for such studies should be consulted. In general, however, organizational procedures will be quite similar. This introductory section states the organization of the research report without concern for data presentation and interpretation. If this part were to be detached from the study the only inconvenience to a reader would be his lack of knowledge regarding what to expect in the study and where to find it.

Preface

The title page for a graduate project usually contains: title of the research, investigator, degree which the candidate is seeking, institution where the work is being completed, and date. In addition, at some institutions the members of a candidate's sponsoring committee also are indicated. Usually this is the policy when individual members do not sign an approval sheet included in the document. When this format is used sponsoring committee members are listed at the top of the title page, as evidenced in Figure 9.

Although it is optional, many investigators like to include an acknowledgement page. In simple and direct terms the researcher expresses gratitude to those who have given him assistance in his project.

One of the most useful areas in the prefatory section is the Table of Contents. Each of the various headings and sub-headings are listed here, by specific page number, thus serving partially as an index. It is better if this table is not finalized until the entire report is completed so that specific page references can be indicated accurately. Evidently this procedure is not always followed as carefully as it should be. This writer, for example, has reviewed some graduate theses and other projects in which page numbers listed in the Table of Contents did not coincide with the actual location of the materials. In addition to chapter headings and sub-headings with page references for each, the Table of Contents lists bibliography and appendices.

Following next, when needed, are List of Tables and List of Figures. Each of these headings should be started on a separate page, the same as would be true when ending one chapter and beginning another. If, for instance, only five tables are to be listed, any remaining space on

Sponsoring Committee: Associate Professor Roger P. Phelps, Chairman; Associate Professor Walter Kob; and Adjunct Professor Alexander G. F. Gode

THE HISTORICAL DEVELOPMENT OF THE DOUBLE BASS

IRVING HERSCH COHEN

Submitted in partial fulfillment of the requirements for the degree of Doctor of Philosophy in the School of Education of New York University

1967

FIGURE 9.   *Thesis Title Page*

that page in the Table of Contents is left blank with the enumeration of figures beginning on another page.

The Main Body

Three sections make up the main body of the study; namely, introduction; presentation and interpretation of data; and summary, conclusions, and recommendations. The introduction contains a brief statement of the same items referred to in the third chapter of this book relative to organization of the research proposal. It will be recalled that these include statement of problem and sub-problems, definition of any terms which are necessary for a clearer understanding, an indication of delimitations which exist in the research, basic assumptions and hypotheses, incidence of the problem, review of related literature, and general overview of method.

In a research proposal, of course, the tentative plan of procedure is postulated. Frequently, as the research proceeds and data are assembled, evaluated, and interpreted, some modification of the original plan becomes necessary. For this reason the suggestion is made that writing of the introductory phase of the actual research report be deferred until all data have been presented and interpreted. The introduction in the research report, to recapitulate, contains the actual statement of the problem and other parts just enumerated even though they may not differ from the way they were listed originally in the research proposal. The section on related literature in the final version of the research report becomes an account of the materials which subsequently proved to be significant to the study. The introduction may be listed as the first chapter or simply as an introduction without any chapter designation. In terms of consistent organization the former is preferable.

The heart of a research report is the middle section which pertains to the presentation and interpretation of data. It is essential that this part be planned and executed meticulously. The organization into chapters is determined largely by the investigator in view of the material to be presented. A rather common organizational scheme is to let each sub-problem constitute a separate chapter. This procedure applies fairly well to research studies which are descriptive, experimental, or analytical. Historical research, and quite commonly philosophical, moreover, may require a more detailed breakdown of one topic into several chapters because of the nature of the material presented. Tables and figures normally appear in the middle section of the report, although there may be instances when incorporating them in the appendix may seem more feasible.

Data may be presented and interpreted both in the same chapter or presentation and interpretation may appear in separate chapters, preferably contiguous, although this procedure lacks some of the "Gestalt" that is so important for clarity in research reporting. The interpretation of data is not to be treated lightly but rather must be given careful attention and deliberation by the researcher, who is better able than anyone else to reveal its significance. Reflective thinking is essential to the interpretation of accumulated data.

The final section of the main research report consists of summary, conclusions, and recommendations. Frequently these three aspects are incorporated into one final chapter. Organized in this way it is possible for one who does not have time to read the complete study to learn about its contents by examining this chapter. The summary, consisting of brief accounts of the important items contained in each chapter, is preceded by a succinct account of the organization of the study. In this way it is not necessary to include a summary at the end of each chapter, as is done sometimes in research studies. A section which combines the summaries of each individual chapter in one place normally is more beneficial and helpful to a reader than are accounts scattered throughout the document. In addition, it eliminates repetition which results when summaries are given at the end of each chapter and again at the completion of the study.

The conclusions section, it has been observed, often proves to be perplexing because the distinction between summary and conclusions or between conclusions and recommendations is not clearly stated. When stating conclusions the researcher simply reports whether or not the hypotheses were sustained or whether satisfactory answers were received to questions raised in the sub-problems. Conclusions should be expressed in a direct manner by statements similar to "As a result of data provided it may be concluded that . . . ." Specific references can then be made to the chapter or section where data upon which the conclusions reached are located. To recapitulate, the summary section rarely abstracts results of the research; the conclusions, derived reflectively, interpret these data or findings.

Recommendations is an important section for potential researchers because it is here that areas needing further study are delineated. Furthermore, an investigator, should he desire to do so, may establish priorities for problems needing further study. In view of his intensive study a researcher is in an enviable position to make such assessments. Recommendations may be predicated on conclusions which have indicated certain hypotheses to be invalid. On the other hand, recommendations can be made on the basis of hypotheses which have been confirmed. Whatever the basis for their determination, recommendations indicate what areas of his research an investigator has reflectively determined need to be pursued further.

Epilog

Two parts make up the epilog of the research report; namely, bibliography and appendix. Either or both of these items actually could be omitted and the value of the data would not be lessened. They are, nevertheless, valuable adjuncts to a study. All materials pertinent to the topic to which reference was made during the course of the research are included in the bibliography. This is not to suggest that every book or article scanned in the hopes of finding something relevant should be accounted for. Some source materials obviously turn out to be of major significance while others may prove to be of minor relevance only. All items listed in footnotes must appear in the bibliography also. Sometimes a distinction is made between primary and secondary sources. Frequently this difference is difficult to establish clearly and as a result materials of the same kind are not grouped under a common heading even though they should be. In this ambiguous type of bibliographical listing books, periodical articles, unpublished materials, and others, all are consolidated alphabetically by author's surname or by title when no author is indicated.

A much clearer and more useful delineation is to list each entry alphabetically by author's surname or title of the item when author is missing, under different categories such as books, periodical articles, newspaper articles, unpublished materials, and other sources of information. No one style of indicating bibliographical references is accepted universally, hence the investigator uses the one which is recommended by his adviser or the local agency responsible for his research. He should be consistent, however, throughout his bibliography regardless of the style he uses.

For a book entry the following is a practical suggestion: surname of author or editor, followed by first name and middle initial; title of publication underlined; edition (if more than one); city of publication; publisher; and publication date. Here is an example: Lundin, Robert W. *An Objective Psychology of Music.* Second Edition. New York: The Ronald Press Co., 1967.

Periodical articles may be listed as follows: author's surname followed by first name and middle initial; title of article in quotation marks; name of periodical underlined; volume number in Roman numerals; date; and pages included in the article. A periodical entry might look like this: Phelps, Roger P. "The Mendelssohn Quintet Club: A Milestone in American Music Education," *Journal of Research in Music Education,* VIII (Spring, 1960), 39-44. In an alternative form a slight change in the manner of indicating volume number, date, and pages included would result in the same article being listed as: Phelps, Roger P. "The Mendelssohn Quintet Club: A Milestone in American Music Education," *Journal of Research in Music Education,* 8:39-44, Spring, 1960. In this somewhat simplified version volume number (placed in Arabic numerals) immediately precedes designation of pages and date of the periodical comes at the end.

Newspapers referred to are listed either simply by title and date, or, in the instance of a by-line article, with that person's surname followed by first name and middle initial, title of article in quotation marks, newspaper title underlined, date, and page or pages used. Examples of these follow:

New York Times, February 24, 1967.

Taubman, Howard. "Computer in Humanities," *New York Times,* June 27, 1967, 36.

Unpublished materials most likely to be used consist of: (1) master's theses or doctoral dissertations, (2) mimeographed papers, (3) typewritten speeches, (4) minutes of meetings of boards of directors, and (5) letters. In the first three instances an author's surname is followed by first name and middle initial, title of item in quotation marks, kind of item or its location, and date (when available). For minutes of boards of directors meetings name of group precedes kind of minutes, date, and form of material. In recording letters, the surname, first name, and middle initial of the individual who wrote the letter appears followed by indication of the kind of letter, and date. These examples, with corresponding numbers, illustrate how the materials just discussed may be listed: (1) Cohen, Irving H. "The Historical Development of the Double Bass." Unpublished doctoral dissertation, New York University, 1967. (2) Choate, Robert A. "Research in Music Education." Paper read at New England Conference on Educational Research, Providence, R. I., November 28, 1964. (Mimeographed.) (3) Phelps, Roger P. "Music in a Scientific Era." Speech delivered at meeting of Rotary Club of Baldwin, N. Y., May 26, 1965. (Typewritten.) (4) Baldwin, N. Y. Educational Assembly. Minutes of Executive Committee Meeting. June 12, 1967. (Typewritten.) (5) Gordon, Roderick D. personal letter, January 10, 1967.

Another source of information is personal interviews, although the validity of data obtained in this way is questioned by some researchers. In descriptive and historical studies, in which an investigator frequently is concerned with the biography of an individual, effective use can be made of information received in this manner because it is often unobtainable in any other way. It is well to admonish, however, that the person being interviewed sometimes may present a biased viewpoint, and even though the interviewer may suspect this he cannot often sustain his contention. In recording an interview the name and title of the person being interviewed precede place and date of interview. An example is: Personal interview with Harold W. Arberg, Music Specialist, Arts and Humanities Branch, U. S. Office of Education, Washington, D. C., June 18, 1965.

The section entitled appendix may be singular or consist of several parts, in which case the plural designation of appendices will be utilized. Material included here is regarded as useful to the study but not absolutely essential in the main body. Each appendix should be indicated by a letter (A, B, C, etc.) if the materials are of different nature. Items of similar content may be labeled A1, A2, A3, etc. The kinds of data normally placed in the appendix consist of lists of individuals, questionnaires and other instruments used to collect data, copies of charters and other legal documents, and other materials too cumbersome to include in the body of the study. Musical examples also may be collected in an appendix, or, if not too numerous, in the appropriate place in the main body where reference is made to them. In the case of analytical research, however, they may be so extensive that the study should be divided into two volumes; the first containing commentary in the usual manner in a research report and the second including music only. The designation of the appendix is centered at the top of the page. Centered one double-space below it is identification of the material presented there, all listed in capital letters. An example of this follows:

APPENDIX A

STATE SUPERVISORS OF MUSIC

MECHANICS OF PREPARING THE REPORT

Certain routine matters relative to the preparation of a report, when considered carefully, enable a researcher to prepare a thoughtful and erudite report. Although minor deviations may be expected from one institution to another, an investigator should maintain consistency throughout his report regardless of which specific style sheet is followed.

The number of copies required and the manner in which the research report is reproduced vary according to the type of research report and the agency to which it is being submitted. Reports of federally-supported research basically follow a specific pattern which is the same regardless of the type of funding, but the number of copies required and other details do differ according to the type. As already noted, the investigator should follow the guidelines pertinent to his type of project when completing this type of research project study.

A graduate student is usually required to submit three copies of his thesis or dissertation "in partial fulfillment of degree requirements." These consist of an original, typed on only one side of paper 8 1/2" x 11" in size, and two carbon or Xerox reproductions. Before a student prepares his second and third copies by Xerox he should determine whether or not these will be accepted by his institution. Because of the clarity of Xerox reproductions many colleges and universities will now permit a student to submit the required number of copies of his research report in this manner along with the original. Carbon copies do have a tendency to smudge if they are handled extensively. Duplicates produced by the Xerox process, in contrast, will remain constant.

A specific weight and grade of paper is usually specified by each individual institution, so the researcher should acquaint himself with these requirements before typing the final version. Frequently 18- to 20-pound watermark bond is suggested for the original and 9- to 12-pound pebbled onion skin for the two carbon copies. A good grade of black, hard finish, medium-weight carbon paper should be used and changed frequently. The final version of the document should contain no strikeovers. Erasures can be made easily and cleanly on bond paper using a good typewriter eraser. Also available now are chemically-coated pieces of paper which vary in size from 1" x 2 1/2" to 2" x 2 3/4" which can be placed directly over the spot containing an error and when the mistake is retyped on it a clean copy results upon which the correct symbol or letter may then be typed.[1]

If a choice exists between using a typewriter containing elite or pica type, the latter is preferable because of its larger size. An electric typewriter produces a copy which is generally superior to that produced by non-electric models.

Theses and dissertations are normally double-spaced throughout except for long quotations, which are single-spaced. Direct quotations of fewer than four lines are included in the double-spaced context of the document and are initiated and terminated by double quotation marks. Quotations extending for more than four lines are single-spaced and set off by double spacing immediately preceding and following them. They are indented four spaces and are not preceded or followed by quotation marks of any kind unless a quotation within a quotation is involved. A quotation within the single-spaced material would, of course, call for opening and closing double quotation marks.

Quotations are identified by superscripts which consist of Arabic numbers placed at the end of the direct or paraphrased quotation. A superscript is raised one-half space above the line of type and the numbers, beginning with "1," appear consecutively throughout each chapter. The numbering scheme for superscripts and complementary footnotes begins anew in each chapter. No marks of punctuation follow the superscript. Direct quotations must be presented as they appear in

---

[1]Ko-Rec-Type, used for original, and Ko-Rec-Copy for carbon copies, are typical of these.

the original; changes are not permissible even though errors are evident. Recognition of errors will be noted by *sic,* which will be mentioned later in this chapter. Failure to quote material exactly as it appears is a weakness observed all too frequently when graduate research projects are examined. Intellectual honesty demands that nothing be changed from the original in a direct quotation. Indirect quotations, or paraphrases, also require that credit be given to the originator of the borrowed material. Recognition need not be given for the sources of ideas which are common knowledge or are part of one's general background. Intellectual honesty, however, should compel an investigator to indicate the source of his information if there is doubt as to whether or not such recognition is necessary. It is better to overuse superscripts than to underuse them.

Marginal delimitations should be adhered to quite strictly. The left hand margin needs to be 1 1/2 inches to allow enough room for binding of the report. The other three margins are frequently specified as 1 inch, but these requirements may vary slightly according to local preferences. Pages will be trimmed slightly during the binding process so a one-inch margin on all sides except the left should be regarded as an absolute minimum. Except for pagination, all commentary, including footnotes, is to fit into this marginal pattern as closely as possible. To make the task of conforming to these limits while typing easier, a guide sheet may be prepared on onion skin and inserted immediately beneath the original copy. Lines outlining the desired margins can be drawn on the guide sheet with India or dark black ink. To type ten or twelve single-spaced consecutive numbers up along the outside of the left guideline, beginning in the lower left hand corner, is helpful to gauge spacing of footnotes. For example, appropriate space can be reserved using the guide numbers to determine where the last line of type of the context should appear when it is known that there will be three footnotes of two spaces each with a single space between them.

The initial and each subsequent. new paragraph should be indented from five to ten spaces according to local specifications. Chapter headings and subheadings should follow a consistent schematic pattern which is in accord with the style sheet being used by the investigator. The suggestions which follow should not be construed as the only way in which these various kinds of hearings may be identified.

Each new chapter is designated by a Roman numeral and a title, both of which are in capital letters and separated by a double space in the following manner:

CHAPTER VII

SUMMARY, CONCLUSIONS, AND RECOMMENDATIONS

Three spaces intervene between the chapter title and the initial line of text.

The first subheading is centered in the middle of the page, underlined, and the first letter of each important word capitalized as follows:

Significance of the Study

Presentation of data then begins on the next line with an indentation consistent with that used throughout the study. The second subheading, known as a side heading, is also underlined and the first letter of each noun, adjective, and verb is capitalized as in this instance:

Use of New Educational Media in the Classroom

The context is then indented and begins on the next line. A third subheading is the paragraph heading. It is indented the same number of spaces as each paragraph, underlined, and followed by a period. Only the first word of the heading is capitalized and, unlike the centered and side headings, the text begins two spaces after the period terminating the title. A paragraph subheading looks like this:

Preparing overhead transparencies. Musical examples may be . . .

If additional subdivisions are needed they should follow the procedure just described relating to centered and side headings, in that order, but without the titles being underlined.

Pages in the prefatory section of a research study are consecutively numbered in lower case Roman numerals (i, ii, iii, etc.) centered at the bottom of the page. No number is recorded on the title page although the numbering of pages actually begins with it. Thus the first number which appears is normally ii. Each page in the main body of the document, including the bibliography and appendix, is assigned an Arabic number. Centered at the top of the page, the pagination sequence begins anew with the main body of material. Although the first chapter actually begins on the first page, the number is not included here. The same is true of each of the other pages on which a new chapter begins; however, these pages are counted in the numbering of the report. Some government reports suggest that the Arabic numbers be centered at the bottom of the page and some style sheets indicate that they should be placed in the upper right hand corner. Pagination for both prefatory and main body material is placed slightly outside the margins, which usually means about three-quarters of an inch from the top or bottom of the page.

Acknowledgement of indebtedness to those who have been quoted directly or indirectly is the main reason for including a footnote. Footnotes are also used to refer the reader to other sections of the document or to include amplifying material which does not belong in the body of the study. All superscripts should be identified at the bottom of the same page by corresponding footnotes. When a superscript would normally appear on the bottom line of a page of text without adequate space to list it in a footnote, the entire line with appropriate superscript and footnote material should be carried over to the next page. All sources listed in footnotes must be included in the bibliography also. When preparing to defend his study in a final oral examination the candidate would be well advised to familiarize himself with the contributions of the individuals he has quoted if he does not already know.

Footnotes are separated from the main body of the study by a line approximately 1 1/2 inches in length, which is one space below the last line of text. The initial footnote begins on the second space below this separating line. In other words, the blank space above and below this line should be the same. The first and each subsequent footnote is indented to correspond to the paragraph indentation and is preceded by an appropriate number which is raised approximately one-half space above the line of type. Neither space nor punctuation occurs between the footnote number and the material which follows. Footnotes are single-spaced but a double space separates each one. A guide sheet, as observed earlier, can be used to assist in setting up footnotes properly.

The manner for recording footnote references follows. Similarities and differences between the procedure for listing the same sources of information in footnotes and in the bibliography may be observed by comparing the examples which follow with their counterparts, noted earlier in this chapter. For a book, the footnote number is contiguous to and precedes the full name of the author or editor (first name, middle initial, surname). Next in order are: title of publication underlined; edition preceded by left hand parenthesis, followed by semicolon; city of publication followed by colon; publisher; date of publication terminated by right hand parenthesis; and location of footnote material. A clarifying example is:

[18]Robert W. Lundin, *An Objective Psychology of Music* (Second Edition; New York: The Ronald Press Co., 1967), p. 61.

Periodical articles follow a similar format to that for listing books; namely, author's full name, title of article enclosed by quotation marks, name of periodical, volume number in Roman numerals, date, and pages cited, as in the following example:

[26]Roger P. Phelps, "The Mendelssohn Quintet Club: A Milestone in American Music Education," *Journal of Research in Music Education,* VIII (Spring, 1960), 41. An optional way to list the volume number, date, and pages included would be:

[26]Roger P. Phelps, "The Mendelssohn Quintet Club: A Milestone in American Music Education," *Journal of Research in Music Education,* 8:41, Spring, 1960.

Newspaper articles are identified in a footnote by type of material, name of newspaper, and date. When a by-line article is used, specific page reference is also included. Examples of these are:

[14]Editorial, *New York Times,* February 24, 1967.

[15]Howard Taubman, "Computer in Humanities," *New York Times,* June 27, 1967, p. 36.

Listed as numbered respectively in the footnotes which follow are unpublished graduate documents, mimeographed papers, typewritten speeches, minutes of meetings of boards of directors, letters, and personal interviews. They are identified by author's full name, title of item, kind of material preceded by left hand parenthesis, location (when appropriate), date followed by right hand parenthesis, and specific page reference (if necessary):

[1]Irving H. Cohen, "The Historical Development of the Double Bass," (unpublished doctoral dissertation, New York University, 1967), p. 65.

[2]Robert A. Choate, "Research in Music Education," (paper read at New England Conference on Educational Research, Providence, R. I., November 28, 1964), p. 3. (Mimeographed.)

[3]Roger P. Phelps, "Music in a Scientific Era," (speech delivered at meeting of Rotary Club of Baldwin, N. Y., May 26, 1965), p. 2. (Typewritten.)

[4]Minutes of Executive Committee Meeting, June 12, 1967, Baldwin (N. Y.) Educational Assembly, (in files of the Board of Education, U. F. S. District No. 10, Baldwin, N. Y.).

[5]Roderick D. Gordon, personal letter, January 10, 1967.

[6]Interview with Harold W. Arberg, Music Specialist, Arts and Humanities Branch, U. S. Office of Education, Washington, D. C., June 18, 1965.

This chapter does not discuss the many intricate aspects of correct punctuation; these should already be part of a researcher's techniques as a result of his experiences in communications skills courses. Some phases of punctuation which seem to be most frequently mishandled, however, deserve review here. More detailed information may be obtained from standard references listed at the end of this chapter.

Many common errors of punctuation occur in connection with quotations. Periods or commas are always placed *inside* the final quotation marks; colons or semicolons outside. Question marks and exclamation points precede the final quotation marks when they are part of the quoted material, otherwise they belong outside.

Commas are used to set off non-restrictive clauses, those which can be omitted without impairing the meaning of the sentence. In this example the non-restrictive clause begins after the first comma: The Music Educators National Conference, which holds its national convention biennially, is the largest subject matter discipline represented in the National Education Association.

Individual elements in a series are separated by a comma as follows:

Wrong: Mary has studied piano, clarinet and violin.

Right: Mary has studied piano, clarinet, and violin.

Parenthetical phrases or words should be set off by commas:

Wrong: John the best bassoonist in the school received a top rating at contest.

Right: John, the best bassoonist in the school, received a top rating at contest.

Semicolons are used to separate various elements in a series which contain commas or other marks of punctuation within, as in this example:

Enrollment in instrumental music classes in the Central Elementary School is as follows: Grade Four, 16; Grade Five, 22; and Grade Six, 31.

Dashes are used rather than parentheses when a parenthetical expression includes within it a comma or some other type of punctuation. A dash appearing in typewritten material consists of two hyphens without any spaces between or on either side of them, as illustrated here: His performance skill on the French horn already is so advanced that he undoubtedly—although he has not expressed an interest yet—will be able to receive a music scholarship at any college or university he desires to attend.

A hyphen is used to join two or more words used as an attributive adjective before a noun as follows: The violin-playing conductor led his ensemble in a performance of Handel's *Concerto Grosso in G Minor,* Opus 6, No. 6.

Words which are divided at the end of a line must be separated correctly. A standard dictionary, such as Webster's, should be used whenever any doubt arises regarding correct word syllabication. Incorrect division of words is an error which is encountered all too often in graduate theses and dissertations. The easiest way to eliminate errors of this type is to avoid dividing words even though space remains at the end of a line. Words involving one division, such as "a-bout," should be written intact on the next line rather than divided at the end of the preceding one. A word division of any kind over a page should be avoided.

Research studies frequently use special symbols or characters which are not included on a typewriter. This is especially true in many musical studies. These insertions may be made by hand with black India ink, or, if the examples are extensive, they may be reproduced from an original copy by some commercial process such as Xerox or ozalid and fastened in with rubber cement.

In the interest of expediency an investigator is sometimes tempted to use abbreviations. Abbreviations, unless in material being quoted, should not be used in the context of a study except for these titles: Mr., Messrs., Mrs., Dr., St., Rev., and Hon. when used in conjunction with a specific name and Sr. and Jr. following a name. In footnotes, however, abbreviations are acceptable and even recommended for clarity.

Foreign words are underlined except those which have become anglicized through common usage. They should be used sparingly to achieve a specially desired effect and not merely so an investigator can display his sophistication. This writer has read, on several occasions, doctoral dissertations in which the candidate has shown gross ignorance of foreign words and phrases by using some of the most unorthodox spellings imaginable.

Round numbers and numbers under one hundred are usually spelled out, although some style manuals recommend that only numbers below ten should be written out. Regardless of which system is used, consistency in style should be maintained throughout. Arabic numerals, however, are used for percentages, precise amounts of money, dates, and street, telephone, and page numbers. A sentence should not be started with a numeral even though numerals are present in the remainder of the sentence. When dealing with percentages the symbol % must not be used; instead, the word "percent" should be written after the Arabic numeral.

Tables and figures need to appear as closely as possible after the page on which reference to them was made. These graphic components need an appropriate reference in the text. The word "TABLE," in capital letters, is centered on a line at the top of the table, followed by an identifying Arabic number. Centered two spaces below this is the caption, also in capital letters. The designation "Figure" is used for any kind of graphic material other than a table. A figure could be a chart, graph, photograph, musical excerpt, or some other type of material. The designation for "Figure" is indicated in capital and lower case letters, followed by an Arabic number, but it is centered two spaces below the figure instead of above it as is true with a table. The caption is centered two spaces below the designation "Figure" and usually consists of a combination of capital and lower case letters.

Among the special Latin terms used in conjunction with footnotes are: *ibid., op. cit.,* and *loc. cit. Ibid.,* which literally means "the same," is used to refer to the same work when there are no intervening citations, as follows:

[1]Ruth T. Watanabe, *Introduction to Music Research* (Englewood Cliffs, N. J.: Prentice-Hall, Inc., 1967), p. 73.

[2]*Ibid.* [This indicates the same source and same page. The term also may be followed by another page number.]

Op. cit., meaning "the work cited before," refers to a source cited previously which has been followed by other intervening citations. When used, *op. cit.* is preceded by the author's surname followed by a specific page reference, as in this example:

[3]Lundin, *op. cit.,* p. 41.

A shortened form of indicating footnote information is preferred by some authorities, in which the previous citation simply might read: Lundin, p. 41. *Loc. cit.,* literally "the same," is used when there are intervening citations between a reference to the same source and same page, and is indicated:

[4]Watanabe, *loc. cit.* [This signifies the same source and same page as the last Watanabe reference. *Ibid.* would be incorrect here because other items have intervened.]

An ellipsis is used in a direct quotation to indicate that material has been omitted. It is indicated by three dots with a space preceding and following each one. . . . When the ellipsis occurs at the end of a sentence an extra dot is added to signify a period. The omission of a complete paragraph is indicated by a line of periods across the page, each followed by one space.

Interpolations are used for purposes of correction or clarification. Interpolated material is placed between brackets [ ], which may be inserted by hand with India ink, or by typewriter using the slash symbol and connecting it above and below with the underscore designation: $\underline{/\ /}$. An interpolation may occur in a direct quotation where material has been omitted and the meaning of the sentence remains obscure unless a word is inserted, as in this example: "The superintendent of schools announced . . . [expanded] music instruction for next year." When erroneous spelling is observed the Latin word *sic,* literally meaning "that is what it is," is interpolated: "Accordian [*sic*] class instruction has been added this year." No correction of errors in a direct quotation is permitted. The investigator merely indicates that he has been perceptive enough to observe them when he uses *sic,* which is underlined because it is a foreign word.

When his study has been completed, an investigator should have it checked by a qualified person who is unfamiliar with its contents. This is in addition to the usual critical evaluation made by a student's adviser and members of his sponsoring committee. This is not to suggest that the candidate in so doing abrogates his adviser or sponsoring committee of responsibility. They check his work frequently and thus can become calloused to it easily. An outside observer will examine it from a fresh vantage point and can sometimes spot deficiencies in logic or content which may have been overlooked by those working closely with the student. In the realm of sponsored research, for example, a project supported by the U. S. Office of Education is usually reviewed by the project officer prior to the researcher's submission of his final report. The project officer's suggestions should then be incorporated in the final version.

Many advisers encourage their advisees to submit thesis or dissertation material a chapter at a time so that the burden of making extensive corrections does not all take place at the end. Thus more attention can be given to minor details when the document is in its final stages. When all corrections have been made the candidate resubmits his document in its entirety to obtain approval so that he may proceed with the typing of the final version.

Proofreading the completed report should be done carefully prior to submitting a research study to a final examining committee, sometimes referred to as "defense of the thesis." On one occasion a two-page list of errors was found by this writer in the final version of a doctoral dissertation which could have been eliminated by careful proofreading.

Obtaining a professional proofreader or copy editor to evaluate his material may be the solution for an individual who has difficulty detecting his own errors.

STYLISTIC CONSIDERATIONS

There is no reason why research reports should be dull and boring. Using a direct and straightforward style in writing can contribute to a more pleasurable experience for the reader. Complicated sentences should not be used assuming that they represent more scholarly writing than do those which are simply structured. Pretentious words sometimes help a writer to achieve variety but they should not be used solely for the purpose of trying to impress a reader with the investigator's sophistication. The style of writing in research reports, although formal, should be intriguing enough to hold a reader's attention nevertheless. Use of active rather than passive voice will contribute significantly to a direct stylistic approach in writing.

Since research reports essentially present an account of what already has taken place, past tense should be used for most of the writing. On occasion, however, present or future tense may be required.

Clichés, colloquialisms, and hackneyed terms are best avoided in formal writing except as they may be needed to illustrate a point. Phrases or words which an investigator repeatedly uses in his report become *passé* and detract from the study. Variety and interest can be maintained throughout by the liberal interspersing of synonyms. A dictionary such as Roget's *Thesaurus* will be an excellent reference for assistance in this regard.

The third person is used for formal writing except when first or second person personal pronouns appear in direct quotations. When a researcher finds it necessary to make reference to himself he may modestly use "this investigator," "this researcher," or some similar phraseology. It is in poor taste to use wording such as "I found."

Correct grammatical construction obviously is a necessity in research reporting. Presumably every student who undertakes to write a thesis or dissertation has already developed competency in expressing himself consistently and clearly. If he has not, a refresher course in written English skills might be helpful. As an example of inconsistent usage, although the practice is quite common, it is generally considered in poor taste to begin a sentence with conjunctive words such as "and" or "but" in formal writing. Conjunctives are used to connect phrases or clauses, not to begin sentences.

Spelling should be orthodox and consistent throughout the document. To substitute "thru" for "through" or "nite" for "night" is inexcusable except when these simplifications appear in direct quotations. If words such as "catalogue" or "esthetic" are used in the first chapter of a report they should not be spelled "catalog" and "aesthetic" in other sections of the study unless there is sufficient justification for making such changes.

There is a tendency for inexperienced researchers to use terms which are absolute. An investigator who makes statements such as "No study of this kind exists," or "Nothing has been written about this subject" places himself in an extremely vulnerable position. It is very difficult to compile a bibliography which is exhaustive and completely accurate because the frontiers of knowledge are continuously expanding. To report "To this writer's knowledge no study of this kind exists" or "This writer has been unable to locate anything written about this subject" is in much better taste. Words such as "never," "ever," and "always," should be used rarely, if at all, because they are expressions of absoluteness.

Precede direct quotations by an appropriate introductory statement. To merely present quotations without some type of introduction results in a disjunct and incoherent narrative style. A reader must not receive the impression that direct quotations are separate from the narrative. They should, rather, be complementary to a smooth narrative flow.

Individuals engaged in the preparation of a research report are sometimes unduly concerned about the number of pages they are expected to produce to make a research study acceptable. The criterion for acceptability ought not be the number of pages assembled but rather what is contained in them. Normally, a concise and well-prepared report of fifty pages is more acceptable than a verbose, incoherent, and redundant one of the same topic of two hundred pages. An investigator should say what he intends in clear and terse language.

When an individual is under pressure to meet a deadline he has a tendency to become careless and overlook minor details. It is the responsibility of an investigator to see that his ultimate product represents the best work of which he is capable. The world of scholarship can hardly condone slipshod work any more than does NASA, where perfection is the hallmark of space technology. All details such as consistency in style of writing, footnotes, pagination, spellings, use of special terminology, and others, should be checked carefully by the investigator, his adviser, and others, to insure that the final report is one which is a credit not only to the investigator and the institution he represents, but also to the entire profession of music education.

Writing a research report can be a very gratifying and stimulating experience. Sharing the results of research is both a privilege and a responsibility incumbent upon every researcher. A researcher's initial reaction to reporting his research findings may be negative. When he reflectively considers what information needs to be transmitted, however, his responsibility for disseminating his findings can become impelling.

The increasing subsidization of music education research is now beginning to manifest itself in the form of several different kinds of grants. Some of the agencies which provide support for music education researchers and procedures for making application for these subsidies are discussed in the next chapter.

QUESTIONS FOR REVIEW AND DISCUSSION

1. Discuss the composition of the three complementary parts of a research report.
2. Compare the format for bibliographical references suggested in this chapter with the one in effect at your institution, and note differences which are evident between them.
3. What is the proper procedure for handling direct quotations of more than four lines? Of fewer than four lines?
4. How may the different types of subheadings discussed in this chapter be identified?
5. What is the purpose for using superscripts and footnotes in a research study? Discuss proper procedures to be utilized with each one.
6. Indicate conditions under which you would use the following Latin terms: *ibid.*, *op. cit.*, and *loc. cit.*
7. What stylistic considerations are important in the proper preparation of a research report?

SUPPLEMENTARY READINGS

ALMACK, JOHN C. *Research and Thesis Writing*. Boston: Houghton Mifflin Co., 1930. Chapters X and XI.

BARZUN, JACQUES, and GRAFF, HENRY F. *The Modern Researcher*. New York: Harcourt, Brace and World, Inc., 1962. Chapters 11-15.

BEST, JOHN W. *Research in Education*. Englewood Cliffs, N. J.: Prentice-Hall, Inc., 1959. Chapter 10.

BORG, WALTER R. *Educational Research: An Introduction*. New York: David McKay Co., Inc., 1963. Chapter 17.

CAMPBELL, WILLIAM G. *Form and Style in Thesis Writing*. Boston: Houghton Mifflin Co., 1954.

GOOD, CARTER V. *Essentials of Educational Research*. New York: Appleton-Century-Crofts, 1966. Chapter 9.

————, and SCATES, DOUGLAS E. *Methods of Research*. New York: Appleton-Century-Crofts, 1954. Chapter 10.

HILLWAY, TYRUS. *Introduction to Research*. Second Edition. Boston: Houghton Mifflin Co., 1964. Chapter 18.

KERLINGER, FRED N. *Foundations of Behavioral Research*. New York: Holt, Rinehart and Winston, Inc., 1965. Appendix A.

KOEFOD, PAUL E. *The Writing Requirements for Graduate Degrees*. Englewood Cliffs, N. J.: Prentice-Hall, Inc., 1964. Chapter 8 and Appendix K.

McGRATH, G. D., JELINEK, JAMES E., and WOCHNER, RAYMOND E. *Educational Research Methods*. New York: The Ronald Press Co., 1963. Chapter 9.

A Manual of Style. Eleventh Edition. Chicago: University of Chicago Press, 1949.

The MLA Style Sheet. PARKER, WILLIAM R. (comp.). Revised Edition. New York: Modern Language Association of America, 1964.

MORGAN, HAZEL B., and BURMEISTER, CLIFTON A. *Music Research Handbook*. Evanston, Ill.: The Instrumentalist Co., 1962. Chapters IV, V, VII-X.

RUMMEL, J. FRANCIS. *An Introduction to Research Procedures in Education*. Second Edition. New York: Harper and Row, Publishers, 1964. Chapter XI and Appendix A.

STRUNK, WILLIAM JR., and WHITE, E. B. *The Elements of Style*. New York: The Macmillan Co., 1962.

TURABIAN, KATE L. *A Manual for Writers of Term Papers, Theses, and Dissertations*. Chicago: University of Chicago Press, 1960.

VAN DALEN, DEOBALD B. *Understanding Educational Research*. Enlarged and Revised Edition. New York: McGraw-Hill Book Co., Inc., 1966. Chapter 15.

WATANABE, RUTH T. *Introduction to Music Research*. Englewood Cliffs, N. J.: Prentice-Hall, Inc., 1967. Chapters 14 and 15.

WHITNEY, FREDERICK L. *The Elements of Research*. Third Edition. Englewood Cliffs, N. J.: Prentice-Hall, Inc., 1950. Chapter XVI.

WISE, JOHN E., NORDBERG, ROBERT B., and REITZ, DONALD J. *Methods of Research in Education*. Boston: D. C. Heath and Co., 1967. Chapter X.

· 12 ·

Subsidization of Research in Music

One of the most significant factors contributing to the increased interest and activity in music research—which is not related to acquiring a graduate degree—is the unprecedented support now available through governmental agencies, private foundations, and other sources. Even though more funds have become available in recent years, they are of no avail unless researchers take advantage of them. Monies appropriated for research do not necessarily have to be spent within a certain fiscal period. If not enough worthwhile proposals are submitted, the funds still remaining are either transferred to other accounts or lie unused. Involvement in research, of course, is predicated on initiative, insight, and creativity on the part of the one engaging in it. Rarely, if ever, are research funds granted without a formal request for them. A potential researcher usually spends considerable time seeking sources of support. On the other hand, *support* for a contemplated project is not guaranteed by a person's aspirations or by his preparation of a sound and elaborate proposal. Currently, only about 20 percent of the proposals submitted are funded by the government. It is unfortunate that limited funds necessitate the rejection of many excellent proposals.

FEDERALLY-SUPPORTED RESEARCH

Federal legislation provided financial support for approximately sixty research studies in music education as of September 1, 1967. These projects represent a wide variety of topics and types of research.[1] There

---

[1]See "Research Projects in Music Education," *Music Educators Journal,* LIV (September, 1967), 60-65, for a listing of these projects by investigator, institution, duration, title, and number.

are basically two kinds of support available, project and program. Projects normally are planned, submitted, and pursued for a relatively short period of time by the person submitting the proposal. Program support, available only to a limited number of proposals in music, is essentially for prolonged activity on the part of colleges or universities, state departments of education, public school systems, and professional and nonprofit organizations.

Federal funds are available for research projects which have relatively fixed time limits. Research of this type may be used to develop or test new educational materials, to analyze or synthesize completed research, to determine educational needs, or critically evaluate issues.

The bulk of support for research in music education has come from the Cooperative Research Act of 1954, Public Law 83-531, and its successor, Title IV of Public Law 89-10, the Elementary and Secondary Education Act of 1965, commonly known by its acronym ESEA. No provision was made for funding music projects in the original Cooperative Research Act. Later the Act was amended and in 1959 Robert G. Petzold, of the University of Wisconsin, at Madison, received the first music grant for his research "The Perception of Music Symbols in Music Reading by Normal Children and by Children Gifted Musically," (U. S. Office of Education, Cooperative Research Project 554).

Prior to an official transmittal to the U. S. Office of Education, the initiator is encouraged to send three copies of a preliminary draft indicating what he proposes to do. The draft should contain the title, objectives, procedures, and significance of the research. If encouragement to proceed is received, the initiator then prepares a formal proposal. The prospective investigator should procure the latest guidelines for preparing the type of research proposal he plans to submit. These guidelines may be obtained from the U. S. Office of Education in Washington or from any of the nine regional offices along with such information as the number of copies to be submitted and deadlines to be observed depending on the type of funding. In addition, a pamphlet which contains helpful information detailing different kinds of federal subsidies available has just been issued.[2]

Small Project Research studies are limited to $8,500 plus overhead, but not to exceed a combined total of $10,000. Proposals may be submitted at any time but projects must be completed within eighteen months. This type of subsidy is appropriate for small-scale postdoctoral or graduate research. A pilot study to determine the feasibility of a more extensive project is possible under a small contract. Experimental

---

[2]*Office of Education Support for Research and Related Activities,* OE-12025 (Washington: U. S. Government Printing Office, 1967).

research, survey and curriculum development, analysis of data and materials, and improvement of instruction also are possible with this kind of support. Examples of research in each of these respective areas, although not necessarily supported by small contracts, are projects by Petzold,[3] Toms,[4] Thomas,[5] Schneider and Cady,[6] and Phelps.[7]

Regional offices now handle Small Project Research as a result of the recent decentralization of the U. S. Office of Education. This step will result in a shorter period of time, usually two to three months, from submission of the proposal to its acceptance or rejection. Funding for accepted proposals also is channeled through the regional offices.

Proposals requesting more than $10,000 normally take from four to five months to process. Basic and applied research, demonstration program, and curriculum improvement are types of research possible with this kind of subsidy. Proposals for all of these programs should be submitted to the Bureau of Research of the U. S. Office of Education in Washington by September 1, December 1, or March 1. Specific guidelines for preparing each of these kinds of proposals are available from the U. S. Office of Education. It is important to follow the most recent guidelines in order that a proposer experience few delays which might be due to lack of current information on deadlines, procedures, and program changes.

Title VII of the amended National Defense Education Act of 1958, Public Law 85-864, another source of funding, provided support for a few research studies in music. Commonly referred to as the "Media Title," Title VII may be used by a music educator to develop and evaluate tape recordings, films, motion pictures, and other educational media or to disseminate information related to new educational media. Research completed by Spohn[8] and Maltzman[9] was supported by NDEA Title VII.

---

[3]Robert G. Petzold, "Auditory Perception of Musical Sounds by Children in the First Six Grades," (U. S. Office of Education Cooperative Research Project 1051, 1966).

[4]John E. Toms, "A Survey of American and British Solo Vocal Literature," (U. S. Office of Education Cooperative Research Project S-133, 1965).

[5]Ronald B. Thomas, "A Study of New Concepts, Procedures and Achievements in Music Learning as Developed in Selected Music Education Programs," (U. S. Office of Education Cooperative Research Project 5-0204, 1966).

[6]Erwin H. Schneider and Henry L. Cady, "Evaluation and Synthesis of Research Studies Relating to Music Education," (U. S. Office of Education Cooperative Research Project E-016, 1965).

[7]Roger P. Phelps, "Seminar in State Music Supervision," (U. S. Office of Education Cooperative Research Project 7-8124, 1967).

[8]Charles L. Spohn, "A Study to Evaluate Two Methods Using Magnetic Tape Recordings for the Self-Instructional Presentation of the Elemental Materials of Music," (National Defense Education Act Research Project 876, 1963).

[9]Edward Maltzman, "National Conference on New Uses of Educational Media in Music," (National Defense Education Act Research Project 5-1410, 1965).

Program support is available to state departments of education, colleges or universities, local school districts, and qualified professional and non-profit organizations, as already noted. The purpose of this type of activity is to give educational benefits or enrichment to large groups. Application and evaluation procedures vary according to the type of funding, so guidelines of this kind should be scrutinized and carefully followed. Since the involvement of music educators in this type of program is more often an indirect and cooperative endeavor than is the case with individual projects, discussion relevant to these titles is included here mainly for purposes of completeness.

The Elementary and Secondary Education Act of 1965, Public Law 89-10, undoubtedly has had a greater impact on education in the United States than any other legislation passed by the Congress. Titles I and III of ESEA are most pertinent to music educators. The purpose of Title I, where the bulk of ESEA funds currently are concentrated, is to provide educational and cultural enrichment to children from low-income families. Allocations for Title I are made to state education departments and vary from state to state according to the number of school-age children from low income families. Local school districts are expected to submit proposals to state departments of education. Title I projects must show evidence of imagination and also suggest practical approaches to meeting the needs of deprived children. Funds for approved projects come from the agency of the state education department charged with such disbursements. Title I funds may be used by music educators in harmony with such purposes as purchasing recordings of classical music, transporting children to concerts, obtaining supplementary musical instructional materials, providing programed instruction, and Saturday morning music lessons.

Title III of ESEA provides for supplementary educational centers and services. Monies available to states under this title are determined by a formula based on school population and total population of the state. Grants under Title III are awarded by the U. S. Commissioner of Education only after proposals have been submitted to the proposer's state department of education for review and recommendation. Supplementary services available under Title III to music educators are organizing summer music camps as an adjunct to regular school programs; establishing materials resources centers containing records, films, slides, and musical scores; providing supplementary performing arts centers; utilizing mobile laboratories in rural areas for languages, library facilities, and music; establishing centers for listening to music after school hours and on weekends; providing concerts by symphony orchestras, opera companies, and other musical groups; presenting lecture-recitals and programs of chamber music with explanatory comments; organizing bands, orchestras, and choruses for preeminently talented children, to meet outside of regular school hours; and workshops and clinics for teachers and students conducted by outstanding performing musicians.

Section 12 of the National Foundation of the Arts and Humanities Act of 1965, Public Law 89-209, also provides limited assistance to strengthen instruction in the arts and humanities in the public schools. Funds are allocated to state departments of education on a matching grant basis, predicated on an approved state plan. An application for funds may be made by a local school district to its state department of education indicating how previously determined weaknesses have been discovered and suggesting the changes in objectives, equipment, or materials necessary to improve programs in the arts and humanities. Among the items of musical equipment which can be obtained under Section 12 are metronomes, tuning devices, recording equipment, folders for music, orchestral and band instruments, portable risers, rhythm instruments, music stands, and storage cabinets.

FOUNDATION SUPPORT FOR RESEARCH

Some subsidies for projects in music are available from private foundations. The format of proposals submitted to a foundation is similar to those submitted to the U. S. Office of Education or any other agency. A foundation proposal should include a clear and concise statement of the problem, objectives, related literature, research procedure, personnel and facilities available, and proposed budget.

There is no easy way to find out which foundations might be interested in subsidizing a specific proposal. An individual seeking support should write to each foundation which, in his opinion, would seem likely to subsidize his proposal, presenting his case as convincingly as possible. The voluminous directory of foundations is a complete and up-to-date compilation of foundations which offer grants in various areas, including music.[10] In addition to identifying the foundations and subject fields in which they offer assistance, the *Directory* indicates to whom applications should be addressed.

The likelihood of obtaining research funds from a foundation is no more certain than receiving funds from any other source. Each proposal must rest on its own merits and the decision to accept or reject will be determined largely on the quality of its organization and its degree of

---

[10]*The Foundation Directory*, Marianna *Lewis* (ed.), (Third Edition; New York: The Russell Sage Foundation, 1967).

relevance to the aims and objectives of the prospective funding agency. The availability of funds is always a significant factor.

An examination of publications of the Music Educators National Conference should make the search for a prospective funding agency easier for a music educator. Agencies which are inclined to be sympathetic to music proposals may be located in the sources listed below.[11]

OTHER SOURCES OF SUBSIDIZATION FOR RESEARCH IN MUSIC

A limited number of postdoctoral awards of short duration are available from the American Council of Learned Societies. Awarded on the basis of a national competition, the music grants are among those given in the general area of humanities.[12]

College and university budgets often include appropriations for research. The amount and kind of support obviously vary among institutions and according to funds available. A prospective researcher should check with the person in charge of such requests at his institution. Larger colleges and universities usually have a research bureau or division; in smaller institutions this responsibility may be charged to the dean or to an assistant dean.

Many local school districts have funds available for research in a topic of immediate concern to the system. Quite understandably the person who engages in the research usually is expected to be associated with the school district which provides the funds. A local superintendent may be responsible for the distribution of research funds or he may delegate this task to one of his assistants.

A state music educators' association occasionally provides limited assistance to a member who may be involved in research activity for the organization. Research of this type frequently falls under the descriptive category and the investigator usually receives no more than a subsidy for expenses incurred in actually conducting the study. Projects of this type are usually undertaken at the request of the association rather than upon the researcher's initiative.

It will be recalled that the third chapter emphasized the importance of a carefully designed research proposal to the ultimate success of a

---

[11]Refer to: *Post-Baccalaureate Grants and Awards in Music* (Washington: Music Educators National Conference, 1963); "Procuring Grants for Research in Music Education," *Music Educators Journal*, XLVII (September-October, 1960), 81-82; Paul R. Lehman, "Sources of Financial Support for Research in Music Education," *ibid.*, LI (February-March, 1965), 82, 85; "Research Funds: A Clarification," *ibid.*, LI (June-July, 1965), 18.

[12]Additional information may be obtained from Council Headquarters, 345 East 46th Street, New York, N.Y. 10017.

project. With subsidized research this becomes even more significant because very rarely will an application for subsidy represent an initiator's first attempt at preparing a research prospectus. Presumably by the time an individual prepares a proposal for research support he will at least have had the experience of organizing and implementing a graduate research study. Lack of such firsthand knowledge, however, should not be regarded as a deterrent to the formulation of an acceptable proposal. On the other hand, as already observed, the organization of a proposal which is justifiable and excellent in all respects is no guarantee that even the most experienced researcher will be successful in obtaining support. Research funds are not as plentiful at this time as they should be. The ratio of proposals rejected to those accepted appears to be a deterrent to some prospective investigators; but this fact does not seem to prevent others from making application.

PREPARATION OF THE INDIVIDUAL RESEARCH PROPOSAL

General guidelines have been established for research proposals submitted to the U. S. Office of Education or to one of its regional offices. These give specific details regarding number of copies required, to whom the proposal is to be submitted, and suggestions regarding format of the proposal, including recommended number of pages. Some minor deviations are permitted depending on the nature of the proposed research. A research proposal submitted to the U. S. Office of Education, or to a regional office, should contain: cover page, abstract or survey of the project, statement of the problem and objectives, procedures for conducting the research, how findings will be disseminated, personnel and facilities, proposed budget, and appended items.

On the cover page is placed the title of the research, the initiator, project director (if different from initiator), signature of official of transmitting agency, proposed beginning and ending dates of the project, total federal funds requested, and date proposal is transmitted.

A one-page abstract should contain: project title; principal investigator; contracting agency; federal funds requested; duration of the activity; and a summary defining purposes and objectives, anticipated contributions to education, and procedures or description of what the research purports to do.

In the statement of the problem and objectives, an investigator indicates concisely the nature of the problem, why the research needs to be done, the objectives, and reviews related literature and research.

Under the procedures section the initiator indicates how the proposal will be implemented, when, and what specifically will be done to accomplish the objectives of the research. Also to be included are statements regarding project evaluation, program arrangements, and any other necessary information which will disclose how objective data are to be obtained.

The manner of disseminating research findings, which has been stressed throughout this book, is an important part of a research proposal. The proposer should indicate how the results of his research will be disseminated and ostensibly what he believes the educational contributions of his research will be.

Careful preparation of the section listing personnel and facilities cannot be dismissed lightly. Name, position, title, experience, and responsibilities to the project have to be listed for every individual and consultant who is to be associated with the proposed research. All personnel who have agreed to serve and their degree of involvement in the project must be indicated. Also listed are consultants who can make valuable contributions to the study, even though they may not have been invited formally. Not to be overlooked are office space for the project director, tentative reservations for classrooms, laboratories, or other facilities needed for the research, and housing arrangements for participants when a conference, seminar, or workshop is involved.

The budget section of a proposal should be prepared preferably with the advice and assistance of some person responsible for administering research projects at the agency which transmits the proposal. The delineation of costs should be reasonable and yet evidence an understanding by the investigator of fiscal responsibility. The initiator lists, in tabular form, estimated federal and local contributions for each item in his budget. The budget includes four categories of costs: direct, indirect, and total costs, and cost sharing, if required.

Direct costs include projected expenditures for personnel, employee benefits, travel, supplies and materials, communications, services, final report costs, equipment, and other direct costs. Personnel expenditure estimates include those for the project director, research assistants, secretary, consultants, and others. To be recorded here for each person involved in the project are percentage of time commitment, annual salary, beginning and ending dates of employment, and, in the instance of consultants, the prevailing local per diem rate of compensation, and the number of days each consultant will be utilized. Social Security, retirement, and other deductions for each individual, based on the prevailing withholding rates in effect at the transmitting agency, will appear under employee benefits. When travel is involved, estimated fares or local mileage rate allowable should be listed for project personnel and consultants. Per diem allowances also need to be indicated.

In calculating this portion of the budget, the proposer is advised, when authorized and applicable, to obtain exemption certificates for federal excise tax on transportation, and state and local sales taxes on housing and meals for each person entitled to receive them. Costs for office supplies and project materials are indicated under the appropriate section. Although not always applicable, communications costs, when necessary to the project, should be delineated as accurately as is possible to estimate. Under the heading of services will be listed estimates for duplicating and reproducing materials and statistical, testing, and other costs. Final report costs are determined on the basis of the number of copies required. This information may be found in the guidelines used in conjunction with preparation of the proposal. When necessary, capital equipment may be purchased with research funds, although it is preferable to rent many items. Questions regarding this portion of the budget should be directed to the appropriate project officer in the U. S. Office of Education or one of the regional offices. Itemize and list any other necessary direct costs and follow this step by obtaining a subtotal of all direct costs.

The second category of the budget contains the indirect costs, or overhead. The basis on which the local overhead is computed, the rate, and period covered, need to be indicated. Overhead includes local agency administrative costs, office space and equipment, utilities, and other services. The local agency official who transmits the proposal should assist with this portion of the budget.

Direct and indirect costs are then totaled in the third part of the budget. The last item, cost sharing, indicates the percentage distribution of proposed federal and local contributions.

The final section of a research proposal, entitled "appended items," includes statements required by the Office of Education and other materials necessary to the project such as data collection instruments. Each proposer must include a brief comment for each of the following: (1) whether or not the proposal or a similar one has been submitted elsewhere; (2) whether or not it is a proposed extension of, or addition to, a previous or current project supported by the Office of Education; and (3) whether or not there has been any previous correspondence with the Bureau of Research regarding the proposal.

After a research proposal has been approved, the contractual arrangements between the sponsoring agency and the U. S. Office of Education are completed. During the course of his investigation the researcher is required to make interim progress reports. Instructions for preparing progress and final reports normally are included with materials forwarded to the investigator after his proposal has been approved for funding. Accompanying the interim and final reports should be a specified number of copies of the ERIC resumé form, which consists of a progress or project summary of no more than 250 words. These resumés facilitate the dissemination of research information through *Research in Education* and other sources.

A formal research proposal, therefore, makes provision for the three significant aspects of successful research which have been emphasized throughout this book; namely, organization, implementation, and dissemination.

With subsidization of music education research on the increase, the future indeed looks bright for an investigator who desires to come to grips with the problems which have plagued music educators for years. The next chapter focuses on some of the promising signs on the horizon for music education research.

QUESTIONS FOR REVIEW AND DISCUSSION

1. Differentiate between program and project support for educational research, giving distinguishing characteristics of each.
2. What kind of research projects are possible with Small Project funding? Give the deadlines for the submission of Small Project proposals.
3. Indicate types of research which may be pursued by grants of more than $10,000. What are the deadlines for submission of these proposals?
4. For what purpose may music educators use Title I ESEA funds? What supplementary services are available to music educators under Title III of ESEA?
5. Discuss in detail the preparation of an individual research proposal for possible federal subsidy.

SUPPLEMENTARY READINGS

BORG, WALTER R. *Educational Research: An Introduction.* New York: David McKay Co., Inc., 1963. Chapter 18.

COURTNEY, E. WAYNE (ed.). *Applied Research in Education.* Totowa, N. J.: Littlefield, Adams and Co., 1965. pp. 278-302.

CULBERTSON, JACK A., and HENCLEY, STEPHEN P. (eds.). *Educational Research: New Perspectives.* Danville, Ill.: The Interstate Printers and Publishers, Inc., 1963. Chapters 17 and 18.

EBEL, ROBERT L. "Some Limitations of Basic Research in Education," *Phi Delta Kappan,* XLIX (October, 1967), 81-84.

FALLON, BERLIE J. (ed.). *Fifty States Innovate to Improve Their Schools.* Bloomington, Ind.: *Phi Delta Kappa,* 1967.

McASHAN, HILDRETH H. *Elements of Educational Research.* New York: McGraw-Hill Book Co., Inc., 1963. Chapter 9.

Research in Education. Washington: U. S. Government Printing Office (November, 1966 to date).

Travers, Robert M. W. *An Introduction to Educational Research.* Second Edition. New York: The Macmillan Co., 1964. Chapter 16.

"Utilizing ESEA Title I Funds," *Educational Equipment and Materials.* (Winter, 1967), 2-4.

• 13 •

Music Education Research and the Future

Any attempt to state categorically what the future may hold for research in music education is, at best, mere conjecture. This is not to suggest that an endeavor to peer into the future is inappropriate for researchers. Quite the contrary, for implicit in the word "research" is the connotation of searching for something new and untried. Many trends are evident which, if they continue, can only suggest an unparalleled growth and development for music education research in the future.

PORTENTS FOR THE FUTURE

There are at least eight definite indications which portend well for the future of music education research. It would be difficult to establish any kind of priority or ranking, because there are definite interrelationships among them. These eight reassuring manifestations are: (1) greater general interest in music education research; (2) the demand for more adequate training in research techniques and principles; (3) more effective organization of non-professional research councils and organizations; (4) the establishment of more specialized and centralized bibliographical centers; (5) more experimentation both inside and outside of the classroom; (6) newer and more effective agencies, procedures, and techniques for the dissemination of research findings; (7) greater subsidization of research by federal and other agencies; and (8) increased cooperation with other agencies involved in research.

Music educators are displaying an unprecedented interest in research now as was noted in the first chapter. Some of the reasons for this interest no doubt are pragmatic; others are philosophical. As findings of research are being distributed more widely, educators are noting in them practical answers to some vexing problems. Thus many find themselves becoming increasingly interested in research, if for no other reason than that in research they have found answers to some of the questions which have been puzzling them. For others at the college or university level involvement in research may result in promotion to a higher professorial rank or in an advancement to a more rewarding salary schedule. Research pursued to receive a graduate degree is even more significant from a practical standpoint. The motive for graduate research in many instances may hardly be regarded as compatible with that of an experienced researcher. The latter feels constrained to advance man's knowledge through research in much the same way that a creative artist composes, because in this way he believes he can best express himself. The researcher, on the other hand, may give bent to his creative urge through the investigations he organizes, implements, and shares with others. Research now has acquired more dignity than it formerly had. In addition, the concept of a researcher who isolates himself in a laboratory has changed to that of one who, as a pioneer in some instances, develops and points the way to new ideas and practices. Although this alteration in thinking has taken place, it may not be as apparent in music education research because the profession does not have to modify a long tradition which revolves around the image of a sequestered scientist in his laboratory.

An increased interest in research has brought a corresponding demand for more training in proper research procedures and techniques. The number of institutions which offer courses in music education research is increasing rapidly. Although most of the courses are graduate student-oriented, a beginning has been made to provide some postdoctoral training. The U. S. Office of Education awarded a grant to Henry L. Cady to hold a conference at Ohio State University in Columbus February 26-March 4, 1967, which included a section related to the training of research workers in music education.[1] The Conference identified many areas needing research and suggested ways in which research findings may be utilized to improve the teaching and learning of music.[2] Symposium on Research in Music Education, also directed

---

[1]"A Conference on Research in Music Education," (U. S. Office of Education Cooperative Research Project 6-1388, 1967).

[2]For a more detailed account see "News of Research," *Journal of Research in Music Education,* XV (Summer, 1967), 165-166.

by Cady, was held at Ohio State University June 23-24, 1967. Generative papers to stimulate discussion were presented which pertained to rationale for research, guidelines for graduate research program development, and projections relative to changes which may be expected in music education research.

A training project in experimental research design, directed by James C. Carlsen, was held at Seattle, Washington March 11-14, 1968, under the sponsorship of the U. S. Office of Education and the Music Education Research Council of the Music Educators National Conference.[3] Fifty-five music educators who are either directing research studies or are pursuing individual research projects were in attendance. Emphasis was placed on designing sound experimental research proposals and on determining appropriate statistical techniques to empirically interpret data. Among the concepts discussed were internal and external validity, analysis of variants interactions in factorial designs, regression discontinuity, analysis of covariance, and multiple comparison techniques.

It is not unrealistic to anticipate projects which are organized, implemented, and disseminated better than many have been in the past as a logical by-product of increased research training. Better music education research can have a salutary effect in decreasing the disdain which has surrounded much of it in the past, as was noted in the first chapter of this book. The corner may already have been rounded, due largely, no doubt, to research training and experience, as evidenced by the sixty projects, noted in the previous chapter, which have been funded through the U. S. Office of Education.

Research groups are becoming more numerous because state research committees or councils have been formed in most of the states affiliated with the Music Educators National Conference. The Music Education Research Council of the MENC has provided encouragement, advice, and assistance in the formation of these councils. In addition, the Council has asked the president of each state music educators' association to name a state research chairman who will be responsible for coordinating research activities within the state and for organizing meetings at the state conventions. Research sessions are now scheduled at each of the six biennial divisional conventions of the Music Educators National Conference, which are held in odd-numbered years. Programs featuring research have been presented for several years at the organization's biennial national conventions, which alternate with the divisional

---

[3]"Special Training Project in Experimental Research Design," (U. S. Office of Education Cooperative Research Project 8-8021, 1968).

meetings. Warren has completed a doctoral study dealing with the history and activities of the Music Education Research Council and its predecessors going back as far as 1918.[4] He points out that the concept of research in music education and the need for it are not novel even though effective organization of such activities has come about only in recent years.

Because the membership of the Music Education Research Council is limited to eighteen members who are elected to a six-year term, the need was recognized for an organization which would be open to all interested music educators. As a result the Society for Research in Music Education, officially organized in 1960, was opened to anyone interested in research. The Society presently includes Life Members and those who hold Special Active Membership in the Music Educators National Conference. Activities of the Society for Research in Music Education are administered by the Music Education Research Council. Among the objectives of the Society are the encouragement of research at all levels of instruction, not only by its members but also by other music educators, and the dissemination of research findings to the profession.

Bibliographical and other pertinent data for music education research studies are now readily available because an ever-increasing number of projects are being stored in repositories such as the Educational Resources Information Center, to be described later in this chapter, and the MENC Historical Research Center. The MENC Historical Research Center was established by the Music Educators National Conference at the University of Maryland at College Park in 1965, having been planned as a center to house materials related to the history of music education. The archives collections will be contiguous and complementary to the preexisting Research Center of the American Bandmasters Association. Materials contained in the MENC Historical Research Center, as noted previously, include early music textbooks; copies of national, state, and local music periodicals; letters, personal effects, speeches, and unpublished manuscripts of leaders in music education, both past and present. The Center promises in the near future to be a unique repository of materials significant to a researcher interested in various phases of the history of music education. Items normally inaccessible or those housed in various places over the country will be assembled in one location. Personal papers, writings, speeches, and other memorabilia of both major and minor figures in music education

---

[4]Fred A. Warren, "A History of the Music Education Research Council and the *Journal of Research in Music Education* of the Music Educators National Conference," (unpublished doctoral dissertation, University of Michigan, 1966).

will be available here. These items may represent valuable primary sources of data to a music researcher, especially one who is preparing a biographical account of a musician who has made outstanding contributions to the profession.

Intensified activity to improve instruction through research and experimental music teaching, both inside and outside the classroom, is in evidence largely as the result of the greater interest in research, already noted, better reporting of research findings, and new educational media, which are offering challenges to music educators. Experimental teaching programs frequently employ new educational "hardware" such as teaching machines. Woelflin, for example, used a teaching machine to determine whether or not this technique was more effective in teaching beginning clarinet fingerings to students than the conventional method wherein the teacher imparts such information.[5] Another investigator, Carlsen, determined that a teaching machine could improve the effectiveness of teaching melodic dictation to college and university music majors.[6] Both Woelflin and Carlsen emphasized that one of the most positive benefits from the use of a teaching machine is to conserve a teacher's time, thus freeing him for other responsibilities.

Another audio-visual device, the tachistoscope, has been used by Hammer[7] and Wiley[8] to improve sight singing and rhythmic sight reading, respectively. The tachistoscope is used rather extensively by reading specialists to improve a person's speed in reading the printed page. It consists of an illuminated device in which it is possible to control the duration of an image flashed on a screen. The subject thus is forced to concentrate on viewing the projected material more quickly as the duration of the image is progressively decreased.

The application of digital computer techniques to music education research is still in its infancy. Nevertheless, many musicians are aware of the seemingly endless possibilities inherent in adapting computer science technology to music. Carthel, for example, used an IBM 1440 computer to ask fifteen high school students to respond to certain musical pitches presented to them.[9] Other studies have been completed in

[5]Leslie E. Woelflin, "Teaching Clarinet Fingerings with Teaching Machines," *Journal of Research in Music Education*, XII (Winter, 1964), 287-294.

[6]James C. Carlsen, "Programed Learning in Melodic Dictation," *Journal of Research in Music Education*, XII (Summer, 1964), 139-148.

[7]Harry Hammer, "An Experimental Study of the Use of the Tachistoscope in the Teaching of Melodic Sight Singing," *Journal of Research in Music Education*, XI (Spring, 1963), 44-54.

[8]Charles A. Wiley, "An Experimental Study of Tachistoscopic Technique in Teaching Rhythmic Sight Reading in Music," (unpublished doctoral dissertation, University of Colorado, 1962).

[9]James T. Carthel, "Music Instruction Through Computer-Assisted Tutorial Interaction," (unpublished master's thesis, University of Texas, 1966).

musicology, largely in the area of bibliography and musical analysis. Roller describes a method he developed to analyze musical compositions using a Control Data 1604 digital computer at Michigan State University.[10] Still in progress at the time of this writing is a project by Lincoln, subsidized by the U. S. Office of Education, which will develop computerized techniques to assist in the indexing of musical themes.[11]

There are several code systems for the representation of musical symbols by the computer because it is capable of handling letters, numbers, and special characters only, not musical symbols. Some of these codes, known as languages, and the place of their origin are: IML and LMT, Princeton University; Plaine and Easie, Queens College, New York; and ALMA, New York University, which is an acronym for Alphanumeric Language for Music Analysis. La Rue and Logemann indicate how a digital computer, using the ALMA system, can expedite the production of a musical thematic catalog.[12]

The utilization of digital computers for music education research and instruction appears to offer many opportunities for the "cybernetic" age at hand. Among the ways in which computers may be used are: (1) relieving the music educator of many tedious administrative and record keeping tasks, (2) providing instantaneous correction for student assignments, and (3) generating and analyzing sound. Closely akin to the latter is electronic music, a field all its own which has excited such contemporary composers as Karlheinz Stockhausen, Pierre Boulez, and Vladimir Ussachevsky, to name a few.[13] The music educator needs to be aware that music is being composed electronically whether or not he accepts it as legitimate music.

The possibility exists now to better disseminate research reports than formerly. This is practicable because music education researchers have not only the more conventional and firmly established process of dissemination through research journals but also the largely untried but highly promising computerized data storage and retrieval systems such as ERIC. Perhaps best known to music educators is the *Journal of Research in Music Education,* a quarterly publication of the Music

---

[10]Gilbert Roller, "Development of a Method for Analyis of Musical Compositions Using an Electronic Digital Computer," *Journal of Research in Music Education,* XIII (Winter, 1965), 249-252.

[11]Harry B. Lincoln, "Development of Computerized Techniques in Music Research with Emphasis on the Thematic Index," (U. S. Office of Education Cooperative Research Project 7-8276. In progress).

[12]Jan LaRue and George W. Logemann, "EDP for Thematic Catalogues," *Notes,* XXII (June, 1966), 1179-1186.

[13]See issues of *Electronic Music Review* and *die Reihe* for detailed information about electronic music.

Educators National Conference, which first appeared in 1953. The *Journal* contains music research articles and reports, reviews of new publications, and news of research activities. State music research journals are published at regular frequency in Colorado, Illinois, and Missouri, and infrequently in Pennsylvania and other states. The amount of duplication between state journals and the *Journal of Research in Music Education* is surprisingly negligible. The state research journals frequently feature research by master's candidates and when doctoral studies are included they usually do not appear in the *Journal*. In his remarks initiating the research news column in the *Journal* this writer observed that state research journals and the *Journal of Research in Music Education* "should supplement and complement one another to the end that the term 'research' will in an active way soon reach the rightful place and understanding that it should have in music education."[14]

A new computerized data retrieval system which appears to have great significance for the future is known by the acronym DATRIX, which signifies "Direct Access to Reference Information: a Xerox Service." Operated by the University Microfilms Division of the Xerox Corporation,[15] DATRIX makes it possible for a researcher to obtain within a few days a computer-produced list of doctoral studies which are pertinent to his topic. Bibliographies sent to the researcher contain title of the dissertation, name of investigator, place where completed, date, and page and volume of *Dissertation Abstracts* where the doctoral study is located. Key word lists are available in three areas but the music education researcher most likely would use the one entitled "Humanities/Social Sciences." Key words which are chosen by the researcher as being relevant to his topic are then fed into a computer which in turn will retrieve every reference in this area beginning with these indicators.

A limited number of research reports of particular significance to music educators have been published by the Government Printing Office in Washington, D. C. and are available from the Superintendent of Documents, where a listing of available titles also may be obtained. A new process employing a high-speed typesetting machine that can compose 1,000 characters a second was put into operation at the Government Printing Office on October 2, 1967. Called Linotron, this process uses a highly advanced television technique to set pages of type from programed computer tapes.[16] With this advanced technological develop-

14"News of Research in Music Education," *Journal of Research in Music Education*, XIII (Spring, 1965), 56. Used by permission of *Journal of Research in Music Education*.

15University Microfilms, 300 North Zeeb Road, Ann Arbor, Michigan 48106.

16*New York Times*, October 3, 1967.

ment the dissemination of information should be even quicker and more effective and comprehensive than it has been in the past.

The Educational Resources Information Center, better known by the acronym ERIC, was established by the U. S. Office of Education in 1965. The ERIC system is composed of Central ERIC in Washington and eighteen external clearing houses which had been established at the time of this writing for different subject areas and located in various parts of the United States. *Research in Education,* the monthly publication of ERIC, which first appeared in November of 1966, contains report and project resumés in abstract form of approximately 250 words. Report resumés signify completed studies and are prefixed by an ED number; project resumés consist of interim reports, indicated by an EP prefix. ERIC has as its objective to obtain, abstract, index, store, retrieve, and disseminate educational research. This computerized system for disseminating research information of various kinds to educators is one of the most complete and comprehensive in existence. Complete texts of documents filed in the ERIC system are available at reasonable prices in either hard copy or microfiche and may be obtained from the ERIC Document Reproduction Service[17] or from any ERIC clearing house.

Approximately sixty projects in music education have received federal subsidy, as related earlier. There is every reason to believe that federal and foundation support will be more pronounced in the future because of an increased interest in research and in applications for subsidy. This increased support will be forthcoming as music educators achieve more experience in writing and implementing research proposals and as grants are awarded solely on the basis of worthiness, regardless of the subject area, rather than on specific allocations to different fields of endeavor.

Cooperation between educators in music and other disciplines appears to be entering a new and potentially beneficent stage. Some cooperative endeavor may be due to the increasing importance placed upon humanities instruction in public schools and colleges and universities. When incorporated in humanities courses music is shown in proper perspective to art, literature, drama, and other disciplines. Another contributing factor is the assumption that knowledge knows no inter- or intra-disciplinary barriers. Such an endeavor is the project known as RILM (Répertoire International de la Littérature Musicale) which, in 1966, was established jointly by the International Musicological Society (IMS), the International Association of Music Libraries (AIBM),

---

17Operated by the National Cash Register Co., 4936 Fairmont Ave., Bethesda, Md. 20014.

and the American Council of Learned Societies (ACLS). RILM is an abstracted, computer-indexed international bibliography of scholarly writings about music. Included are articles, books, dissertations, reviews, essays, catalogs, iconographies, and other pertinent musical items which have appeared since January 1, 1967. *RILM Abstracts*,[18] first published in August of 1967, is the quarterly journal of RILM and includes abstracts of up to 150 words related to various items of current music literature.

Phi Delta Kappa is a professional education fraternity for men oriented toward service, leadership in education, and educational research. Its official publication, *Phi Delta Kappan,* contains articles of consequence to music educators on occasion. The organization publishes annually a listing of doctoral dissertations, reports, and field studies in education completed or underway, entitled *Research Studies in Education.* Other publications of significance appear from time to time. Phi Delta Kappa basically is interdisciplinary in philosophy and coverage so attention to a specific subject area is infrequent. Applications of concepts and philosophies presented in its publications must be made by each individual as they are appropriate for him.

The importance of research to the future progress of music education is evident. Research in music education undoubtedly is at a higher peak now than ever before, both quantitatively and qualitatively. This is due to at least four reasons which are interrelated. First, exacting standards for subsidized research have resulted in projects of consistently high quality. The demand for excellence has compelled researchers to set exacting standards not only for themselves but also for those whose research they supervise. A third factor is the ever-increasing trend for music educators to seek additional graduate instruction. This in turn has caused institutions of higher learning to either inaugurate music research methodology courses or upgrade those already in existence. Finally, as music educators begin to realize that the application of research findings can make their teaching easier and more effective, they engage in it themselves or encourage others to do so.

Music education optimistically stands on the threshold of even greater research opportunities in the future. Members of the profession, realizing that research holds the key to the destinies of untold numbers of youngsters whose lives they are helping to shape, appear poised and ready to face the future with confidence. It is imperative that this quest for answers to problems proceeds with dispatch and precision to the end

---

[18]Available from the International RILM Center, Queens College, Flushing, N.Y. 11367.

that the researcher may attain his avowed goal of making the world a better place in which to live.

QUESTIONS FOR REVIEW AND DISCUSSION

1. Discuss the eight indications listed in this chapter which suggest that a brilliant future is assured for music education research.
2. Which of the eight manifestations noted in the previous query seem to have the most significance for a potential or fledging researcher? Why?
3. What are some of the ways in which computers may benefit music educators and researchers?

SUPPLEMENTARY READINGS

BOWLES, EDMUND A. (ed.). *Computers in Humanistic Research.* Englewood Cliffs, N. J.: Prentice-Hall, Inc., 1967. Section V.

BURKE, ARVID J., and BURKE, MARY A. *Documentation in Education.* Fourth Edition, Revised. New York: Teachers College Press, Teachers College, Columbia University, 1967. Chapter 23.

CONDON, THOMAS J. "Goals for Humanistic Research with Computers," *ACLS Newsletter,* XVIII (April, 1967), 1-7.

COURTNEY, E. WAYNE (ed.). *Applied Research in Education.* Totowa, N. J.: Littlefield, Adams and Co., 1965. pp. 303-333.

FLANAGAN, JOHN C. "Functional Education for the Seventies," *Phi Delta Kappan,* XLIX (September, 1967), 27-32.

"Future of the Computer Tutor," *EDUCOM,* II (September, 1967), 5-8.

HAMMER, HARRY. "The Tachistoscope in Music Reading," *The American Music Teacher,* XVII (September-October, 1967), 39, 48.

HUTCHESON, ROBERT J., JR. "Programmed Instruction and Music Education," *Missouri Journal of Research in Music Education,* II (Autumn, 1967), 9-52.

"Information Storage, Retrieval, and Dissemination," *Educational Researcher,* XVIII (Supplement 1967).

KERLINGER, FRED N. *Foundations of Behavioral Research.* New York: Holt, Rinehart and Winston, Inc., 1965. Appendix C.

KUHN, WOLFGANG E., and ALLVIN, RAYNOLD. "Computer-Assisted Teaching: A New Approach to Research in Music," *Bulletin of Council for Research in Music Education,* XI (Fall, 1967), 1-13.

LUND, DIANE. "New Teaching with Chorus and Baroque," *Minnesota National Laboratory News Bulletin,* V (Summer, 1967), 4-7.

McGRATH, G. D., JELINEK, JAMES E., and WOCHNER, RAYMOND E. *Educational Research Methods.* New York: The Ronald Press Co., 1963. Chapter 11.

PHELPS, ROGER P. "Some Observations Relative to Research in Music Education," *Colorado Journal of Research in Music Education,* II (Spring, 1965), 5-7.

ROBINSON, DONALD W. "The USOE and Research in Education," *Phi Delta Kappan,* XLVIII (September, 1966), 2-5.

The Rotarian, CXI (October, 1967), 16-31.

Rummel, J. Francis. *An Introduction to Research Procedures in Education.* Second Edition. New York: Harper and Row, Publishers, 1964. Chapter X.

Sax, Gilbert. *Empirical Foundations of Educational Research.* Englewood Cliffs, N. J.: Prentice-Hall, Inc., 1968. Chapter 13.

Scientific American, CCXV (September, 1966).

Travers, Robert M. W. *An Introduction to Educational Research.* Second Edition. New York: The Macmillan Co., 1964. Chapter 15.

"Writings on the Use of Computers in Music," Berlind, Gary (comp.). Institute for Computer Research in the Humanities, New York University. (Mimeographed.)

Index

229

DATE DUE